THE MEDIEVAL CHURCH
OF
ST ANDREWS

collegium S.

franciscanorum
ædes.

domus
vrbis

dominicanorum
ædes.

Ecclesia Parochia
ciuitatis.

collegium

The
Medieval Church
of
St Andrews

Edited by

DAVID McROBERTS

BURNS
GLASGOW
1976

First published 1976

Printed in Great Britain by
JOHN S. BURNS & SONS
25 Finlas Street, Glasgow. G22 5DS

EMO. AC RMO. DNO.
DNO. GORDON IOSEPH GRAY
S.R.E. PRESB. CARD.
TITULI SCAE. CLARAE AD VINEAM CLARAM
ARCHIEPISCOPO
SCI. ANDREAE ET EDINBURGENSIS
UNIVERSITATIS SANCTIANDREAE
ARTIUM MAGISTRO ET S.S. THEOL. DOCTORI
QUI
ANNO AB INCARNATIONE MCMLXIX
LARGITORE PAULO VI ROM. PONTIFICE
DE URBE IN PATRIAM ASPORTAVIT
TANQUAM REGULUS ALTER
INSIGNES RELIQUIAS
DIVI ANDREAE
APOSTOLI CHRISTI AMABILIS
REGNIQUE SCOTIAE PATRONI
ATQUE
PROTECTORIS CAELESTIS

FOREWORD

Books on St Andrews are numerous but it is remarkable that, apart from George Martine's *Reliquiae Divi Andreae*, published in 1797, no volume has ever been devoted expressly and exclusively to the ecclesiastical pre-eminence of the city, which was the principal centre of the Church in medieval Scotland. Again, apart from some valuable studies of its architectural history, it is extraordinary how limited has been the literature on the metropolitan cathedral in spite of the fact that this was the largest building ever erected in medieval Scotland and was, in many respects, the most important building in the kingdom, being the main seat of jurisdiction of the Ecclesia Scoticana, a cultural centre of widespread influence and a focal point of national sentiment.

The present work will help to remedy such defects in the bibliography of St Andrews. The book is based on the original research of several experts (some of whom have made a lifelong study of St Andrews). The early centuries of Church life in Kinrimund are investigated afresh: the architectural history of the great church is elucidated: the position of the Augustinian canons as the cathedral chapter and the personalities of some bishops and administrative personnel are examined: and from scraps of evidence scattered widely in late medieval documents, an attempt has been made to reconstruct something of the appearance and day-to-day life of the cathedral in its heyday and to reassess the central place that it held in the affections of the Scottish people throughout the Middle Ages.

In addition to the writers, whose scholarly research appears in these pages, we gratefully acknowledge the help we have received from many institutions and individuals. In particular we have to thank the Trustees of the National Library of Scotland for permission to publish for the first time the sixteenth-century panoramic view of St Andrews from the unique copy in the National Library. For photographs and blocks, kindly made available by the Department of the Environment, we are indebted to Mr Stewart Cruden, Inspector of Ancient Monuments for Scotland and to Mr Richard Fawcett. In the case of the line illustrations, the site plan on page 13 and the plan of the cathedral at the end of the book were drawn by Mr W. Murray Jack, of St Andrews, from original surveys prepared for the Royal Commission on the Ancient Monuments of Scotland by Mr C. S. T. Calder with additional information supplied by the contributors of the present work. The reconstructions on pages 17, 19 and 25 were drawn by Mr John Purves of St Andrews from details supplied by Mr R. G. Cant, the dimensions being derived from surveys of the east and west gables of the cathedral prepared by Mr R. Campbell for the National Art Survey of Scotland. Lastly we have to thank the Very Rev. Anthony Ross, OP, for compiling the index which makes the volume so much more useful to scholars.

CONTENTS

FOREWORD vii

THE CELTIC CHURCH IN KINRIMUND 1
MARJORIE O. ANDERSON

THE BUILDING OF ST ANDREWS CATHEDRAL 11
RONALD G. CANT

DAVID BERNHAM, BISHOP OF ST ANDREWS, 1239-1253 33
MARINELL ASH

'KIN, FREINDIS AND SERVANDIS,' THE MEN WHO
    WORKED WITH ARCHBISHOP DAVID BEATON 45
MARGARET H. B. SANDERSON

'THE GLORIOUS HOUSE OF ST ANDREW' 63
DAVID MCROBERTS

THE AUGUSTINIAN CHAPTER OF ST ANDREWS 121
MARK DILWORTH, OSB

ST ANDREWS IN THE JOHN LAW CHRONICLE 137
JOHN DURKAN

APPENDICES:

    I. THE SIXTEENTH-CENTURY PANORAMIC VIEW
        OF ST ANDREWS 151
    DAVID MCROBERTS

ix

II. COMPARATIVE INTERIOR DIMENSIONS OF
SOME OTHER MEDIEVAL CATHEDRALS   153
RONALD G. CANT

III. A ST ANDREWS PILGRIMAGE CERTIFICATE
OF 1333 AT SAINT-OMER   155
DAVID MCROBERTS

IV. THE DEPENDENT PRIORIES OF ST ANDREWS   157
MARK DILWORTH

V. BISHOP KENNEDY'S MACE   167
DAVID MCROBERTS

INDEX OF PERSONS   173

LIST OF ILLUSTRATIONS

SIXTEENTH-CENTURY PANORAMIC VIEW OF ST ANDREWS
Frontispiece

Reproduced from National Library of Scotland, Ms Acc. 2887, by kind permission of the Trustees of the National Library of Scotland.

PLATE I. ST ANDREWS: CATHEDRAL AND PRECINCTS FROM THE AIR .... *facing* p. 4

Block by courtesy of the Department of the Environment. Crown copyright reserved.

PLATE II. THE ST ANDREWS SARCOPHAGUS ...... *facing p.* 5

Block by courtesy of the Department of the Environment. Crown copyright reserved.

PLATE III. THE TWO CATHEDRALS AT ST ANDREWS *facing p.* 20

Block by courtesy of the Department of the Environment. Crown copyright reserved.

PLATE IV. THE WEST FRONT OF ST ANDREWS CATHEDRAL
facing p. 21

Block by courtesy of the Department of the Environment. Crown copyright reserved.

PLATE V. SOUTH WALL OF NAVE: ST ANDREWS CATHEDRAL .... *facing p.* 24

Block by courtesy of the Department of the Environment. Crown copyright reserved.

PLATE VI. ST ANDREWS CATHEDRAL: THE EAST GABLE
facing p. 25

Block by courtesy of the Department of the Environment. Crown copyright reserved.

PLATE VII. THE PONTIFICAL OF BISHOP DAVID BERNHAM
facing p. 32

Bibl. Nat. Paris, Ms Latin 1218, fo 4.

PLATE VIII. THE PONTIFICAL OF BISHOP DAVID BERNHAM
facing p. 33

Bibl. Nat. Paris, Ms Latin 1218, fo 2.

PLATE IX. FOURTEENTH-CENTURY TOMBSTONE: ST ANDREWS CATHEDRAL .... *facing p.* 52

Picture by courtesy of the Department of the Environment. Crown copyright reserved.

PLATE X. COAT OF ARMS OF THE ISLE OF MAN: ST ANDREWS CATHEDRAL .... *facing p.* 53

Picture by courtesy of the Department of the Environment. Crown copyright reserved.

THE MEDIEVAL CHURCH OF ST ANDREWS

PLATE XI. TOMBSTONE OF JOHN GALYCHTLY OF EBRUKS
facing p. 68
Block by courtesy of Proceedings of the Society of Antiquaries of Scotland.

PLATE XII. HENRY WARDLAW, BISHOP OF ST ANDREWS, 1403-1440 .... *facing p.* 69
Picture by courtesy of the Department of the Environment. Crown copyright reserved.

PLATE XIII. WILLIAM SCHEVEZ, ARCHBISHOP OF ST ANDREWS, 1476-1497 .... *facing p.* 84

PLATE XIV. A ROYAL DIRGE .... *facing p.* 85
Ost. Nationalbibliothek Wien, Cod. 1897, fo 141v.

PLATE XV. SIGNATURE OF JOHN HEPBURN, PRIOR OF ST ANDREWS .... *facing p.* 100
St Andrews University Library.

PLATE XVI. ALEXANDER STEWART, ARCHBISHOP OF ST ANDREWS, 1504-1513 .... *facing p.* 101
Bibliothèque municipale, Arras.

PLATE XVII. CELEBRATION OF LOW MASS ...... *facing p.* 116
Reproduced from National Library of Scotland, Ms Acc. 6236, fo 45v, by kind permission of the Trustees of the National Library of Scotland.

PLATE XVIII. DAVID BEATON, CARDINAL ARCHBISHOP OF ST. ANDREWS, 1539-1546 .... *facing p.* 117
St Mary's College, Blairs.

PLATE XIX. SEAL OF CARDINAL DAVID BEATON *facing p.* 132

PLATE XX. JAMES STEWART, PRIOR OF ST ANDREWS, 1538-1570 .... *facing p.* 133
From the portrait at Darnaway Castle.

PLATE XXI. TOMBSTONE OF JOHN WINRAM, ST ANDREWS
facing p. 148
St Leonard's College Chapel, St Andrews.

PLATE XXII. OBIT OF ARCHBISHOP JOHN HAMILTON, 1571
facing p. 149
Scottish Catholic Archives, Edinburgh.

PLATE XXIII. EARLY THIRTEENTH-CENTURY HEAD OF CHRIST .... *facing p.* 164
Picture by courtesy of the Department of the Environment. Crown copyright reserved.

PLATE XXIV. BISHOP KENNEDY'S MACE .... *facing p.* 165
Picture by courtesy of the Royal Scottish Museum.

PLAN OF THE MEDIEVAL CATHEDRAL OF ST ANDREWS
at end of volume

THE CELTIC CHURCH IN KINRIMUND

by

MARJORIE O. ANDERSON

The last bishop in St Andrew's church of Kinrimund to bear a Celtic name died in 1093. The church and bishopric were not securely established again until 1144, and then on very different lines. It will be convenient to speak of Kinrimund until 1093 as 'Celtic,' and of St Andrews from 1144 onwards as 'medieval,' with an intervening half-century of disintegration and experiment.

That there was a monastery at Kinrimund in the time of the Pictish kings, before the middle of the ninth century, is proved by an entry for 747 in the Irish annals: *Mors Tuathalain abbatis Cinrighmonai*.[1] This is an almost unique instance of interest shown by the annals in a Pictish religious house, all the more remarkable because it was probably written in north-east Ireland, not in Iona.[2]

The name of the place must be older than 747, in meaning if not in its Irish form: 'head of king's (*or* royal) mount.' The anonymous author of a St Andrews *historia fundationis* in the mid-twelfth century, whom I shall call 'the Augustinian,'[3] says that *Rymont* or *regia mons* had been a *regia urbs* before the monastery was founded;[4] a statement too readily suggested by the name to carry much weight. The foundation legend in both its versions names a Pictish king as the founder. If he is to be identified with a historical king at all, he must be one of the two whom we know as Angus I (729?-761) and Angus II (820-834). The earlier Angus, in whose reign the abbot Tuathalan died, has the more obvious claim. Both were over-kings of the Picts, and each of them was primarily king of Fortriu, a province roughly equatable with southern Perthshire.[5] Fife, being contiguous to Fortriu and separated from the rest of the country by the firths of Forth and Tay, may have been in some special way subordinate to kings of Fortriu. But it is possible that the *rig* in virtue of whom Kinrimund got its name had been kinglets of Fife, or even of some still more local unit corresponding to an Irish *tuath*. The place, though fairly accessible by both land and sea, is not an obvious one for a royal fortress. The name *Cursus Apri*, by which a territory round Kinrimund

---

1. A. O. Anderson, *Early Sources of Scottish History* (*ES*), i, 238.
2. See M. O. Anderson, *Kings and Kingship in Early Scotland* (1973) (*KKES*), 18f.
3. Skene's *Chronicles of the Picts and Scots* (*PS*), 183-193, from Harleian MS 4628. The first part (to top of p. 188) is the B version of an earlier foundation legend for which see M. O. Anderson, 'St Andrews before Alexander I,' in *The Scottish Tradition* (essays in honour of R. G. Cant, 1974), 6ff. The latter part was composed between 1144 and the death of David I in 1153.
4. PS, 188. For possible implications of *urbs*, see Barrow, *The Kingdom of the Scots*, 66.
5. See *KKES*, 140f. Angus I is nowhere entitled 'king of Fortriu,' but his brother and successor Brude is so entitled in the Irish annals.

was known, tempts one to imagine that kings may have stayed there for the pleasure of hunting wild boar.[6]

The *cenn-* of Cennrigmonaid, if taken literally, would suggest that the principal church (whether or not it contained relics of St Andrew in 747) was on the headland above the harbour. This headland, now known as the Kirkhill, was the site of a medieval church of culdees, and some of the apparently Christian burials that have been found there were possibly older than the eighth century.[7]

The B version of the foundation legend names seven churches which it says were built at or soon after the foundation in addition to the *basilica* of St Andrew. Monasteries containing several churches were not unusual in Ireland.[8] When the legend was written, old buildings or burial grounds may have been still visible or actually in use. One church bore the name of St Regulus, the legendary bringer of St Andrew's relics, whose story may, for all we know, have overlain and effectively obliterated the cult of some local saint.[9]

What could be the site of one church of the Pictish period lies about 175 yards (160 metres) south-west of the Kirkhill. Here a solid stone ' shrine' nearly four feet long, shaped like a house or church, was found with associated skeletons in 1895. Further burials were found nearby in 1969. The ' shrine,' which can be linked with a ' large class of Anglo-Danish " hogback " tomb-covers,'[10] may be as early as 800.

The more famous ' sarcophagus' shrine, nearly six feet long, built of richly carved stone panels and corner-posts, may also belong to the first half of the ninth century, though not all scholars accept so early a date.[11] It came to light in 1833 when a deep grave was being dug in the Cathedral burial ground.[12] The unusual depth at which it was found, with its top apparently at least seven feet below the 1833 ground level, suggests that it had been buried deliberately, unlike most of the grave-stones of the Celtic period. The depth would probably be consistent with its having been buried like an ordinary coffin under three feet or so of earth in, say, the twelfth century.[13] We cannot very well assume that the place where it was found was close to the church where it originally stood. It is sumptuous enough to have been transferred from an old building to a new one.

---

6. See below. An alleged early name of the district was *Muckros, nemus porcorum (PS,* 185); but Irish *mucc* and Latin *porcus* normally mean a domestic pig.
7. References in *Scott. Trad.,* 1.
8. See Máire and Liam de Paor, *Early Christian Ireland* (1964), 54ff.
9. See Dowden in *PSAS,* xxvii, 247-254.
10. Charles Thomas, *The Early Christian Archaeology of North Britain* (1971), 150; references in *Scott. Trad.,* 2; *St Andrews Citizen,* 20 December 1969. The ' shrine' is kept in St Leonards School.
11. Isabel Henderson favoured an eighth-century date in *The Picts* (1967). 88 (cf. 149-157, and references ibid., 172). See also George Henderson, *Early Medieval* (1972), 126.
12. David Hay Fleming, *St Andrews Cathedral Museum* (1931), Celtic Monuments section, pp. 3ff.
13. In the twelfth century the shrine would be regarded as obsolete. A portable shrine, of unknown age but with a Gaelic name *Morbrac,* was still in use in the early thirteenth century *(St A. Lib.,* 329).

In any case we do not really know where it was found in 1833. A paper read in 1854 implied that it was within the area of the medieval cathedral.[14] John Stuart[15] a little later said that it was 'about thirteen yards north from the tower of St Regulus' chapel' (the eleventh-century church of St Andrew), that is about the southern edge of the area where so many tomb-stones of the Celtic period have been unearthed. But the earliest printed account to define the spot put it 'a little west of St Regulus' Tower.'[16] It is worth noting that about nine yards west of the tower is a tomb-stone erected in the 1880s in memory of five members of the family of Robert Landale of Grange, the first of whom died, and presumably was buried there, in 1833.

The land called Kinrimund, as it was defined in the twelfth century, extended to more than thirty acres.[17] All the sites I have mentioned lie within an area of about ten acres in the north-east, comparable with the areas enclosed by monastic *valla* at Iona and Clonmacnoise.[18] The boundary of the Pictish monastery, according to version B of the foundation legend, was marked with stone crosses. The shaft of a free-standing cross, possibly a boundary-marker, was built into the east end of the cathedral and may belong to the Pictish period. Its decoration includes human and animal figures and has been described as 'a blending of Pictish and Northumbrian elements, with the Northumbrian predominating.'[19]

The next time we hear of Kinrimund after 747 is in the lifetime of the king Constantine, son of Aed, when Scottish kings had been ruling over the old kingdom of the Picts for more than fifty years. Early in Constantine's reign, about 906, at an assembly held near Scone, a bishop called Cellach joined with the king in promising certain rights to churches. It is clear from the Scottish Chronicle's account that his authority extended far beyond his own church, though perhaps not necessarily beyond the old Pictish kingdom.[20] Cellach's was the first name in a late-medieval list of bishops of St Andrews known principally through Bower and Wyntoun.[21]

At the end of a long reign, in the 940s, Constantine retired into religion (*baculum cepit et domino servivit*).[22] The place of his retirement is described thus in the eleventh-century ' Prophecy of Berchan ': ' the abbey-church on the brow (*or* brink) of the wave. In the house of the

14. George Buist in *PSAS*, i, 234.
15. *Sculptured Stones of Scotland*, i (1856); quoted by Hay Fleming, p. 7.
16. Leighton's *History of Fife* (1840); quoted by Hay Fleming, p. 3.
17. *St A. Lib.*, 127, 143. See R. G. Cant, in St Andrews Preservation Trust's *Annual Report*, 1970, 12.
18. Charles Thomas, pp. 30f.
19. Cecil L. Curle, in *PSAS*, lxxiv, 107, where (and also on p. 110) for ' church of St Mary on the Rock ' read ' east gable of the Cathedral.' The stone is Hay Fleming's no. 19.
20. KKES, 251. Cellach's standing was possibly the same as that of the ' bishop of Fortriu ' at Dunkeld who died in 865.
21. *Chron. Bower*, VI24 (i, 339 and note). See Haddan and Stubbs, *Councils*, ii, 173f.
22. *KKES*, 251.

apostle he will die.'[23] This is made more explicit by a note in a regnal list which says that he became ' abbot of the *keledei* of St Andrew.'[24] If that is true, it may mean that the king served God, not in the church of St Andrew itself, but in a separate church of *céli dé* (culdees) within the monastery of Kinrimund. This interpretation is permitted by Berchan's word *recles*, here translated ' abbey-church,' since a more usual meaning in the eleventh century would seem to be a small church or oratory or even a living-cell.[25] But the note in the regnal list may contain an anachronism. When it was written, regular ' Celtic ' religious life at Kinrimund, other than that of the *céli dé*, had probably been long forgotten. However, it is likely enough that *céli dé*, who originated in a reforming movement among Irish monks in the eighth century, were established in Kinrimund by the middle of the tenth.

Constantine's son and successor, Indulf, died ' in the house of the same holy apostle ' as his father. And a royal Irishman died there ' on pilgrimage ' in 965.[26]

It may have been in this period or a little earlier that burials marked by small stone slabs, decorated in relief, were being made in the area just east of the medieval cathedral site, perhaps extending into the site itself. Nearly twenty slabs or pieces of slabs of the Celtic period have been found here, some of them apparently *in situ*. As far as can be judged from the not very precise locations given in Hay Fleming's catalogue, the eastern limit of the area is about sixty feet east of the east end-wall of the cathedral, and the southern limit forty-eight feet north of the eleventh-century church (' St Rule's ').[27] Other stones of the same kind have been found on the Kirkhill, about seventy yards east and a little north of ' St Rule's '; but there seems to be no proof that any of them was *in situ*, and they could have been carried there as building material.

The decoration on all these stones tends to be stereotyped, and there is a notable lack of human and animal figures. Pictish ' symbols ' are entirely wanting, but it must be remembered that these are not very common in Fife.[28] It is doubtful whether any of the stones can belong to the Pictish period. R. B. K. Stevenson would date them at earliest in the late ninth and early tenth century.[29]

Leaving aside the fact that king Constantine was said to have been abbot of the *céli dé*, not ' abbot of Kinrimund,' it is quite possible that by the middle of the tenth century the original monastic establishment had become more or less secularized, and that there was no longer a religious abbot. At several other places in Scotland where there had been

23. *ES*, i, 448.
24. *KKES*, 267, 274f, 283, 288, 291; on the date of the note, 52.
25. See Royal Irish Academy, *Contributions to a Dictionary of the Irish language*.
26. *ES*, i, 471f.
27. Hay Fleming, nos. 3, 27, 30, 32-36, 43-48, 50, 60, 62.
28. Distribution maps 3 and 4 in *The Problem of the Picts*, ed. F. T. Wainwright (1955).
29. Ibid., 126.

PLATE I. ST ANDREWS: CATHEDRAL AND PRECINCTS FROM THE AIR.

PLATE II. THE ST ANDREWS SARCOPHAGUS.

In the year 1833, somewhere between St Rule's tower and the east gable of the medieval cathedral, were unearthed the remains of a richly carved sandstone tomb or shrine made in imitation of an antique sarcophagus. The tomb is 176cm. x 93cm. x 71cm high (excluding the restored cover or roof). It is thought to be the work of Pictish craftsmen and to date from about the year 800 AD. The decoration has parallels in Carolingian and Mercian art and in the Book of Kells. The large figure of David rending the lion's jaws may symbolize a Pictish king, perhaps the occupant of the shrine or its donor.

old monasteries, for instance at Abernethy and Brechin, we find in the twelfth century completely secular families bearing the title of *ab* or *abbas,* and sometimes traces of an *abthaine,* land that had been held by the monastery in the person of the abbot.[30] At St Andrews, in spite of a relatively full record, there are no such survivals, from which it may be inferred that the title ' abbot of Kinrimund ' had disappeared at an early date. The abbatial office, it seems, must have been absorbed in that of the bishop.[31] This development was possibly connected with the special status of the bishop of Kinrimund, to which we shall return later.

Several of the names in the St Andrews episcopal list are found also in more reliable sources, notably the Scottish Chronicle[32] and the Irish annals, though as the see is never named in these sources there is room for doubt as to whether all the early bishops were really in Kinrimund.[33] A group of *notitiae* relating to the *céli dé* of Loch Leven, written up in medieval St Andrews, names three eleventh-century ' bishops of St Andrews ' among their benefactors.[34] It also names Fothad son of Bran (Fothad I) as the bishop of St Andrews who took the Loch Leven *céli dé* under his protection by an arrangement described as *precarium,* a technical term possibly chosen by the St Andrews editor. If there is no mistake here the arrangement would have been made shortly before 955.[35]

The next bishop after Fothad, Cellach II, is said by Bower to have been ' the first to go to Rome for confirmation.' The claim suggests that there may have been some attempt in the second half of the tenth century to bring the church in Scotland into line with Roman ideas of ordination.[36] It is worth remarking that in the same reign, that of Culén son of Indulf (966-971), in which the Scottish Chronicle enters Cellach's accession, it tells us that Leot and Sluagadach (of whom unfortunately we know nothing) went to Rome.[37]

When Maelduin died in 1055 he was described as *ordan Gaedel o cleircib,* ' the glory of the Gaels from [their] priests.'[38] The annalist entitles him *epscop Alban,* and at 1093 Fothad II is called *ardepscop Alban,* ' high bishop of Alba.' The equivalent Latin title was said to have been inscribed on a book-shrine which there seems as good reason to attribute to Fothad II as to the tenth-century Fothad I.[39] The writer whom I have called ' the Augustinian ' said that he had found the title

---

30. At Armagh a father-to-son family of abbots can be traced after 966 (Kathleen Hughes, *The Church in Early Irish Society* (1966), 245f.).
31. See Gordon Donaldson, ' Scottish bishops' sees before the reign of David I,' in PSAS, lxxxvii, 113.
32. *KKES*, 251f.
33. Donaldson, 110.
34. *St A. Lib.,* 113ff.
35. Haddan and Stubbs, *Councils,* ii, 147f.; *Scott. Trad.,* 3. On *precarium,* see Ducange.
36. Donaldson, 117.
37. *KKES*, 252.
38. *ES,* i, 599. Cf. R. I. A. *Contributions* under *ord(d)an.* The translation in Haddan and Stubbs, ii, 174, is faulty
39. *Scott. Trad.,* 4.

B

in Latin (*summi archiepiscopi sive summi episcopi Scotorum*) ' in ancient as well as modern writings.'[40] The ' ancient writings ' were perhaps a version of the episcopal list, possibly already making the claim reported by Bower that every bishop in the list had been *primus et praecipuus in regno*.

The *Alba* of 1055 presumably meant the whole of the king's dominions north of Lothian and Strathclyde, but how long the bishops in Kinrimund had held this position it is impossible to say. We have seen that Cellach I's standing may have been something more limited. By Maelduin's time the kingdom included ' Lothian ' in its most extended sense,[41] and the bishop's immediate sphere of authority may already have extended to the Tweed, as did the medieval diocese.

The episcopate of Fothad II (c 1059-1093) coincided almost exactly with the reign of Malcolm III. He is described in one of the Loch Leven notes as *vir piissime recordationis cuius vita et doctrina tota regio Scotorum [= Alba above] feliciter est illustrata.*[42] It was believed at York in the first half of the twelfth century that Fothad II had professed subjection to the archbishop of York ' by counsel and command of Malcolm king of Scots and queen Margaret.'[43] If this is true, Malcolm, under the influence of his queen, must have conceded the claim made by York in 1072,[44] a claim which was stubbornly resisted by their son Alexander I.

It was almost certainly in the episcopate of Fothad II that a new church of St Andrew was built, a little to the south of the old burial ground and very probably on or near the site of an older church. The new church has been known since the sixteenth century as ' St Rule's ' or ' St Regulus.'[45] The relics of the apostle enumerated in the B version of the foundation legend[46] had probably been acquired by Kinrimund long before this church was built. Perhaps we may think of it as the *basilica sancti Andree apostoli* in Scotland that is compared with Jerusalem and Rome as a place of pilgrimage by the author of a Life of St Cadog in the eleventh century;[47] and it must have been in existence when queen Margaret endowed her ferry and hostels at the Forth for pilgrims to St Andrew's shrine. The design of the building reflects the king's connections with England. Though extremely small by the standards of a century later (*modica nimis, permodica*)[48] it is still impressive.[49] A parish church which is believed to have stood some sixty feet to the north,

40. *PS*, 190.
41. M. O. Anderson, ' Lothian and the early Scottish Kings,' in *SHR*, xxxix, 110.
42. *St A. Lib.*, 117, where the name is corrupted to *Modach*.
43. James Raine. ed., *Historians of the Church of York and its Archbishops*, ii, 363; Haddan and Stubbs, ii, 160. Cf. Raine, 126; A. O. Anderson, *Scottish Annals from English Chroniclers*, 131.
44. Haddan and Stubbs, ii, 159.
45. See Boece. *Historiae* VI 15. In the fifteenth century it was still ' the old church of St Andrew ' to distinguish it from the medieval cathedral; cf. *Scott. Trad.*, 4
46. *PS*, 183.
47. *Vitae Sanctorum Britanniae*, ed. Wade-Evans, 80, 82.
48. *PS*, 190; *St A. Lib.*, 122.
49. See Ronald G. Cant, ' The Building of the Cathedral,' below.

within the southern part of the old burial ground, may possibly have been there in the Celtic period.[50]

By the time of bishop Fothad II the church of Kinrimund was no doubt very wealthy, though we have scarcely any knowledge of its endowments except what can be inferred from medieval records. The nucleus was a generous tract of surrounding land known as the *Cursus Apri* said by the Augustinian to have been granted by the Pictish founder. Originally perhaps a boundary following the line taken by some legendary boar-hunt, it is used in the medieval period as a name for the land itself. It is sufficiently well defined for us by the names of places that are said to be within it.[51] These lie within the modern parishes of St Andrews and St Leonards, Cameron, Dunino, Ceres, and Kemback, forming a compact area about eleven miles by six. In the B version of the foundation legend the original *parochia* is the whole of Fife east of a line from Largo through Ceres to Naughton on the firth of Tay, an area which, though the definition looks arbitrary, would actually include many of the Fife lands of the medieval bishops. The legend names three other places, Forteviot on the Earn, 'Monichi' (perhaps near Monifieth in Angus[52]), and Kindrochet in Braemar (in the medieval diocese of Aberdeen), in a way that suggests some special relation to Kinrimund. All may have had churches dedicated to St Andrew, as Kindrochet certainly had. And all perhaps were, or had been, royal residences.

The medieval diocese of St Andrews was curiously intermixed with those of Dunkeld, Dunblane, and Brechin, and it has been convincingly suggested that the contorted boundaries were drawn so as to enclose scattered possessions of the four Celtic monasteries.[53] In the twelfth century and later we hear of ancient dues owed to the bishop of St Andrews from places between Tay and Dee.[54] Monymusk, beyond the Dee and in the medieval diocese of Aberdeen, had ties with the bishops of St Andrews that went back at least as far as the reign of Malcolm III.[55]

South of the Forth also ancient dues of cain and conveth were owed to bishops of St Andrews by a number of churches. Miss Ash draws attention to a tripartite division of demesne lands of the medieval bishops in Lothian, where baronies were based on Kirkliston (in West Lothian), Stow (Mid Lothian), and Tyningham (East Lothian). The last two at least were ancient ecclesiastical sites, and all could have come into the

---

50. Hay Fleming, pp. 32, 34.
51. The Augustinian shows that lands with which bishop Robert endowed the new priory in 1144 (see *St A. Lib.*, 122f.) lay within the *Cursus Apri*. A terrier of lands in the *Cursus*, drawn up in the thirteenth century, was printed in Pinkerton's *Enquiry* (2nd edn., 1814), 469f.
52. Skene, in *PSAS*, iv, 306; W. J. Watson, *Celtic Place-Names of Scotland*, 331.
53. Donaldson, 113.
54. For many of the references on which this and the next paragraph are based, I am indebted to an unpublished thesis by Marinell Ash: *The Administration of the Diocese of St Andrews*, 1202-1328 (Newcastle-upon-Tyne, 1972), chapter VIII, part 6.
55. See *RRS*, i, no. 47.

possession of bishops of Kinrimund before 1000 through the extension of the Scottish king's dominions.[56] Fothad II, we know, enjoyed *servitium* from Broxmouth, a few miles from Tyningham.[57]

By Fothad's time the church of St Andrew at Kinrimund was probably being served by secular, very possibly married, clergy. The *céli dé* formed a distinct community. They too may have abandoned life-long celibacy,[58] though even about 1144 they apparently lived apart from their wives ' after becoming Keledei.'[59] In the eleventh century they may have had a small church of their own, possibly on the Kirkhill where their later church stood.

Another group which must have been present in the eleventh century was that of the scholars, students for the priesthood presumably. They were still present as a body in 1120 when *scholastici* turned out to welcome Eadmer, bishop-elect.[60] Early in the thirteenth century *pauperes scolares* of St Andrews were claiming a right to ' ancient cain.'[61]

One other institution we know of is the *hospitale*. In 1144 it had only room for six guests, and perhaps it had always been small, though not without endowments including a share of the altar of St Andrew.[62] It may have occupied the same site as the Augustinians' *hospitale* which replaced it, just inside the western boundary of twelfth-century Kinrimund, and outside the cathedral and priory precinct.

In the same year, 1093, in which bishop Fothad died, Scotland lost king Malcolm III, queen Margaret, and their eldest son. During the uncertain years that followed, and throughout the reign of Edgar, the see was left vacant. Soon after Alexander I became king in 1107, he showed a real desire to bring the church in Scotland more into line with the rest of western Christendom, though his schemes for St Andrews foundered on his absolute refusal to allow the claim of York or Canterbury to superiority over Scottish bishops. We now find for the first time a Kinrimund bishop being denoted by the name of his see. A letter from Anselm, archbishop of Canterbury, in 1108, speaks of the elect *episcopus ecclesiae Sancti Andreae de Scotia.*[63] This was Turgot of Durham who occupied the see uneasily from 1109 until shortly before his death in 1115. There followed a five-year interregnum during which the revenues were administered by William, a monk of Bury St Edmunds, on behalf of the king and with severe detriment to the church.[64]

---

56. See M. O. Anderson in *SHR*, xxxix, 100ff.
57. See A. A. M. Duncan in *SHR*, xxxvii, 118ff.
58. Cf. Kathleen Hughes, *u.s.*, 227
59. *PS*, 189.
60. Haddan and Stubbs, ii, 200.
61. *St A. Lib.*, 316f.
62. Ibid., 123; *PS*, 189.
63. Haddan and Stubbs, ii, 172. Fothad II was alleged by a York writer to have called himself *Scottorum episcopus in sede Sancti Andreae apostoli* (ibid., 160).
64. Eadmer (ibid., 199; Anderson, *Scottish Annals*, 142).

In 1120 Eadmer of Canterbury (whose narrative is a principal source for these affairs) was elected bishop, but when he and the king could reach no agreement over Eadmer's relations with Canterbury the king renewed his commission to the monk William, and a month later ' such lands of the bishopric as remained had been wholly drained ' (*funditus evacuatis*). Although a compromise then allowed Eadmer to take possession of his see, the king so undermined his authority, and so despoiled the episcopal revenues, that in the following year (1121) Eadmer returned to Canterbury.

The Augustinian, on the other hand, speaks of Alexander as a generous benefactor. It seems that towards the end of his life the king must have regretted the damage done to his chief bishopric. This must, I think, be the period the Augustinian had in mind when he described an evil state of affairs that had existed at Kinrimund ' until the time of king Alexander ' and his benefactions.[65] There was then no resident [Roman] priesthood, no one to serve the altar of St Andrew or to say mass except when king or bishop was present. The *céli dé*, having no church of their own, were allowed to say mass in their own way in a ' corner ' of St Andrew's church, no doubt at a side altar as the Irish at Toul were allowed to do in the tenth century.[66] There were five individuals (*personae*) living entirely secular lives, who nevertheless had rights in the altar offerings and who must surely have represented, if they were not actually descended from, ordained priests of an earlier time. They treated their shares of the altar as heritable property, their only service being to render some hospitality to pilgrims and guests. Two of these shares, pertaining to two ' personages,' were among the endowments of the Augustinian priory in 1144.[67]

It was to put an end to this state of affairs that Alexander decided to found a religious house in Kinrimund, and to endow it by ' restoring ' the *Cursus Apri* with which the church had been originally endowed and which had since been ' taken away.'[68] A few months before his death in 1124 he caused Robert, prior of his Augustinian foundation at Scone, to be elected bishop, though difficulty over the claims of York caused the consecration to be postponed for three or four years. Robert was for many years short of revenue, but he contrived to enlarge the fabric of the church[69] by using his own share of the altar offerings together with *oblationes* which were now reclaimed from lay hands. If the meaning is that these also were altar offerings, the lay hands were presumably those of the five *personae*. He did not think it expedient to use the episcopal revenues, such as they were, for the endowment of a body of regular

65. *PS*, 189f.
66. Kathleen Hughes, *u.s.*, 253f.
67. *St A. Lib.*, 123.
68. *PS*, 190, reads *ex integro instituit*. The reading in *Chron. Bower*, *ex integro restituit*, seems preferable. The context seems to require that the Harleian MS's *oblata* be read as *ablata*.
69. During this period, 1127-1144, the *Kin-* of *Kinrimund* was replaced by *Kil-*, ' church ' (*Scott. Trad.*, 1).

clergy; and the *Cursus Apri* lands which king Alexander had intended for that purpose, and which were not counted as episcopal property,[70] were still partly alienated. Robert seems to have recovered them piecemeal as their lay possessors died off.[71] At last in 1144, under persuasion from king David, he used some of these lands to endow a priory of Augustinian canons.[72]

---

70. *de episcopatu non erat* (*PS*, 193).
71. Reading *obeuntibus* for the MS's *abeuntibus* (ibid.).
72. *St A. Lib.*, 122.

THE BUILDING OF ST ANDREWS CATHEDRAL

by

RONALD G. CANT

I

To understand how St Andrews cathedral came to be planned and constructed it is necessary to consider what Bishop Robert and his companions found in the way of ecclesiastical buildings when they came to the ancient religious settlement of Kinrimund in 1127.[1] According to their own account, by this time only one church was in actual use here, and beyond reasonable doubt this was the still surviving building known since the later Middle Ages (quite erroneously) as ' St Rule's chapel.'[2] There is now fairly general agreement that it can be dated to the eleventh century, in all probability the 1070s, and that it was intended primarily as a ' reliquary church ' consisting of a dignified but relatively small chapel (26 by 20 feet in internal dimensions) with a quite remarkably tall western tower (108 feet in height, not counting the spire, and 14½ feet square on plan). Within the chapel, and in close association with its principal altar, the relics of the apostle would be preserved, while the tower would serve as a landmark to guide pilgrims to this focus of the cult of Scotland's patron saint.[3]

When ' St Rule's ' was built there were probably several other churches in Kinrimund.[4] If so, all had passed out of use by 1127 and must have been regarded as beyond the possibility of repair or improvement. At all events, despite the quite serious structural problems involved, it was decided to enlarge ' St Rule's ' to serve as the cathedral and priory church of the new ecclesiastical order.[5] To effect this, an arch was formed in the east gable leading into a deep apsidal sanctuary (approximately 24 by 16 feet) while another arch was driven through the west wall of the tower similar to that already in existence in its east wall and a nave added (perhaps some 60 by 27 feet in internal dimensions). The choir (as it had

---

1. Robert, then prior of the Augustinian abbey of Scone, had been nominated to the bishopric by King Alexander I shortly before his death in 1124. He is generally thought to have been consecrated by the archbishop of York in 1127 and to have taken up residence in Kinrimund this same year. The ecclesiastics who accompanied him would almost certainly include some Augustinian canons from Scone to serve the principal church of the most important religious centre in Scotland. See G. W. S. Barrow, *The Kingdom of the Scots* (1973), 172.
2. This ' Augustinian account,' identified as such by Professor Barrow in 1952 (*Kingdom of Scots*, 222) is in *Chron. Picts-Scots*, 191-3. See article on ' The Celtic Church in Kinrimund,' by Dr Marjorie O. Anderson, above.
3. The dating of the building here is in accordance with the re-interpretation advanced by H. M. and Joan Taylor in Nora K. Chadwick (ed.), *Celt and Saxon* (1963), 216-20, and *Anglo-Saxon Architecture* (1965), 711-12, although the 1070s appear a more likely period than anything earlier. With this amendment the account in *Hist. Mon. Comm. (Fife)* (1933), 228-30, still provides a valuable description of the building.
4. See article by M. O. Anderson, above.
5. When Bishop Robert proceeded to the organisation and endowment of the priory in 1144 he stated that he had been ' concerned to enlarge the church, hitherto somewhat small (*permodica*) for divine worship ' (*St Andrews Liber*, 122-3).

11

become) would contain stalls for the Augustinian community, comparatively small in these early days, and one might assume that the nave was intended for use as a parish church, but this was not so either here or in the later cathedral. Instead, the parish of Kinrimund or Kilrymont, including the bishop's new ' burgh of St Andrew,' was served by a church of Holy Trinity (perhaps the successor of a Celtic foundation) situated only a short distance to the north-west of ' St Rule's.'[6]

As thus reconstructed and enlarged, ' St Rule's ' comprised nave, central tower, choir, and sanctuary. With a total internal length of approximately 125 feet (38.4 metres) it was a fair-sized church for its date and location and one of some architectural distinction but yet appreciably short of what might be thought appropriate, in the longer run, for the principal centre of the Scottish church.[7] It may accordingly be assumed that it was the intention of the new ecclesiastical authorities to proceed in due course with the construction of a ' definitive ' cathedral in the grand European manner.

When Bishop Robert carried the ' burgh of St Andrew ' into the second phase of its development, probably in the 1150s, with two wide streets converging towards the east, this may well have been done with the creation of a new cathedral in view.[8] But he died in 1159 and the actual foundation of the building was the work of his successor Bishop Arnold in 1160.[9] The site was on the level ground to the north-west of ' St Rule's ' (and Holy Trinity) and just east of the square in which the two main streets of the burgh met. Although the precinct—and indeed the whole east end of the extended town—remained outside the burgh jurisdiction, and the boundary between ' St Andrews ' and ' Kilrymont ' was apparently still well understood around 1200,[10] the name of the old religious settlement began to fall out of use thereafter and the name of the patron saint came to be applied to church, precinct, bishopric, and burgh alike.

II

The new cathedral was designed on the cruciform plan accepted as the almost invariable norm for all major medieval churches. Like many of its particular period, it was a somewhat elongated structure, overall and

---

6. The Augustinians seem to have been somewhat disinclined to become directly involved in parochial responsibilities, at least in their early days. See J. C. Dickinson, *The Origins of the Austin Canons* (1950), esp. 241; also I. B. Cowan, ' The Religious and the Cure of Souls in Medieval Scotland ' in *Scot. Church Hist. Soc. Recs.*, XIV (1966-68), 215-30. The site of the church of Holy Trinity, appropriated to the priory c 1160 (*St A. Liber*, 132), was midway between ' St Rule's ' and the later cathedral (W. E. K. Rankin, *The Parish Church of the Holy Trinity, St Andrews* (St Andrews Univ. Publns., LII, 1955), 14-19.
7. In their first form Glasgow cathedral and Holyrood abbey were unaisled cruciform structures, the former some 112 feet and the latter perhaps 140 feet in length. See R. A. Ralegh Radford, *Glasgow Cathedral* (1970), 17, 38, and J. S. Richardson, *The Abbey and Palace of Holyroodhouse* (1971), 14 and plan.
8. See R. G. Cant in *St Andrews Preservation Trust Annual Report and Year Book for 1973* (1974), 12.
9. *Chron. Wyntoun*, IV, 426-7.
10. *St A. Liber*, 151

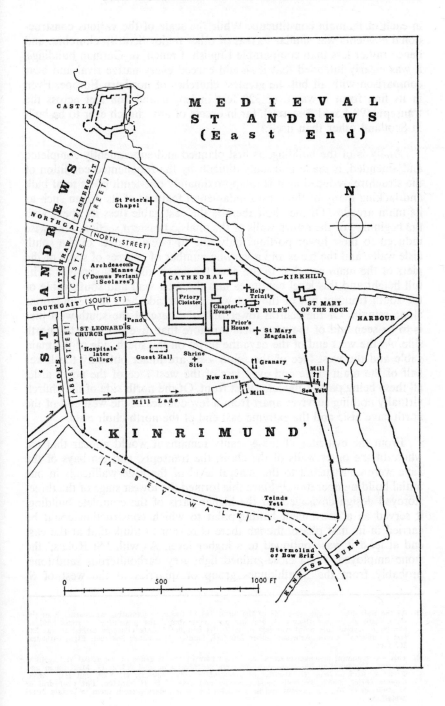

in each of its main constituents. While the scale of the various constructional elements was similar to that of other major Scottish churches, and hence rather less than comparable English, French, or German buildings, it was clearly intended that it should exceed every native rival and bear comparison with all but the greatest churches of northern Europe. Even in its first form it was over 320 feet in length and 168 feet across the transepts (98.4 x 51.2 metres), far in excess of any church ever to be built in Scotland other than itself.[11]

Analysis of the building, as first planned and subsequently completed and amended, is made unusually difficult by the fragmented condition of the structure, reduced as it is to approximately one-tenth of its total bulk and lacking many of the most fundamental features of its design such as its main arcades. Of the choir there is the east gable (less its apex) with the beginning of the return walls of the unaisled eastern section, otherwise reduced to their lower portions only, the first few courses of the south aisle walls, and the bases and a varying number of courses of some of the piers of the main arcades. In the nave the south aisle wall survives to its full height and this level continues into the west wall and south gable of the south transept but of the east wall and arcade here the foundations alone remain. Of the central tower only the base of the south-west pier is to be seen and of the nave piers no more than five bases on the north side. At the west end of the nave the turret on the south side of the main gable and the west face of the south aisle are intact but only the lower half of the main gable and even less of the west face of the north aisle, all these being part of the later west front. Of the north side of the church virtually nothing survives apart from a few courses of the west end of the north nave aisle and the extreme east end of the north choir aisle.

From the evidence of these scanty remains it would appear that the whole of the outer walls of the choir, the transepts, and ten bays of the nave were constructed to the general level of the aisle wallheads in one initial building operation.[12] Since this formed the lowest stage of the three-storeyed design envisaged for the higher parts of the complete building, it served as a convenient halting-point to which construction could be carried in its first phase, though there is reason to think that at the east end at least it was continued to a higher level. As with ' St Rule's,' the stone employed was a close-grained light-grey carboniferous sandstone, probably from the Strathkinnes group of quarries to the west of St

11. As the wall-shaft on the west side of the tenth bay of the nave (counting westwards) is of the same form as those further east, and not an ' angle-shaft,' the possibility of some kind of extension beyond this point was left open. In its completed state Glasgow cathedral was 285 feet in internal length, Arbroath abbey 280 feet, Dunfermline abbey 268 feet, Elgin cathedral 263 feet.

12. This was common medieval practice, confirmed here by the evidence of the actual architectural remains. The building has been authoritatively described and analysed in D. MacGibbon and T. Ross, *Ecclesiastical Architecture of Scotland* (3 vols., 1896-7), II, 5-29, and *Hist. Mon. Comm. (Fife)*, 230-7. To both these accounts and that of S. H. Cruden, *The Cathedral of St Andrews* (1970), the present article is indebted even if differing from them in certain interpretations.

Andrews.[13] This was cut as squared *ashlar* to the proportions usual for the time and laid in regular courses packed with a rubble core. Included in the lower courses of the masonry of the east gable were fragments of Celtic carved work.[14]

This eastern gable of the church was flanked by square angle-turrets planned to contain newel-stairs linking the upper levels of triforium, clerestory, and parapet walk when these came to be built. Similar turrets were located at the north-west corner of the north transept and the south-west corner of the south transept. Here the stair survives, beginning at ground level, and it is likely that a similar arrangement would prevail in the north transept. As was not uncommon with great churches of its period, the east end projected for two unaisled bays beyond the remainder of the choir, and its solid side walls continued westwards for one further bay.[15] As a result the eastmost bays of the choir aisles were enclosed on the north, east, and south, facilitating their use as chapels. The remaining five bays to the west were planned to be divided by arcades supporting the triforium and clerestory of the main choir structure. Each of the transepts was given an eastern aisle which, for the three bays that projected north and south of the choir aisles, provided accommodation for further chapels. The nave was to be aisled in continuation of the choir.

This early work is in a mature but rather austere romanesque style employing a panelled design for each bay, inside and out, with a single rather high round-headed window as the main architectural feature. These windows were framed externally by banded nook-shafts with foliated capitals supporting the outer arch.[16] This design was carried up into the ' triforium stage ' of the north and south walls of the unaisled eastern section of the choir and the initial construction would also seem to have comprised the whole of the intervening east gable.[17] Here the two lower stages were designed with a group of three romanesque lancets and it has usually been accepted that a similar arrangement continued into the next stage (corresponding to ' clerestory level ').[18] In actual fact the sur-

---

13. The quarries cover a wide area with distinct variations of colour and quality of stone. The rubble infilling and some of the ashlar, especially in later work, is a creamy-brown sandstone of rather poorer quality from the coastal outcrops nearer at hand. In 1435 the priory obtained permission to take stone from the quarry at Kinkell (*St A. Liber*, 423). The romanesque ashlar was dressed with diagonal ' droving,' the transitional and gothic work with vertical, but the original face of the stone has generally weathered away. In consequence of this, only one mason's mark has been identified, on the first pier of the north choir arcade from the crossing. This takes the form of a five-pointed star drawn with a continuous interlacing line.

14. See article by M. O. Anderson, above.

15. The whole three eastmost bays may initially have projected clear of the main body of the choir, for the east walls of the aisles merely ' butt ' against the side walls of the main structure. Even so, the plan must have been amended to its present form before building was very far advanced, quite possibly to secure a more satisfactory arrangement of the chapels here, and a limited structural tie was provided by the angle-shafts for the aisle vaulting.

16. The stones forming the bands were ' dooked ' into the wall behind instead of forming an integral part of it as was the case in most other churches.

17. This conclusion is suggested by the homogeneity of the romanesque design of all the architectural details involved, including the flanking turrets. The apex of the gable, the line of which is indicated by the deep grooves cut in the stonework of the turrets to house the timbers of the main roof, is likely to have been completed later. It probably contained a wheel window, although in practical terms this would light no more than the loft above the choir vault.

18. MacGibbon and Ross, *Eccl. Arch.*, I, 9, 10.

viving evidence indicates that while the central window here might well have been of similar dimensions to those below, the flanking windows were of lesser width and height.[19] This was clearly done so as to fit the design under the choir vault which would accordingly seem to have been envisaged from the inception of the building.

The completion of this first stage of the work appears to have occupied some thirty years, to about 1190.[20] Thereafter the great piers and arches of the crossing were probably completed as an abutment for the arcades and superstructure of the choir and transepts and perhaps the first four bays of the nave. The crossing arches, intended to support the mass of the central tower (which would very likely only be carried to just above the level of the main roofs at this stage) were carved with Norman ' dog-tooth ' ornament of truly monumental scale.[21] On the other hand, the piers of the choir arcades and the few surviving fragments of the cleres-tory adjoining the east gable are of transitional character, turning from romanesque towards early gothic, and strongly resembling corresponding portions of the nave of Jedburgh abbey.[22]

Like St Andrews, Jedburgh was an Augustinian house. While the choir, crossing, and outer walls of the remainder of its church were completed in the romanesque style (about 1180), the arcades and super-structure of the nave are transitional work of the 1190s approximately contemporary with that at St Andrews. The dimensions and spacing of the piers are almost exactly the same in each case, and although those at St Andrews must have been slightly higher, both are of ' composite ' construction, the four major members being of identical ' keel-shaped ' section. At Jedburgh, the four minor members are also keel-shaped while those at St Andrews are round, but the resemblances so far outweigh the differences that the design of the abbey nave may be taken as a reasonable guide to that of the cathedral choir.

The arches of the Jedburgh arcades are pointed and moulded to correspond to the profile of the supporting piers, but in the case of the triforium the twin pointed openings are subsidiary elements within arches of semi-circular form. At clerestory level there is a divergence of design arising from the fact that the St Andrews choir was vaulted whereas the Jedburgh nave had a timber roof. Thus in the latter the windows are twin lancets set within a uniform arcaded treatment within and without. At St Andrews, however, the vaulting dictated that each bay had a single tall lancet window, its inner arch being considerably ' stilted ' above the

19. The relationship of the three tiers to one another, shown as virtually uniform by MacGibbon and Ross, op. cit., 10, was actually of considerable architectural subtlety.
20. The date is suggested by the stylistic changes in the structure.
21. D. Hay Fleming, St Andrews Cathedral Museum (1930), 179 and fig. 108, where the opinion of Thomas Ross is given that the surviving details ' formed part of a diagonal arch under the great tower.' Since it is unlikely that the tower was vaulted, they may more probably have been incorporated as composite elements in the main arches of the structure.
22. Jedburgh abbey is described and illustrated in MacGibbon and Ross, Eccl. Arch., I, 398-416, and Hist. Mon. Comm. (Roxburgh) (1956), I, 194-209.

ST.ANDREWS
CATHEDRAL
East Gable
Interior

Conjectural
Reconstruction
of Original
Design

0   5   10   15   20   25 feet

columns supporting it and the smaller arches on each side and its outer arch interrupting or varying the sequence of the ' blind ' arcading at this level.[23]

Between the inner clerestory arches and the main wall was the usual wall-passage, still visible where it emerges from the angle-turrets at the east end. Below these openings, and like them linked by wall-passages crossing the base of the windows in the upper part of the east gable, are similar openings at triforium level, but the passages here would be limited to the unaisled eastern section of the choir. When the aisled section further west was reached the space over the aisle vaults and under the outer timber roof would allow for the customary ' triforium-gallery ' and obviate the need for wall-passages.[24]

In a conventual church of this period the aisleless eastern section of the choir was normally designed as a *presbytery* containing the high altar. Such may well have been the original intention and just possibly the initial arrangement at St Andrews when the building was first brought into use, but from an early date and perhaps from the outset this part of the church served as a ' reliquary chapel ' of the patron saint.[25] As an ornamental embellishment the lower part of the walls was lined with arcading, apparently of the same form as that on the west wall of the south transept where the semi-circular arches are interlaced in a manner much favoured in late romanesque work.[26] Above this the main tier of windows seems to have been set in a pillared arcade like that in the south transept but unstilted. By contrast, the triforium consisted of relatively plain windows, one in each bay, linked by a wall-passage. The design of the choir clerestory and of the east gable has already been discussed. If the use of the east end as a reliquary chapel is accepted the high altar is likely to have been placed against a *reredos* screen clear of the entrance to this chapel and the flanking chapels in the east ends of the choir aisles. Westwards of the high altar, on the south side of the choir, would be the bishop's throne, and west of this again on both sides the canons' stalls. These would be ' returned ' against the *pulpitum* or choir screen which probably stood in the eastern arch of the crossing.

This was as much of the structure as was strictly necessary for it to be brought into use as a cathedral and priory church, perhaps about the year

---

23. In the interior this arrangement is akin to that of the choir clerestory at Jedburgh (see note 28 below). At St Andrews, however, the treatment has a definite functional basis, whereas at Jedburgh it is more a matter of design.
24. The point is elaborated to this extent in view of the statement in *Hist. Mon. Comm.* (*Fife*), 234, that ' the nave triforium, unlike that in the choir, had no passage.' In actual fact the arrangement of the triforium gallery in the nave must have been very similar to that throughout the greater part of the choir.
25. See chapter by David McRoberts on ' The Glorious House of St Andrew,' below.
26. The arcading seems to have been removed in the course of Prior Haldenstone's reconstruction, but the bases of the pillars and traces of the arch ' springers ' survive. The height of the arcading as indicated by the latter is inconsistent with the ' ingoes ' or embrasures below the main windows in the side walls, but the stonework here appears to derive almost entirely from a nineteenth-century repair, as may the architectural treatment. There are vestiges of similar arcading in the wall of the *slype* adjoining the south transept.

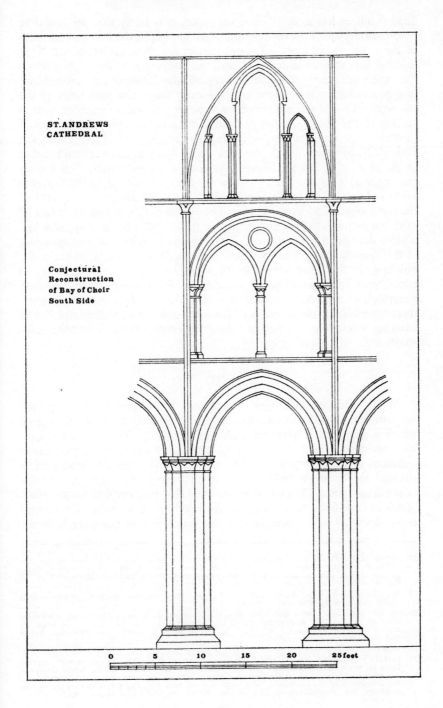

ST.ANDREWS
CATHEDRAL

Conjectural
Reconstruction
of Bay of Choir
South Side

0   5   10   15   20   25 feet

1230,[27] but as has already been suggested, it is likely that this building phase also included the completion of the transepts, the four eastern bays of the nave, and at least the lower part of the great central tower. That this last was vaulted is doubtful, and the high roofs of the transepts and the nave were clearly of timber. As regards the design of the ' croce-kirk,' it appears that in their main and triforium stages the west sides of the transepts followed the pattern of the flanking walls of the unaisled eastern section of the choir. On the east sides the arcades and triforium would probably resemble the corresponding western section of the choir. On both sides, however, the clerestory is more likely to have resembled that in the choir of Jedburgh, likewise supporting a timber roof. This has on the inner side of the wall-passage an open arcade of pointed arches alternately stilted to frame the windows.[28] Of the design of the bays of the nave arcade and superstructure completed in this period, little can be said, but as the latest part of the fabric to be completed it may have had a more developed gothic form.[29] The south nave aisle shows the springing of the vaulting that probably extended throughout the whole aisles of the building. If the construction of these vaults was, as seems likely, in accordance with the original intention of the builders, their insertion nevertheless involved a considerable alteration of the pre-existing structure, especially at the junction of the nave and the south transept.[30] The vaulting was of ' quadripartite ' design springing from composite wall-shafts with ' curly-kail ' caps.

III

While work on their new church was proceeding in this way, the Augustinians would continue to occupy ' St Rule's,' to the south side of which a group of conventual buildings, probably of timber, may have been attached.[31] In accordance with established practice, the permanent buildings of the priory would be grouped round a square cloister court situated in the angle between the south transept and the nave of the ' definitive ' church. If so, it is remarkable that no provision to this effect seems to have been made in the initial building phase. While the roman-esque doorway in the first bay on the south side of the nave is in the

27. Bishop Malvoisin, who was responsible for the completion of this eastern part of the new cathedral, was buried within it in 1238 (*Chron. Wyntoun*, V, 94, 95). His predecessor, Roger Beaumont, who died in 1202, was the last bishop to be buried in ' the old church ' as ' St Rule's ' came to be called after ' the new church ' was brought into use (ibid., 58, 59).
28. *Hist. Mon. Comm.* (*Roxburgh*), I, 209 and fig. 234. At St Andrews, however, the intermediate arches may quite possibly have been omitted.
29. On the other hand, when this work was being completed, it was evidently not considered necessary to alter the romanesque design of the nave aisle windows, as occurred when the remainder of the nave was put in hand. If so, the design of the arcades and superstructure may well have been more conservative.
30. Noted in MacGibbon and Ross, *Eccl. Arch.*, II, 14.
31. In 1144 x 1153 King David I authorised his sheriff there to provide the canons with material from his wood of Clackmannan ' for their buildings ' (*St A. Liber*, 183-4). While this grant was subsequently renewed, at the time in question, between the completion of ' St Rule's ' and the foundation of the ' definitive ' cathedral, it must have been for the temporary conventual buildings. The ' Augustinian account ' (*Chron. Picts-Scots*, 191) speaks of a cloister, c 1144.

PLATE III. THE TWO CATHEDRALS AT ST ANDREWS

Like several other ecclesiastical centres in Europe, St Andrews had two cathedrals. A large cathedral was constructed to satisfy the aspirations of the high Middle Ages but ancient historical association and innate piety demanded that the smaller and more ancient cathedral should also be preserved. Here we see the ruined east end of the large medieval church and, in the background, the remains of the small earlier cathedral with its lofty tower. In medieval records the smaller church is usually referred to as ' the old church ' but Hector Boece speaks of it as the church of St Rule—*diui Reguli templum*—and this title has been adopted by many modern writers.

PLATE IV. THE WEST FRONT OF ST ANDREWS CATHEDRAL.

The fragmentary remains of the west front of the cathedral as reconstructed by Bishop William Wishart (1271-1279).

appropriate position for the east processional door of a cloister, it was designed as though to stand in the open instead of under the cover of a cloister walk.[32] Moreover, when the cloister came to be inserted, this involved the raising of the sills of the aisle windows of the nave and those in the west wall of the south transept.[33] Most remarkable of all, the night stair leading down into the transept from the dormitory on the upper floor of the east cloister range, cuts across the design of the wall-arcading and has all the appearance of a clumsy afterthought.[34]

In view of the uneasy relations that developed between the bishop and the Augustinians, to which Professor Barrow has directed illuminating attention,[35] the possibility suggests itself that the former may have been contemplating providing his cathedral with a chapter of secular canons, perhaps drawn from the ' Culdees.' This would then have left the Augustinians permanently in their temporary quarters at ' St Rule's.' In the outcome, however, they moved into accommodation in the cloister court attached to the ' new church ' by Prior John White (1236-58),[36] and although the ' Culdees ' continued to claim a share in episcopal elections throughout the thirteenth century, they did so as the corporation of ' the Collegiate Church and Chapel Royal of the Blessed Mary of the Rock ' located outside the precinct to the north-east. Indeed, the policy of the two bishops, Roger Beaumont (1198-1202) and William Malvoisin (1202-38), whose antipathy to the Augustinians was most apparent, seems to have been directed to this end rather than to intrude the ' Culdees ' into the cathedral at their expense.

While this alternative possibility, and the supporting evidence, deserve careful examination, it is very difficult to believe that the work on the new cathedral from 1160 onwards had been done without the participation of the Augustinians or the intention that they should occupy the building when complete. Although the bishops continued to play a leading part in advancing the work, its actual organisation and the supervision of construction rested with the officer concerned with such matters in

---

32. This is suggested by the surmounting ' weather-table ' designed to throw water off the top of the structure, as pointed out many years ago by Dr J. S. Richardson, but it may be that this was no more than a convention of design.

33. As originally designed, the windows evidently ran down to the level of their inner sills, giving a proportion not unlike those in the east end of the church. While the infilling has been faced with ashlar on the outside, the alteration is quite apparent in the construction of the masonry and in the inside there is little more than a rough rubble backing, doubtless intended to be concealed by plaster.

34. Although all previous accounts identify the night stair with the newel access-stair in the south-west corner of the transept, such an arrangement would not only be dangerously inconvenient but at variance with accepted practice. In any event part of the foundation of the night stair is still to be seen, with the entry to the access stair clearly passing under its southern end, and the mutilation of the arcading forms a line corresponding to the normal positioning of a night stair.

35. G. W. S. Barrow, ' The Clergy at St Andrews ' in Kingdom of Scots, 210-32.

36. Chron. Bower, I, 368.

21

C

corporations of regular clergy, the sacrist.[37] And throughout the period of the building of ' the new church ' there are records of grants by successive bishops, Malvoisin included, to the priory canons for this purpose.[38] Thus the initial omission of provision for conventual buildings must have been due to no more than a misunderstanding, not without parallels elsewhere, between the builders and their clients, or to the fact that the early Augustinians did not envisage a claustral arrangement such as was eventually provided.

When the Augustinians prepared to move into their new quarters (around the year 1250) they would find, in addition to the architectural deficiencies already mentioned, and presumably by now resolved, that the nave of the church as constructed to date was not long enough to provide an abutment for the west range of the cloister court. It was accordingly decided to add four bays to the west end of the nave (possibly in accordance with an earlier intention) giving it fourteen bays in all and the complete church the remarkable length of 391 feet (119.2 metres).[39] The necessity for this work should have been apparent as soon as the claustral buildings were put in hand, since cloister courts were almost invariably square on plan with the chapter house situated in the centre of the east side just beyond the end of the south transept and so dictating the dimensions of the court.

By this time medieval ecclesiastical architecture had moved fully into its gothic phase but in the relatively simple form known as ' First Pointed.' The conventual buildings of the priory had been designed in this style

---

37. Bishop Richard (1163-78), in fulfilment of the responsibility on him ' to provide for the advancement of the work on the new church of St Andrew,' and in exercise of his powers as feudal superior of the burgh, forbade its officers or burgesses to detach masons, hewers, quarriers, or others engaged on the building without the express permission of the canon in charge of the work (*St A. Liber*, 338). The sacrist commonly bore the additional title of ' master of the fabric ' and although no early instances of this seem to have been recorded, in 1435, under Prior Haldenstone, Robert Brog, a canon of the priory, was ' sacrist and master of the fabric ' (ibid., 419), while in the cathedral museum is the tombstone (long preserved in St Leonard's church) of John Ruglyn, ' canon and master of the fabric,' 1502 (*Hist. Mon. Comm. (Fife)*, 248).

Direction of construction and repair (under the master of the fabric) was the responsibility of a master-mason, and it seems just possible that ' Master Walter, mason,' who witnessed a charter by David earl of Huntingdon to the priory 1189 x 1199 (*St A. Liber*, 239), may have been directing work on the building at this time. At a later date the famous John Morrow (or Jean Moreau) ' had in keeping all mason work of St Andrews ' and several other important churches (see J. S. Richardson, *The Medieval Scottish Stone Carver* (1964), 36, 44, 57-8), but the actual construction would be undertaken by ' working stone-masons ' of the type represented by the early fifteenth-century effigy in the cathedral museum (Richardson, *op. cit.*, 15, plate 17; Fleming, *Cath. Museum*, 56-8 and fig. 89).

38. Bishop Malvoisin was concerned in a double grant, from the rectory of Scoonie church and the whole of the Whitsun ' processional offerings ' in the diocese (*St A. Liber*, 160, 161). The second grant had been made earlier by Bishop Richard (above, note 37) without the specific assignment now made ' to the fabric of the new work of the church of St Andrew,' but he had in fact donated land on the western outskirts of St Andrews for this purpose (ibid., 141). Under Bishop David Bernham (1239-53) the Scoonie grant was extended to include the entire rectory (ibid., 168). Further grants towards the fabric included the rectories of Lathrisk and Forgan (ibid., 173, 174) under Bishop Gamelin (1255-71), while the burning of the cathedral in 1378 led to the assignment of several other rectories already appropriated to the priory to the ensuing reconstruction.

39. As already mentioned (above, note 11), the ten-bay nave was not ' definitive ' but seems to have been laid down with some kind of eventual extension in view. Indeed, the foundations westwards of this point could well date from the initial building phase. In this connection, it might be regarded as significant that the well sunk within the structure for use by its builders is exactly midway between the east gable and the west gable-line of the fourteen-bay nave. In the British Isles, only Norwich cathedral achieved a nave of equal constructional extent, even if the actual length is slightly greater (250 feet to 230 feet) through the use of a larger ' building module.'

which was now employed in the extension and completion of the church. As part of this work the aisle windows of the nave from the fifth to the tenth bays inclusive (counting from east to west) were rebuilt in gothic form, as was the west processional door from the cloister.[40] These alterations may well have been contemporaneous with the claustral buildings. But the construction of the main arcades and the upper parts of the nave seems to have been delayed until the time of Bishop William Wishart (1271-9) who must thus take the credit for advancing towards a conclusion a project on which his predecessors had been engaged for well over a century.[41]

Scarcely had the west front of the church been completed when it was blown down by a gale, and when it was rebuilt it was withdrawn two bays to the east, so reducing the nave to twelve bays, the minimum necessary to give a firm abutment to the west range of the cloister.[42] The side walls of the discarded bays were then used to support a three-arched vaulted porch or *narthex* across the lower part of the new front. This feature, almost without parallel in medieval Scottish church architecture, would do something to redeem the relative plainness of the principal front of the cathedral.[43] What form it may originally have been intended to take is unknown, although a church of its importance might have been expected to terminate in twin western towers.[44] As completed, however, the west front above the narthex showed little more than a cross-section of the building, the high central gable being flanked by octagonal turrets and the 'lean-to' outline of the aisles. The turrets contained newel-stairs giving access to the upper parts of the structure, but only the northern stair began at ground level.

In view of the extensive rebuilding of the nave that took place a century after its completion and the almost total disappearance of its

---

40. The rebuilding of these windows seems to have been done in association with the raising of their sills. By contrast with the earlier infilling of the windows further to the east, the work here was done, inside as well as outside, in good ashlar. Despite this, the alteration is perfectly apparent in the stonework, especially on the inner face. There were also adjustments of the buttress details on each side of the tenth bay. Interestingly the panel design of the earlier bays was continued in the interior of the new work, but as this abutted on the adjoining conventual buildings there were no windows and in the eleventh and twelfth bays the panels were eventually modified into blank arched recesses; the first design is more evident in the abandoned thirteenth bay. One slight difference of design is that in the new work the wall-shafts have a fillet on the central member.
41. *Chron. Wyntoun*, V, 127, speaks of Wishart as having caused to be built ' ner al the body of the kyrk,' that is the nave, the work beginning at ' the thride piller fra the chaunscellar dur.' The latter term referred to the entry to the ritual choir of the church in the *pulpitum* which in Wyntoun's time (in the early fifteenth century) still stood on the eastern side of the crossing. Hence Wishart's arcades probably continued westwards from the third bay of the south arcade but, since the arcade no longer exists, we cannot be certain of this.
42. *Chron. Bower*, I, 360-1
43. On this and certain other points relating to the nave, see the article by D. Hay Fleming in *Proc. Soc. Antiq. Scot.*, XLIX (1914-15), 209-21. The statement in *Hist. Mon. Comm. (Fife)*, 234, that the narthex was two bays in depth is unsupported by the architectural evidence which suggests that it was of one bay. The only other examples seem to have been the galilee at Melrose abbey in its earlier form (*Hist. Mon. Comm. (Roxburgh)*, ii, 267 and fig. 350) and the simple lean-to construction across the west front of Dundrennan abbey (J. S. Richardson, *The Abbey of Dundrennan* (1937), 8). At Culross abbey the west end of the nave may have formed some kind of vestibule (*Hist. Mon. Comm. (Fife)*, 72).
44. While such a consideration might have been one of the reasons inclining the original builders to leave the west end of the nave incomplete, the remains of the fourteen-bay plan do not seem to indicate any provision for towers and the collapse of the front suggests that its design was probably not unlike its replacement. It may be worthy of note that the nave of Norwich cathedral was finished without towers.

main arcades and superstructure, it is difficult to determine the details of its early design. It clearly included the customary three storeys, the form of the main arcade, triforium, and clerestory being indicated, in part at least, by the fragments attached to the west gable. These confirm that the piers were of composite form, the major members being of semi-circular section, the minor strongly keel-shaped, and the caps bell-shaped like those surmounting the wall-ribs of the two westmost bays of the south aisle. With slight variations of detail the general effect of the arcades would be not dissimilar to those of the nave of Dunblane cathedral, generally accepted as being approximately contemporary in date.[45] The triforium seems to have contained two twin-arched openings in each bay as in the choir of Glasgow cathedral, also of this period,[46] but the clerestory windows, although linked by a continuous wall-passage, were apparently separate two-light openings similar to those in the aisles.[47] The aisles were ceiled with simple, quadripartite vaulting but the main nave was finished with an open timber roof that may have resembled the choir roof of Glasgow cathedral in its original (thirteenth century) form.[48] In the interior of the west gable, just over the main doorway, was an arcaded gallery similar to those at Arbroath and Holyrood abbeys and presumably intended to serve a like purpose in the observances of Palm Sunday.[49] In addition to the west door there was a north doorway to the nave,[50] possibly with a porch, immediately opposite the west processional door, as was commonly the case with conventual churches. There might also have been a door in the end of the north transept.

With the whole building now available for use, a rearrangement took place in the lay-out of its eastern half by moving the 'ritual choir' towards the west. At a later date the *pulpitum* was evidently located in the western arch of the crossing so that the canons' stalls, as in many other conventual churches, stood under the tower and in the western part of the structural choir. And considering the importance of their corporate worship in the life of the cathedral such a reallocation of space might be thought only right and proper. While the aisles of the choir, the transepts and nave provided space for chapels associated with subsidiary altars,

45. MacGibbon and Ross, *Eccl. Arch.*, II, 86-112, esp. 96, where an elevation of a bay of the nave is given in fig. 516.
46. The design of the choir triforium is discussed and illustrated by John Honeyman in G. Eyre Todd (ed.), *The Book of Glasgow Cathedral* (1898), 263-5. See also MacGibbon and Ross, *Eccl. Arch.*, II, 160-203, P. MacGregor Chalmers, *Glasgow Cathedral* (1914), and R. A. Ralegh Radford, *Glasgow Cathedral*.
47. While this suggestion is to some extent conjectural, the space occupied by the window in the bay design is comparable to that of the aisle windows and would necessitate the use of a central mullion.
48. The original nave roof was burned in 1378. Its replacement may also have resembled the choir roof at Glasgow as remodelled in the early sixteenth century when the open trussed construction of cusped section was given a more simple gothic curve and lined with boarding ornamented with moulded ribs. See W. T. Oldrieve, 'The Ancient Roof of Glasgow Cathedral' in *Proc. Soc. Antiq. Scot.*, L (1915-16), 155-72; also Chalmers, *op. cit.*, 60, and Radford, *op. cit.*, 32.
49. See R. L. Mackie and S. H. Cruden, *Arbroath Abbey* (1954), 34 and note. At St Andrews the gallery continued beyond the central nave, the south aisle (and perhaps the north aisle too in its day) having an arched aperture at this level at the west end just below the line of the vault.
50. *Chron. Wyntoun*, V, 127.

PLATE V. SOUTH WALL OF NAVE: ST ANDREWS CATHEDRAL.

The wall of the south aisle of the nave still survives at St Andrews. As in other medieval monastic sites in Scotland, this wall survives because it protected the cloister garth which the post-Reformation occupants had transformed into dwelling houses and gardens. Between the eighth and ninth bays of the wall (from the west) there is a change in the style of architecture used, the Romanesque giving way to early Gothic.

PLATE VI. ST ANDREWS CATHEDRAL: THE EAST GABLE.

The interior of the eastern gable of the cathedral shows traces of the original design which w
replaced by the new fenestration of Prior Haldenstone's reconstruction. The massive rema
of the tomb of Archbishop James Stewart show the floor level of the chapel of the relics
remodelled by Haldenstone. The chapel would be screened off from the church by the h
altar and its retable. The three steps which led up to the vanished high altar indicate the fl
levels of sanctuary and choir. The broken remains of the tomb of Archbishop William Sche
can be seen in the centre in front of the altar steps.

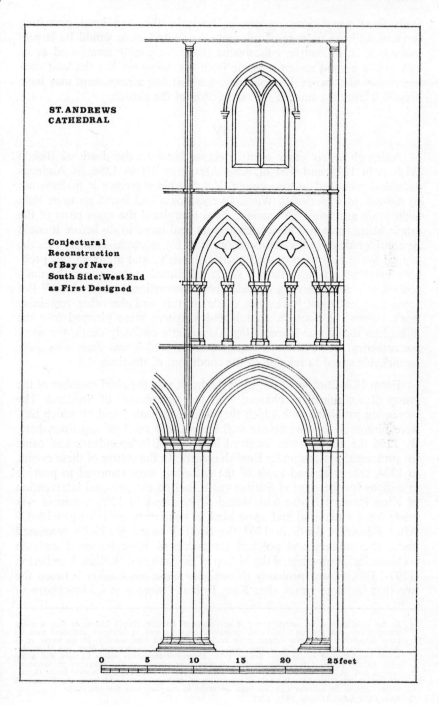

ST. ANDREWS
CATHEDRAL

Conjectural
Reconstruction
of Bay of Nave
South Side: West End
as First Designed

0   5   10   15   20   25 feet

apart from processions on greater festivals, the occasional preaching services, and the passage of pilgrims, the central nave would be largely unused. It is, of course, conceivable that it originally terminated at its east end in a rood screen separate from the *pulpitum*, but the later conjunction of the two at this point suggests that this arrangement may have prevailed from the time of the completion of the church.

IV

Although seven years were to elapse between the death of Bishop Wishart in 1279 and that of King Alexander III in 1286, St Andrews cathedral remained unconsecrated. Yet this circumstance is perhaps not so difficult to understand. Wishart's episcopate had lasted no more than eight years and while he seems to have completed the main parts of the fabric, there must still have been a great deal more to do before it could be considered ready for consecration. It is, for example, unlikely that the central tower had been carried to its full height, and although this probably involved no more than a single additional storey above the main roofs it was nevertheless a considerable constructional undertaking.[51] But some progress must have been made on this and the other remaining work before the Scottish church and kingdom were plunged into the difficulties that ensued from King Alexander's untimely death, for when the cathedral was eventually consecrated in 1318 it was done with quite remarkable speed in relation to the conditions of the time.

From 1286 Bishop Fraser of St Andrews was the chief member of the group of six guardians charged with the government of Scotland. The increasing problems with which they were confronted and by which they were ultimately overborne are well known and need no repetition here. By 1296 the country was involved in a war of independence and came for prolonged periods under English control. In the course of these events, in 1304, the outer lead roofs of the cathedral were removed to provide munitions for the siege of Stirling castle, but on the personal intervention of King Edward I who had visited St Andrews in 1296, payment was made for the material and some kind of temporary covering provided.[52] After Edward's death in 1307 the Scottish cause gradually recovered under the military and political leadership of King Robert I and the ecclesiastical leadership of the bishop of St Andrews, William Lamberton (1297-1328). It was probably through the close association between the two that just four years after King Robert's victory at Bannockburn in

---

51. So far as is known, no central tower of any medieval Scottish church had more than a single storey above the roofline. The most ambitious example was at Glasgow cathedral with its lofty fifteenth-century spire replacing an earlier timber and lead version. If the tower at St Andrews ever had a spire it is also likely to have been of timber and lead, but if so this would be destroyed in the great fire of 1378. Thereafter the tower seems to have had a flat roof. In the siege of the castle in 1547 cannon were placed on the tower of St Salvator's college and on ' the Abbey Kirk,' that is almost certainly the cathedral central tower (Knox, *History*, I, 95; Pitscottie, *History*, II, 89). Such an arrangement would imply the absence of spires, that of St Salvator's having been destroyed in the course of the operations.
52. *Bain's Calendar*, II, nos. 1654, 1687.

1314, steps were taken to consecrate the cathedral of the nation's patron saint in a ceremony that was to be, in part at least, a vindication of Scottish independence. In preparation for the occasion the accustomed crosses would now be incised in the appropriate places on the outside and inside of the building. Those on the exterior of the choir and south transept may still be seen to the remarkable scale of 31¼ inches (79 cm.) in overall diameter.[53] With all in readiness the great church was at long last consecrated by its own bishop in the presence of the king and all the major dignitaries of the Scottish church and kingdom on 5 July 1318.[54]

Complete now in all its parts, the immense cruciform building, 357 feet (109 metres) in internal length, comprised an aisled nave of twelve bays, a massive central tower, twin four-bayed transepts, each with three eastern chapels, an aisled choir of six bays, and at its east end beyond the high altar the reliquary chapel of St Andrew. Although perhaps lacking the superlative architectural qualities of its rivals at Glasgow and Elgin, it far exceeded both in scale, above all in sheer length.[55] Furthermore, the discipline of form imposed on it by its original designers meant that even after all the changes of detail bound to occur in a building under construction over so prolonged a period, it retained a majestic uniformity and simplicity of outline. These qualities must have been particularly apparent to pilgrims approaching St Andrews whether by sea or land and to the citizens of the burgh, the main streets of which were directed towards the church which gave the town both its name and its special importance in the Scottish and European scene.

But the cathedral did not stand alone as a building. National shrine and centre of the most important diocese of the *Ecclesia Scotticana* as it might be, it was more immediately the church of the priory of Augustinian canons who worshipped within its walls, who constituted its chapter, and whose conventual buildings formed an integral part of its architectural design.[56] As has been noted, the buildings were arranged around a square cloister court, having the nave of the church on its north side and linked to it by east and west processional doorways. The buildings on the east side of the court formed a continuation of the south transept. Exactly midway in this range, in accordance with convention, was the chapter house, a compact vaulted compartment entered from the cloister by a fine early gothic doorway. About the time of the consecration of the cathedral, however, this original chapter house became a vestibule to a new and rather larger building projecting to the east, erected at the expense of Bishop Lamberton in co-operation with Prior John of Forfar who was buried within it on his death in 1321.[57]

---

53. The consecration cross on the west front of Holy Trinity church (completed in 1412) is 18¼ inches in diameter and the examples on St Salvator's church (completed in 1460) are 16¼ inches.
54. *Chron. Wyntoun*, V, 370-3; *St A. Liber*, xxvi.
55. Above, note 11.
56. These buildings are described in *Hist. Mon. Comm. (Fife)*, 235-7.
57. *Chron. Bower*, I, 362, 365.

To the north of the old chapter house (between it and the south gable of the church) was the customary *slype* or passage leading from the cloister to the graveyard. To the south was a three-bayed vaulted apartment probably serving as a vestry but which might have been ' the prior's chamber' before a separate lodging was built further to the east. South of this chamber was the day stair leading up to the dormitory and then the six-bayed vaulted *calefactory* or warming-house. Occupying the whole upper floor over these apartments was the dormitory or *dorter* with the *rere-dorter* at its south end. On the corresponding level on the south side of the court, and likewise above a vaulted undercroft, was the largest apartment of the group, the great refectory or *frater*. On the west side was the *Senzie House* with certain more miscellaneous apartments.[58]

To the east of the buildings surrounding the cloister court was the Prior's Lodging, perhaps the ' great chamber' built here around 1270 by Prior John of Haddington.[59] To the north-east of this was ' the old church,' as ' St Rule's ' was now termed, by this time probably shorn of its nave and hence returned virtually to its original state. Its precise use at this time is a matter of conjecture, but the veneration in which it was held is perhaps indicated by the fact that it continued to feature in the design of the chapter seal.[60] Between it and the cathedral and destined to persist here for a century more was the parish church of Holy Trinity.[61] To the south-west of the main group, across the roadway leading through the precinct from the town to the harbour, was an arcaded guest hall thought to have been built by Prior White about 1250.[62] Further to the west was the ancient pilgrim hospital or hospice with a chapel, appropriately dedicated to St Leonard, that served as a second parish church.[63] Elsewhere within the precinct were numerous other buildings, many of them connected with the work of what was an important economic and jurisdictional organism as well as a religious community. Surrounding the entire group was a wall (of which more will be said later), some ten feet high, three-quarters of a mile in length, enclosing within its circuit an area

---

58. *Senzie* is old Scots for synod. George Martine, describing the buildings in the 1680s (*Reliquiae Divi Andreae* (1797), 188) mentions ' senzie-house, senzie-hall, and senzie-chamber.' The last of these seems to have been at the south end of the west range running north and south. The Senzie hall may have been at the north end of the range running east and west immediately adjacent to the cathedral nave. In the mutual wall here, on the upper level above a vaulted undercroft of two dates, are the remains of a sequence of stone stalls that might have been designed to accommodate the dignitaries of the St Andrews diocesan synod.
59. *Chron. Bower*, I, 368-9
60. Fleming, *Cath. Museum* (fig. 127) illustrates a fifteenth-century example representing the church with choir, tower, and nave as in the twelfth-century seals. The removal of the nave may have occurred after the consecration of the new cathedral. Much romanesque masonry, possibly from here, is incorporated in the fabric of the Pends which dates from the mid-late fourteenth century.
61. The building was replaced by a great new aisled edifice in the centre of the town in 1410-12 but the old building continued in use for various purposes for some time thereafter (Rankin, *Holy Trinity*, 18-19).
62. *Chron. Bower*, I, 368. It was improved and enlarged around 1400 by Prior James Bisset (*op. cit.*, I, 372). See also *Hist. Mon. Comm (Fife)*, 240.
63. J. Herkless and R. K. Hannay, *The College of St Leonard* (1905). The arrangement for the use of the chapel for parochial purposes would seem to have been made by the priory in fulfilment of a papal authorisation of 1198 to build a second parish church (*Cal. Papal Letters*, I, 5). Thus, remarkably, the parochial needs of the burgh of St Andrews and its extensive landward parish were served until 1412 by two relatively small buildings situated not in ' St Andrews' but ' Kilrymont.'

of thirty acres and the most splendid ecclesiastical precinct in medieval Scotland.[64]

V

The buildings of the cathedral and priory have been described as they existed at the death of Bishop Lamberton in 1328. Although he had brought the church to the point when it could be consecrated, the extensive repairs effected on other parts of the fabric in the time of Prior William of Lothian (1340-54) suggest that these had not yet fully recovered from the vicissitudes of the preceding period, for ' he covered the whole dormitory with a handsome roof of timber below and of lead above; he also roofed the old church, the east chamber, and four parts of the cloister, and many other buildings.'[65] So matters seem to have remained until the great fire that devastated the cathedral in 1378, towards the close of the long episcopate of William de Landallis (1342-85).[66]

The damage caused by this conflagration, a type of calamity to which great medieval churches were particularly prone, seems to have been on a very extensive scale. Some accounts, indeed, speak of the ' destruction ' of the cathedral.[67] The timber and lead roofs were certainly destroyed, but beyond this much of the stone fabric was rendered unstable, necessitating massive reconstruction.[68] Particularly formidable was the rebuilding of one side of the central tower, the most vulnerable part of a cruciform church through problems of thrust as well as sheer weight. From a consideration of the structural problems involved and of the remedies taken to resolve them, it was the west side which was affected, the first arches of the nave arcades being filled up with solid masonry to give more adequate support.[69] At the same time the flanking arches to north and south, framing the entries to the nave and choir aisles from the transepts, were considerably contracted. In the transepts themselves the arches of the eastern chapels had to be underpinned while the pillars supporting them were replaced, an undertaking so precarious that it would presumably precede the work on the tower.

In the nave a similar reconstruction is said to have affected no fewer than nine pillars of the south arcade counting from the west end, the new piers being carved with the coats of arms of the lords who contributed to

---

64. *Hist. Mon. Comm. (Fife)*, 240-3. The area enclosed was slightly less than that of ' Kilrymont (in its more precise sense), involving a recession of the boundary behind the line of Abbey street and the eastern part of South street.
65. *Chron. Bower*, I, 369.
66. Ibid., I, 364, 371.
67. *Cal. Papal Letters*, IV, 244.
68. The details are given in *Chron. Wyntoun*, VI, 309-311. To assist in the reconstruction King Robert II paid for two masons who worked here from at least 1381 to 1384 (*Exch. Rolls*, III, 70, 674).
69. There is a suggestion of a similar infilling in the first arch of the south choir arcade by doubling the thickness of the ' screen wall ' which formed a backing to the canons' stalls in the centre and to the sequence of episcopal monuments facing the aisles (although not in the arch in question).

their cost.[70] That the work may have included parts of the vaulting of the south aisle is suggested by the fact that the supporting wall-shafts opposite the second to the seventh piers, unlike their neighbours, have no caps. So comprehensive a rehabilitation would imply that the entire arcade and superstructure might have had to be rebuilt, and although there is no specific mention of a comparable reconstruction of the north arcade and aisle vault, there are strong indications that this may have been the case. The base of the third pier from the west end incorporates a large section of a pier comparable in form to the surviving responds of the earlier arcade at the west end of the nave. Similar fragments seem to be incorporated in the fifth and sixth pier bases while the lowest course of the infilling in the final bay before the crossing continues into the base of the eleventh pier. Opposite the fifth pier, one of the sequence of late buttresses added to the western half of the north aisle wall contains significant fragments of vaulting ribs, and part of a fine thirteenth-century capital was also found here.[71]

Work on the nave at this time also included the rebuilding of much of the west front. The narthex seems to have been removed, revealing the somewhat inadequate scale of the main doorway when deprived of this embellishment. Above the doorway the earlier arcaded wall-passage was blocked up, perhaps to strengthen the construction, its place being taken in the exterior design by an ornamental 'blind arcade' similar to that over the outer arch of 'The Pends' or vaulted gatehouse of the priory built about this same time on the south side of the cathedral square.[72] Immediately over the arcading in the cathedral west front was a pair of three-light traceried windows and above them another pair of two-light windows with a wall-passage linking the turret stairs at clerestory level, and in the apex of the gable a wheel-window or perhaps a *vesica* or 'pointed oval.'[73]

Bishop de Landallis died while this work was only partly complete. Closely associated with him in its direction was his prior, Stephen Pay, and it may well have been because of his experience in this field, and its continuing importance, that he was (rather unusually) elected bishop in 1385.[74] But on his way by sea to obtain papal confirmation—and quite possibly financial aid additional to that already assigned for the rebuilding

70 *Chron. Wyntoun*, VI, 311. Among the carved fragments in the cathedral museum is what appears to be part of a late gothic pier having attached to it a shield displaying the arms of the Isle of Man. This might very probably relate to John Dunbar, earl of Moray (1372-91), whose grandfather Thomas Randolph had been granted Man, with Moray, in 1312.
71. Much of the new work, including the pier section with the Man shield, is executed in a close-textured brown sandstone. The moulded detail of the buttress bonded into the earlier buttress opposite the first pier indicates that contrary to the impression given by the foundations further east, the new buttresses were designed with considerable skill. See again article by D. Hay Fleming mentioned in note 43.
72. *Hist. Mon. Comm. (Fife)*, fig. 393. The details actually differ in certain respects.
73. In the reconstruction of the likely appearance of the front by Thomas Ross in *Trans. Scot. Ecclesiological Soc.*, VII (1924-27), frontispiece and 93-4, a wheel window is shown, an interpretation that is followed in *Hist. Mon. Comm. (Fife)*, 235.
74. This is in fact the only instance of a prior of St Andrews succeeding to the bishopric or archbishopric although John Hepburn was elected (unsuccessfully) in 1514.

in 1381[75]—he was taken prisoner by the English and died shortly thereafter. There then ensued the three important episcopates of Walter Trail (1385-1401), Henry Wardlaw (1403-40), and James Kennedy (1440-65). All were men of distinction, much involved in affairs of state, and in the case of Wardlaw and Kennedy in the development of the new university of St Andrews.[76] Hence the direction of building schemes affecting the cathedral and priory fell to an even greater degree than usual to the priors of the period.

The repairs on the church were apparently still in progress under Prior James Bisset (1393-1416), who is said to have completed the roof of the nave, the roofs of the choir and transept having been already replaced under Bishop de Landallis. He also equipped the choir with stalls, presumably in replacement of others destroyed in the fire.[77] The ' ritual choir ' in which these were placed now came to extend (if it had not done so before) into the space under the central tower as far as the stone *pulpitum* in its reconstructed western arch. But as this painstaking and prolonged rehabilitation was nearing completion in 1409 the gable of the south transept was blown down by a gale.[78] There is mention of stones crashing through the roofs of the dormitory, the chapter house, and the transept chapel-aisle, and in the church indeed the work involved not only the rebuilding of the gable but parts of the side walls including the southmost arch of the arcade opening to the chapels. The remaining respond here indicates the use of cylindrical piers in the new work after a fashion that became increasingly common in Scottish ecclesiastical buildings of the fifteenth century.[79] A contemporary St Andrews example is the parish church of Holy Trinity as rebuilt in the centre of the city in 1410-12 in terms of an agreement between the priory (as rector) and the town council.[80]

Bisset's successor as prior was James Haldenstone (1418-43) who, among other work, was responsible for the reconstruction of the principal remaining feature of the cathedral, the great east gable. Although he is credited with rebuilding it and the adjoining vault ' from the foundations,' this was clearly not the case.[81] What he actually did was to replace the two upper tiers of romanesque lancets here with a single large three-light window, its sill being kept just clear of the roof of the triforium wall-passage where it emerged from the angle-turrets and its apex rising to the full height of the vault.[82] Otherwise the gable is as it left the hands of

---

75. *Cal. Papal Letters*, IV, 244. See also *St Andrews Copiale*, 114-8, 452.
76. The university came into being in 1410. The ceremonies attending its formal inauguration, following the receipt of the papal bulls early in 1414, took place within the priory refectory and the cathedral (*Chron. Bower*, II, 445-6).
77. *Chron. Wyntoun*, VI; *Chron. Bower*, I, 372. See also article by David McRoberts, below.
78. *Chron. Bower*, II, 444.
79. The St Andrews example has analogies with the western responds of the nave arcade of the church of the Holy Rude at Stirling. See MacGibbon and Ross, *Eccl. Arch.*, III, 318, and *Hist. Mon. Comm. (Stirling)*, I, 135 and pl. 25.
80. Rankin, *Holy Trinity*, 22-8.
81. *Chron. Bower*, I, 375.
82. In the reconstruction the string-course between the old triforium and clerestory stages was economically re-used below the new window.

its first builders save for the addition of immense angle-buttresses to sustain the thrust of the vault. This is likely to have formed part of Haldenstone's work, and since it and the insertion of the new window must have involved the erection of scaffolding round the entire gable, it could well have given the impression of a more thorough-going reconstruction. It was also probably at this time that the arcading along the lower part of the interior walls was removed in the course of a comprehensive refurnishing of the reliquary chapel of St Andrew.

Elsewhere within the church Haldenstone was responsible for numerous other embellishments and improvements, but the most striking structural development in the interior, the rood loft and rood altar at the east end of the nave, was the creation of his colleague William Bower, a canon of the cathedral and vicar of St Andrews from about 1410 to 1440.[83] In most churches the rood screen, with or without an associated loft, stood slightly to the west of the choir screen, but the two were sometimes combined, and this seems to have been the arrangement here.[84] The third marquis of Bute, who did so much in the 1890s to reveal, interpret, and enhance the remains of the cathedral and priory, envisaged the rood loft as ' a permanent stone gallery of one arch crossing the nave.'[85] It is more likely to have formed an extension of the stone choir screen so as to occupy the whole first bay of the nave, now walled up on each side in the manner already described. On the ' solid platform ' so provided would stand the rood altar with the great rood itself above.

After Prior Haldenstone, while repairs to the fabric and furnishings of the cathedral continue to be recorded, no changes of significance seem to have been made to the structure, even after 1472 when the bishopric was raised to the dignity of an archbishopric with the authority, long desired, of primate and metropolitan of the Scottish church.[86] The few identifiable architectural developments of the period seem to date mainly from the time of Prior John Hepburn (1482-1522). He is chiefly remembered for his refounding and partial rebuilding of the old hospice and church of St Leonard as a college of the university in 1512[87] and for his work on the priory precinct wall which he virtually doubled in height and equipped with a formidable sequence of turrets and gateways.[88] But he also concerned himself both with ' the old church ' and the cathedral proper. At the former he reconstructed the space within the ground floor of the tower as a vestibule to the chapel in a style that suggests that he was also responsible for remodelling the inner arch of the east processional door of the cathedral nave in the elliptical form still to be seen.[89]

83. *Chron. Bower,* I, 375-6.
84. A supporting consideration for such an arrangement here was that there was no need to provide a ' parish altar ' for the nave, a function sometimes fulfilled by the rood-altar.
85. MacGibbon and Ross, *Eccl. Arch.,* II, xvi.
86. Theiner, *Monumenta,* 465.
87. Herkless and Hannay, *Coll. of St Leonard; Hist. Mon. Comm. (Fife),* 245-8; R. G. Cant, *St Leonard's Chapel, St Andrews* (1970).
88. *Hist. Mon. Comm. (Fife),* 240-3.
89. The small doorway leading from outside the west front of the cathedral southwards into the west claustral buildings has an arch in the same style on its south side.

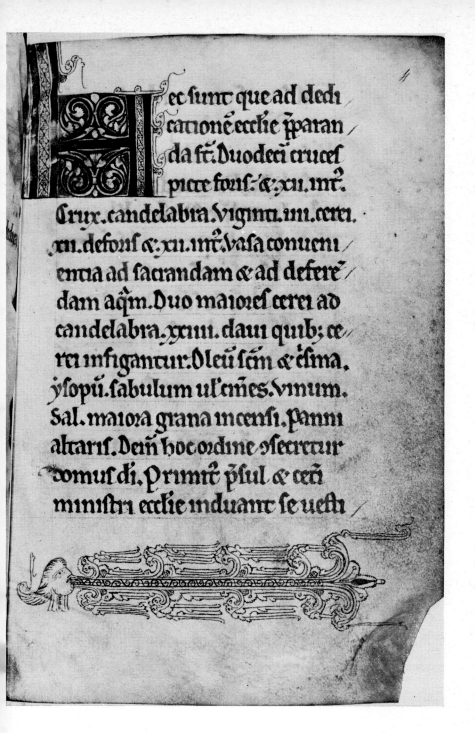

PLATE VII. THE PONTIFICAL OF BISHOP DAVID BERNHAM.

This pontifical (Bibl. Nat. Paris, Ms Latin 1218) was used during the thirteenth century by bishops of St Andrews, David Bernham and William Wishart. It is not unlikely that this was the actual ritual book used at the consecration of St Andrews cathedral on 5 July 1318. The page illustrated (fo 4) lists the various items which should be made ready for the proper consecration of a church.

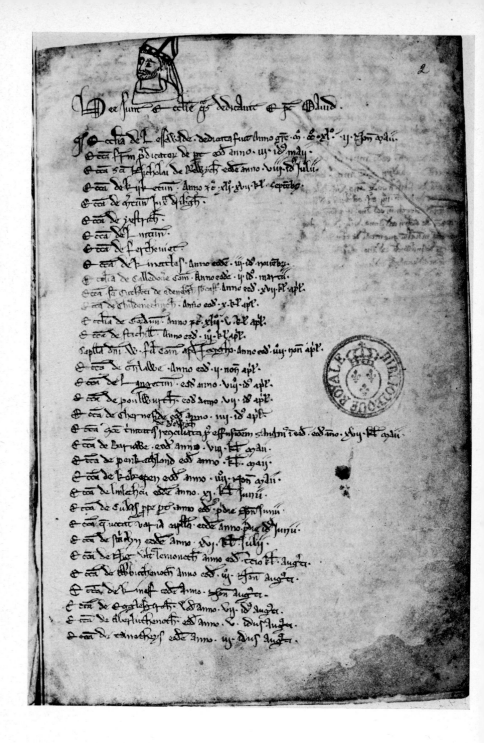

PLATE VIII. THE PONTIFICAL OF BISHOP DAVID BERNHAM

Beginning on fo 2 of the manuscript (Bibl. Nat. Paris, Ms Latin 1218) there is a list of 140 churches consecrated by Bishop David Bernham (1239-1253). The contemporary drawing in the top margin is presumably intended as a portrait of the bishop.

DAVID BERNHAM, BISHOP OF ST ANDREWS, 1239-1253

by

MARINELL ASH

David Bernham was the first native-born bishop of St Andrews since the death of Fothad, the last Celtic bishop, in 1093. In a very real sense he represents the coming of age of a new national church in Scotland within the body of western Christendom. His predecessor, William Malvoisin (1202-1238), was the last, and perhaps the greatest, in the line of Anglo-Norman bishops which had begun with the ineffective appointment of Turgot in 1107. Malvoisin, with his close personal and family ties with England and France, was responsible for bringing the reorganization of the diocese along western lines to a successful conclusion. He also created an effective temporal administration and forged links with many of the major new forces at work in the western church. Above all, he was concerned with the definition of the respective jurisdictions represented in the diocese: episcopal, capitular, archidecanal, monastic. Malvoisin had attended the fourth Lateran council and made at least one other journey to the papal court. He regularly referred questions to the papal court for advice or decisions. During his episcopate both major mendicant orders were introduced into Scotland, as well as the austere Valiscaulians. The bishop completed the building of the choir of his cathedral church in a transitional Gothic style, completing the building programme begun by bishop Arnold in the early 1160s.

This French bishop attracted into his household a number of young Scottish-born clerks who were to provide the next generation of leaders in the Scottish church. Among these clerks was David Bernham, who appears in the bishop's household by about 1225. He was university trained, although whether at Oxford and/or Paris is not known.[1] At some time between 1225 and 1235 he became vicar of Haddington: he retained the seal he used as vicar as his *secretum* during the early years of his episcopate.[2] The living was a wealthy one, valued at forty merks, four times the minimum stipend allowed by the statutes of the Scottish church. The sources of this stipend were subject to an exhaustive inquest shortly after David obtained the benefice.[3] From this inquest it appears that the vicar had a number of chaplains to help in the running of the parish, but it cannot be assumed that Bernham was a total absentee, for he

---

1. A nephew, William Bernham, was a student at both Oxford and Paris. See N. R. Ker and W. A. Pantin, ' Letters of a Scottish Student,' *Oxford Formulares*, ii (Oxford History Society, 1942).
2. Stevenson, *Illustrations*, no. 17; W. Greenwell and C. H. Blair, *Catalogue of Seals in the Treasury of the Dean and Chapter of Durham* (Newcastle-upon-Tyne, 1911-21), nos. 3643 and 3620. It is described as an antique gem with the legend ' memento domine David.'
3. Stevenson, *Illustrations*, no. 17.

33

belonged to the post-Lateran council generation of clergy who, as bishops, were to grapple with the problem of ensuring the proper serving of parish churches by suitable and resident clergy.

In another sense, Bernham's presentation to Haddington was apposite, for he was returning to south-eastern Scotland where his family had its roots. The story of Bernham's family provides a glimpse into the changing social history of thirteenth-century Scotland: the rise of a native-born urban burghal class. Yet there can be no doubt that much of the Bernham family's rise was tied less to economic success than to the advancement of David's career. The future bishop had probably been trained in law. Thus in 1230 he acted as a judicial agent for Holyrood abbey.[4] By 1235 he had become royal chamberlain and his brother Robert proudly styles himself as the chamberlain's brother, when he granted a fishing net on the Tweed to Melrose abbey.[5] By 1238 brother Robert had become mayor of Berwick,[6] and in 1249 was one of the twelve Scottish knights who met the English representatives to draw up the Border laws.[7] Bernham's career in the church was paralleled by the family's tradition of pious donations to religious houses. Various members of the family witnessed charters to Coldstream priory.[8] Later generations of the family included a benefactor of Arbroath abbey in 1268,[9] and a prioress of North Berwick in 1291.[10]

David Bernham became precentor of Glasgow in the last years of the 1230s.[11] His provision to St Andrews in 1239 was essentially a royal appointment. The independent postulation by the cathedral chapter of Geoffrey, bishop of Dunkeld, was disallowed by Gregory IX, who ordered a new election.[12] Bernham, the royal nominee, was chosen in an election which included representatives of the culdees.[13] Proctors were sent to Rome to secure approval of the new election, but only one delegate reached Rome alive. The bishops of Glasgow, Caithness and Brechin were ordered to enquire into the election.[14] Bernham was consecrated by the bishop of Glasgow on 22 January 1240-1.[15]

It was the beginning of a remarkably active episcopate, but even before his consecration Bernham had been involved in a controversy which foreshadowed one of the major themes of his career as bishop:

4. Durham Dean and Chapter, Miscellaneous Charter 1017.
5. *HBC*, 178; *Melr. Lib.* i, no. 178.
6. Durham Dean and Chapter, Miscellaneous Charter 619, printed in Raine, *North Durham*, no. 72.
7. *APS*, i, 83.
8. *Cold. Cart.*, nos. 48-52.
9. British Museum, Additional MS 33245.
10. *CDS*, iii, no. 508.
11. *Glas. Reg.*, i, no. 171; D. E. R. Watt, *Fasti Ecclesiae Scoticanae Medii Aevi* (St Andrews, 1969), 157.
12. *Vet. Mon.*, no. 98; *CPL*, i, 178.
13. For the rôle of the culdees in this election, see G. W. S. Barrow, ' The Cathedral Chapter of St Andrews and the Culdees,' *Journal of Ecclesiastical History*, iii (1952).
14. *Vet. Mon.*, no. 100; *CPL*, i, 178.
15. *ES*, ii, 516.

the provision of absentees to parochial livings. Gregory IX had, apparently, ordered Jedburgh abbey to appoint one of his clerks to a living said to be in their gift. The provision was opposed by proctors for the bishop-elect and the abbey, who appeared before John le Romeyn, sub-dean of York, acting as a papal delegate.[16] Bernham's proctor claimed that the living in question, Aberlemno, which was situated on episcopal demesne, was also in the bishop's gift. Le Romeyn found against the bishop-elect.

Also while he was still elect, Bernham had probably attended the legatine council held by cardinal Otto at Edinburgh on 19 October 1239.[17] The business of the council is not known for certain, but it almost certainly included discussion of the papal campaign against Frederick II and the re-issuance of all or part of the cardinal's London constitutions of 1235. The first provision of the London council was a statute ordaining that all churches were to be properly consecrated.[18] Late in the spring of 1240 bishop Bernham embarked on the first visitation of his diocese, which in the first nine years of his episcopate was combined with the dedication of over one hundred and forty churches.[19]

These dedications have caused a good deal of misunderstanding: in the vast majority of cases they seem to have been what might be called 'conditional' dedications, where knowledge of the original ceremony of dedication was uncertain or lost. The question of recording church dedications was a serious one; it was a problem dealt with several times in the legislation of the thirteenth-century English church.[20] The dedications have tended to obscure the wide ranging activities and interests of this reformist bishop.

There can be little doubt that Bernham consciously modelled his activities on those of Robert Grosseteste, bishop of Lincoln. If Bernham had studied at Oxford he would have known the future bishop of Lincoln: among the *magistri* who appear in David's household is master Peter Ramsay, later bishop of Aberdeen, who had succeeded Grosseteste as rector of the Franciscans at Oxford.[21] The influence of Grosseteste was also apparent in Bernham's initial visitation of his diocese, which paralleled Lincoln's exhaustive initial visitation of his see. Above all, Grosseteste's influence is clear in the pastoral legislation of bishop Bernham. In the

---

16. *Historic Manuscripts Commission*, xiv, appendix 3, 183-4; see also *RRS*, ii, no. 525.
17. Robertson, *Concilia*, i, lvii; *ES*, ii, 515.
18. F. H. Powicke and C. R. Cheney, *Councils and Synods with other Documents relating to the English Church*, ii (Oxford, 1964), 245-6.
19. They are listed and discussed in *Pontificale Ecclesiae S. Andreae: The Pontifical Offices used by David de Bernham, Bishop of St Andrews*, ed. C. Wordsworth (Edinburgh, 1885) and D. E. Easson, 'Church dedications in Scotland Seven Hundred years ago,' *Transactions of the Scottish Ecclesiological Society*, 13 (1939-40). A 'life' of the bishop also centres almost exclusively on a discussion of the dedications and the Lothian constitutions, W. Lockhart, *The Church of Scotland in the Thirteenth Century*, 2nd ed. (Edinburgh, 1892).
20. Powicke and Cheney, *Councils*, 172, 211.
21. 'When divine providence ordained that Master Robert should be promoted from his chair as professor to an episcopal throne, he was succeeded as lecturer by Brother Peter who later became a bishop in Scotland.' Thomas of Eccleston, *De Adventu Fratrum Minorum in Angliam* (London. 1964), 41. There is no other contemporary bishop named Peter in Scotland. Watt, *Fasti*, 1-2.

preamble to his Lothian constitutions of 1242 there occurs the phrase:
'. . . ad pastorale spectat officium . . .' The most recent occurrence of
this variant of papal phraseology had been in Grosseteste's letter to his
archdeacons issued following his diocesan visitation: ' Quia ad pastoris
spectat officium hiis qui ignorant et errant condolere et gregem sibi com-
missum pervigilare.'[22]

Before Bernham was able to act on the information gained by his
first visitation, however, he had to attend the council called to meet in
Rome in the late spring of 1241. With the bishop of Glasgow he had left
Scotland by the turn of the year, but because of imperial threats they
did not join the flotilla carrying delegates to the council, which was
captured by imperial ships off Elba on 4 May 1241.[23] Bernham was at
Durham by late June and had returned to Scotland by August.[24]

The bishop soon returned to his dedicatory activities which were to
continue until Bernham again went abroad to attend the council of Lyons
in 1245. In May 1242 the bishop issued a set of constitutions for the
archdeaconry of Lothian.[25] It seems probable that there was a corresponding set of constitutions for the northern archdeaconry of St Andrews,
for the statutes copied into the lost great register of St Andrews cathedral
priory are described merely as ' Constitutiones Davidis episcopi de
regendo clero.'[26]

A definitive study of the sources and interrelationships between the
various sets of statutes enacted by the thirteenth-century Scottish church
is still to be done. At present it is only possible to note, in general terms,
some of the possible connections between the diocesan and national legislation of Bernham's time.[27] The Lothian constitutions gave practical
expression to many of the more general statutes enacted by a national
council which met at Perth on 2 June 1242. At this meeting the prelates
' with the king's consent and in his presence made good acts for reforming
the abuses and securing the clergie in their possessions and rights.'[28]

After the legatine council of Perth, bishop Bernham returned to
dedicating churches. This activity reached its peak during 1243 when he
dedicated forty-nine churches, compared with a total of fifty-nine in the
two previous years. Thereafter the bishop's dedicatory activities declined:
he dedicated fifteen churches in 1244, five in 1247, three in 1248 and in
1249.

By the summer of 1245 Bernham was on his way to the council of
Lyons. Although this meeting enacted reforming legislation, its main

---

22. Powicke and Cheney, Councils, 203.
23. ES, ii, 527.
24. Priory of Finchale, ed. J. Raine (Surtees Society, 1837), no. 183
25. Robertson, Concilia, ii, nos. 109-39; Patrick, Statutes, nos. 109-39.
26. St. A. Lib., xxvi, no. 19.
27. I have discussed this relationship in some detail in The Administration of the Diocese of St
Andrews, 1202-1328 (University of Newcastle-upon-Tyne Ph.D. thesis, 1972), 35-7.
28. G. Martine, Reliquiae Divi Andeae (St Andrews, 1797), 226. In my thesis I have suggested
that most, if not all, of the first twenty-five statutes of the Scottish church are the product
of this meeting, 37-9.

business was concerned with the papal conflict with Frederick II. A crusade against the emperor was discussed, as well as the relief of the Holy Land and the defence against the Tartar threat. Bernham's seal, styling himself ' Bishop of the Scots ' was appended to the proceedings of the council issued at the final meeting on 17 July 1245.[29]

During this visit to Lyons a number of Scottish problems were brought to the papal court for determination. Among the most important papal bulls relating to Scotland from this time was the reissue of the bull of Clement III which included the provision that papal judges delegate were to hear Scottish cases in Scotland or Durham or Carlisle diocese, but not in York.[30] Bernham's experience at the hands of John le Romeyn may have been one of the reasons for the reissuance.

There can be little doubt that Bernham's relationship with his royal patron, Alexander II, was close. One project in which the two men were closely concerned at the time of the council of Lyons was the canonization of the king's ancestor, Margaret of Scotland. As part of the preliminaries to the canonization and the creation of a cult centre at the royal abbey of Dunfermline a bull was issued allowing the abbot of Dunfermline to wear the mitre.[31] The new saint was canonized in September 1249, shortly after the death of Alexander II.[32] In the following year the ceremonial translation of the saint was held at which the bishop and the young king Alexander III were present.[33]

In return for these papal favours, Scotland was expected to support the crusades against the Hohenstaufen and in the Holy Land. In 1246 master Marianus, papal chaplain, was given authority to deduct for three years half of all the revenues of benefices in England, Scotland and Wales in which the incumbent resided for less than six months.[34] In 1247 the bishop of Dunkeld was delegated to collect a twentieth of church revenues for the crusade.[35] Two years later, Bernham and the bishop of Glasgow were appointed collectors of the Holy Land subsidy.[36] By mid-century money was being disbursed to Scottish crusaders bound for the Holy Land.[37] On the whole, Scottish efforts on behalf of a crusade were concentrated on the Holy Land, yet at the same time money collected in Scotland was being diverted to Henry III's Sicilian ventures.[38]

It is against this international background that the national role of the bishop must be viewed: for the Scottish church was very conscious of its place in western Christendom. Bernham's relationship with his royal

29. C. Burns, ' Scottish bishops at the General Councils of the middle ages,' *IR*, 16 (1963), 137.
30. Public Record Office, London, Papal Bull 21 (21) (a), printed in *Foedera*, i, 263.
31. *Vet. Mon.*, no. 113; *CPL*, i, 215.
32. *Dunf. Reg.*, nos. 290, 281, 285.
33. *Chron. Wyntoun*, ii, 250.
34. Public Record Office, London, Papal Bull 21 (8).
35. *CPL*, i, 237.
36. Ibid., 243.
37. Ibid., 261.
38. Ibid., 263.

D

patron was an expression of an ancient national identity in which sacred and secular authority were inextricably bound up with one another. Bernham still bore the ancient title, *Episcopus Scottorum.* The bishop of St Andrews was in many ways the ecclesiastical counterpart of the king of Scots. Without his support, royal authority was incomplete, a fact given ceremonial expression in St Andrews' traditional role in the enthronement of the king of Scots. Thus a close association between king and bishop was, to say the least of it, of mutual advantage.

The successful canonization of St Margaret is but one example of what this meant in practical terms. Another example was the reorganization of the ' culdees ' of St Andrews into the collegiate church of St Mary of the Rock. The story of this creation has been told by Professor Barrow.[39] Its main immediate importance is the light it throws on the bishop's relationship with his cathedral chapter. Bernham's election had been carried out by the chapter, with representatives of the culdees. The growth of this rival corporation was rightly regarded by the chapter as a threat, but until the end of Bernham's episcopate it was not a threat which they were able to counter. In the early part of the thirteenth century the chapter had been in a precarious financial state and, moreover, had failed to establish the right to carry out independent episcopal elections. From the time of Bernham onwards capitular ' election ' really meant ratification of a royal nominee. With the election of prior John White (1225-1258), however, there was a marked improvement in the priory's position. The basis of this change was a thorough reorganization of the priory's lands and possessions and the redefinition of the corporation's rights. In 1248 in a papal confirmation drawn up from a priory memorandum, Innocent IV confirmed for the first time since 1206 the chapter's right to bring the culdees under regular rule and to take over their prebends.[40] This was a forlorn hope. Instead, at some time between 1248 and 1253 the culdees moved from their corner of the cathedral church to the church of St Mary of the Rock outside the cathedral precinct.[41]

It is clear that there was little love lost between Bernham and his regular chapter. Bernham by training and disposition would favour a corporation of secular priests to balance the reviving power and fortune of St Andrews priory. Letters of papal protection to the college were issued in 1249, and the cathedral chapter seeing this as a threat to their position, obtained papal letters to the effect that this protection did not prejudice their rights.[42] The chapter then attacked the college at its most vulnerable point, by obtaining a final reissue of the right granted by successive popes that vacant prebends were to be filled by Augustinian canons.[43] Early in 1250 a complaint was raised at the curia over a prebend

39. See Barrow, ' Culdees.'
40. *St. A. Lib.*, 101.
41. Barrow, ' Culdees,' 36.
42. National Library of Scotland, MS 15.1.18, no. 32.
43. *Vet. Mon.*, no. 145.

left vacant by the death of Gilbert, which the culdees were said to have withheld from the chapter. The case was remitted to the priors of Kirkham and St Oswalds in York diocese (in apparent contravention of the indulgence of 1245), who found in favour of the chapter. On 7 November 1250 at Inverkeithing the abbot of Dunfermline and the treasurer of Dunkeld confirmed and published the sentence and made further enquiries into the activities of the culdees.[44]

A face-saving solution out of this impasse was found which was almost entirely in favour of the chapter. In 1251 Richard Weyrement, a culdee, acting on his own behalf appeared with the chapter's proctor before the English cardinal of St Laurence in Lucina. There, Weyrement, ' mindful of the favours he had received from the chapter ' (which doubtless included the capitular living of Tannadyce which he held), resigned the vacant prebend to the cardinal, who in turn granted it with all its rights to the chapter.[45]

In the next engagement the chapter was defeated only by circumstance. The bishop and provost of the culdees were cited by the chapter to appear before the pope by 13 July 1253 to answer yet another charge concerning vacant prebends and their fruits.[46] This action came to nothing because of the death of bishop Bernham. The struggle between the chapter and the culdees reverted to electoral rights, which then became subsumed by the political disruption of the minority of Alexander III and the exile of bishop Gamelin.

There seems to be some significance in the fact that the chapter's ' offensive ' against the culdees did not begin until about the time of the death of Alexander II. Without the backing of his royal patron, Bernham's authority was weakened. The chapter took advantage of this fact, and might well have succeeded if national events had not overtaken them.

There is, in fact, a sense of weakness and unhappiness hanging over the last years of Bernham's episcopate. The death of the king was a great dividing line in the bishop's career. Immediately following the king's death, however, he performed St Andrews' traditional role in the installation of the new monarch. An attempt was made to delay the ceremony until the young king could receive the accolade of knighthood, presumably at the hand of Henry III. Nevertheless, Bernham performed the ceremony of enthronement on 13 July 1249, five days after the king's death.[47] As one of the new king's advisors Bernham may well have had a hand in advising Alexander how to deal with any claims the English king was likely to make to overlordship of Scotland, including the attempt

---

44. Ibid.
45. Ibid. and National Library of Scotland, MS 15.1.18, no. 30. See also Barrow, ' Culdees,' 28-9 and note 2, and 29. Cardinal John's chaplain was Richard, a canon of St Andrews, ES, ii, 572, n. 6.
46. St. A. Lib., 26.
47. Hailes, Annals, i, 194-5.

to exact an oath of fealty at the marriage ceremony with princess Margaret at York in December 1251.

By the time of the marriage the split in the factions surrounding the king was clear. It is a convention—if not an accurate one—to term the factions ' Comyn/patriotic ' and ' Durward/English ': Bernham belonged to the former.[48] At the time of the marriage the Comyn party were in the ascendant after an initial eclipse, but whatever his party, for a man like Bernham who had laboured so closely with his king to enhance the authority of his church, the disruption of the minority must have been disheartening and disturbing. The great ceremony marking the translation of the relics of St Margaret contrasted starkly with the issuance in the same year of the *gravamina* of the Scottish church to the new king.

At some time during the first year and a half of the new reign a council of the Scottish church was held at Edinburgh. After the meeting, certainly by the end of 1250, Bernham, Albin, bishop of Brechin and master Abel, archdeacon of St Andrews, drew up a letter to the king which contained the substance of the council's complaints.[49] The *gravamina*, like its predecessors in England, was an expression of the church's concern with the conflict of jurisdictions between church and state.[50] The council had produced a series of ordinances and, although not all were written down at the time of the meeting, it seems likely that some of them found their way into the general legislation of the Scottish church.[51] The essence of the council's complaint was that ecclesiastical persons were being deprived of possessions granted to their churches in alms in contempt of an ordinance confirming the liberties of the church made at the council in the presence of the king and his counsellors.

The complaints of the church are more fully spelled out in a letter of Innocent IV to the bishops of Lincoln, Worcester and Lichfield, issued on 31 May 1251, ordering them to enquire into the wrongs committed against the church by the advisors of the young king.[52] The charges include one that the king's ministers have ordered bishops to revoke excommunications and other ecclesiastical sentences, and another that the church was being despoiled of its possessions by hearings before secular courts. There are other charges as well, but all of them centre on the common factor that secular jurisdiction was impinging on ecclesiastical prerogatives.

It is impossible to determine how much these complaints were connected with the political factions surrounding the king. To a certain extent they were the result of the political instability of the time. But the

---

48. For the background to the minority, see D. E. R. Watt, ' The Minority of Alexander III of Scotland,' *Transactions of the Royal Historical Society* (1971).
49. National Library of Scotland, MS 15.1.18, no. 16, printed in Robertson, *Concilia*, ii, 241-2, and translated in Patrick, *Statutes*, 211-12.
50. See W. R. Jones, ' Bishops, Politics and the Two Laws, The Gravamina of the English Clergy, 1237-1399,' *Speculum*, 41 (1966).
51. See my thesis, 47-50, for a discussion of this point.
52. Robertson, *Concilia*, ii, 242-6; Patrick, *Statutes*, 212-17.

fact that the letter to the king specifically mentioned the despoliation of the prior of St Andrews suggests that these difficulties extended well beyond immediate politics. St Andrews priory tended to support the Durward faction, yet at a time when the Durwards were in the ascendant the prior of the house claimed to have been dispossessed of certain goods as the result of changes made by the king's counsellors. It seems that despite the political divisions within the kingdom, and their respective allegiances, the leaders of the Scottish church were still able in the early 1250s to ignore their political differences in defence of their prerogatives and possessions.

Gradually, however, politics seem to have overcome this unity, for nothing further is heard of the *gravamina*. There is no evidence to suggest that the English bishops ever acted upon the papal letter.[53] By the end of 1251 the fortunes of the Comyn faction were in the ascendant. By the end of the year the bishop was again numbered among the king's counsellors.

David Bernham remained active in the running of his diocese until the time of his departure to the king's marriage at York in Christmastide 1251. Thereafter no surviving evidence tells of his actions, yet he may well have continued to travel about his diocese for he died at Nenthorn in the Merse on 26 April 1253 and was buried at Kelso abbey.[54]

His pontificate had been one of crucial importance for the Scottish church. The coming together in defence of their rights evidenced by the *gravamina* of the Scottish church provides practical evidence of what the ' coming of age of the Scottish church ' meant. The bishop also had influence beyond the bounds of Scotland. His Lothian constitutions became widely known and were eventually borrowed in part for the 1350 constitutions of Sodor and Man.[55]

But perhaps Bernham's deepest influence was upon his own diocese. His dedications indicate a man who was greatly concerned for the life of his diocese. He must have had a deep knowledge of the multifarious life of his see. There is about his activities a sense of purpose: a desire for order and efficiency, for the better ordering of Christian life and practice. This can best be seen in the changing history of the bishop's own household, as it developed to meet the needs of the bishop.

David Bernham's pontificate marks a turning point in the history of the episcopal administration at St Andrews. Malvoisin's household represented the final development of the large, rather amorphous household which had characterised the administration of the Anglo-Norman bishops of St Andrews. It was not unusual for minor servants to witness charters in the twelfth century, including bakers, cooks and brewers.[56]

---

53. There is, in fact, no evidence that the letter ever reached the bishops. Hailes *Annals*, i, 195-6.
54. Dowden, *Bishops*, 15.
55. Patrick, *Statutes*, 57 and note 2.
56. *Scone Liber.*, no. 40, National Library of Scotland Minto Charters, Box 30, Bundle 212, no. 7.

By the time of Malvoisin these minor servants appear less frequently and the witness lists to charters reflect more strongly the episcopal administration which had grown up in the twelfth century. Bishop Richard (1163-1178) was the first bishop to be provided to St Andrews from royal administration. He would be familiar with the division of royal administration between the chapel under the chancellor and the *camera regis* under the chamberlain. A similar division occurred in the bishop's administration: the earliest reference to the episcopal chapel at St Andrews occurs in 1166.[57] Under Richard there is a growing distinction between *clerici* and *clerici episcopi* which reflects the split in personnel between the regular staff of the chapel and those clerks more closely associated with the bishop.

Ironically, it was an absentee bishop, Roger (1189-1202), who was responsible for a number of further innovations which David later used. Roger was not only appointed from being royal chancellor, he was related to the Scottish royal family. A large number of *magistri* appear in his household, many of them coming from the estates of his family, the earls of Leicester. But his most significant innovation was the introduction of the office of Official, who first appears at St Andrews c 1193-4. The Official was the bishop's judicial ordinary, delegated by the bishop to act on his behalf. Roger's chancellor, Geoffrey of Cranford, introduced a number of diplomatic innovations, such as full dating of charters, but this was dropped when he left the episcopal chancery.[58] Full dating of charters was reintroduced to the St Andrews chancery in the last years of bishop Malvoisin.

Under bishop Malvoisin there was a growing distinction between *clerici* and *capellani*. The latter were a more select group, priests in attendance on the bishop, while *clerici* were usually tonsured clerks employed in general clerical duties.[59] These *capellani* performed such duties as acting as the bishop's personal chaplain, overseeing the work of the chancery or carrying specially delegated jobs, such as local enquiries. Under Malvoisin only eight *capellani* appear as witness or agents, as opposed to over three dozen men described as *clerici*.

Bishop David inherited the administration created by his predecessors and changed it yet again to meet the new conditions of his episcopate. He was responsible for stream-lining his administration, almost (from the point of view of the administrative historian) to the point of obscurity. The bishop quickly created a small, fairly constant, group of professional servants and administrators who were apparently in fairly regular personal attendance on the bishop. The administrative duties formerly carried out by the *capellani* were instead exercised by this ' inner circle '

57. Stevenson, *Illustrations*, no. 6; *Holy Lib.*, Appendix II, no. 4. The latter text differs in some respects from the Harley charter printed by Stevenson.
58. G. W. S. Barrow, *Scottish Royal Ecclesiastical Policy*, 1107-1214 (University of Oxford B.Litt. thesis, 1950), 228-9. It is suggested here that this practice was a borrowing from English royal practice.
59. C. R. Cheney, *English Bishops' Chanceries* (Manchester, 1950), 9

of highly trained men. With the exception of Master Alexander of Edinburgh, they all appear as witnesses to an episcopal charter issued in the first year of Bernham's episcopate: ' Hiis testibus . Magistro Petro de rameseya . Magistro Hugone de meleburn . Magistro Alexandro de sancto martino . Magistro Waltero de mortuomari . Domino Roberto persona de methfen . Rogero de suleby . Hugone de strivelin . Gilberto . Jacobo clericis nostris et multis aliis.'[60]

The charters witnessed by this group fall almost entirely within the period 1240-8, the period coinciding with the most active part of the episcopate, before the accession of king Alexander III. By 1250 a number of these clerks are found holding prebends in the new collegiate church of St Mary of the Rock.

There were a number of other administrative changes, all indicating a strong desire for mobility and efficiency. The first example of letters patent by a bishop of St Andrews was issued in the first year of Bernham's episcopate in the course of a visit to Coldingham priory.[61] Officials were apparently only appointed for the periods when the bishop was to be abroad: 1240-2 and 1245-8.[62] Another instance of this efficiency in administration was the changing rôle of the *capellani*. In his confirmation of the freedom of the burgh of St Andrews which was probably issued early in his pontificate, two chaplains appear.[63] They disappear thereafter until one, Gilbert, reappears a decade later in the foundation charter of Scotlandwell (see below). The place of these two chaplains is taken by one of Malvoisin's *capellani*, Robert rector of Methven, who appears over the first eight years of Bernham's episcopate as episcopal chaplain and penitentiary.[64]

At the end of Bernham's active first eight years the numbers of the bishop's ' inner circle ' contracts and the number of *capellani* increases again. This move towards what may be termed a more ' domestic ' household is reflected in the witness list to the grant of the hospital of Scotlandwell to the Trinitarian friars on 2 January 1250-1: ' Magistris Willelmo de Cunningham; Alexandro de Edeneburgh . Dominis Roberto . Radulfo . Gilberto . Jacobo . Capellanis . Galfrido . Waltero . Gilberto . clericis nostris.'[65]

It is, of course, notoriously difficult to use witness lists as evidence for administrative changes, but it is virtually the only evidence available. Furthermore, the evidence of subsequent episcopates suggests that Bernham's successors followed his innovations. For the next eighty years rarely more than one chaplain and three or four clerks witness episcopal

60. *St. A. Lib.*, 164.
61. Durham Dean and Chapter, Miscellaneous Charter 1320, printed in Raine, *North Durham*, no. 479.
62. Watt, *Fasti*, 323.
63. Scottish Record Office, B65/1/1 f. xxxv r, no. 3 (The Black Book of St Andrews).
64. Ibid., *St. A. Lib.*, 165 (without designation), *Dunf. Reg.*, no. 117, *Pais. Reg.*, 119. As penitentiary, *St. A. Lib.*, 169 (1246)
65. Scottish Record Office, RH 6/48

acts. Thus Bernham created the administrative tradition of having a small, regular and highly competent group of agents responsible for the issuance and authentication of episcopal documents. They may well have been the men most constantly in attendance on the bishop. Behind them, however, lay a large anonymous episcopal chancery staff. From what we know of modern bureaucracy, it seems unlikely that the absolute numbers involved in episcopal administration declined in the thirteenth century. Instead, as administration became more efficient, sophisticated and far-reaching, the size of the administrative staff required by the bishops of St Andrews must have increased. But this point can only be argued by analogy, for the documents are silent.

So the episcopate of David Bernham was one of great importance for St Andrews diocese and for the Scottish church. His national significance rested less in what he did (although that was considerable) than in what he represented. He was a native-born churchman, a townsman, who was also a churchman and a bishop; a member of an international aristocracy. He was strongly influenced by the reforms and changes taking place in the church and attempted to act upon them within his own national and diocesan framework. To do this he built upon the achievement of his Anglo-Norman predecessors. R. L. G. Ritchie once called the greatest of these pioneers, bishop Robert (1127-1159) ' Scotland's Lanfranc.' It is, therefore, no invidious comparison to call bishop David Bernham ' Scotland's Grosseteste.'

'KIN, FREINDIS AND SERVANDIS'
The men who worked with archbishop David Beaton

by

MARGARET H. B. SANDERSON

When James Beaton, sixth archbishop of St Andrews, died on 14 February 1538-9, his nephew who succeeded him as primate of Scotland was at the height of a career which owed as much to his own confident astuteness as to his uncle's early patronage, and had up until then been almost entirely secular in character and experience, although financed from ecclesiastical revenues. Born into a family tradition of royal and diplomatic service, he took his master's degree and a post-graduate course in civil law and went on to serve his political apprenticeship in the train of John, duke of Albany, in the interests of Scotland at the French court, an environment which fulfilled his love of grandeur and gave to his political experience a European dimension lacking in that of many of his countrymen. During king James V's adult reign he became a trusted ambassador and indispensable royal servant, making a place for himself in the central administration. But, whatever career might be chosen by a younger son in a laird's large family, the problem of finding enough to live on meant taking part in the scramble for ecclesiastical livings whether he had a vocation for the church or not. David Beaton's career was advanced by his uncle's patronage and his own and his family's record of royal service—often the surest way to ecclesiastical preferment—and was financed from the revenues, consecutively, of the canonry of Kinkell, the chancellorship of Glasgow and the rich abbacy of Arbroath, resigned to him by his uncle in 1524. Throughout this period his connection with the institutional church was financial and material, although he kept a firm hand on the running of his Arbroath estates, and he remained un-ordained to major orders.[1]

His greatest diplomatic success, the negotiation of the king's marriage to Mary of Lorraine in the winter of 1537 and following spring, took place at a watershed in his career, about the time he became a genuine churchman. During 1537 he was made administrator of the metropolitan see for his ageing uncle. At about the same time came rewards from the French king, who had already granted him letters of naturalisation, for whom ' Monsieur d'Albrot ' represented the stability of Franco-Scottish alignment. On 5 December 1537, on the nomination of Francis I, Pope Paul III provided him to the bishopric of Mirepoix. Consecrated some-time between late July and mid-August 1538 and raised to the cardinalate

---

1. Glasgow university, Vatican transcripts, Reg. Supp., 2020, fos 173r-v; I am grateful to Dr I. Cowan and Mr T. Smyth for this reference.

45

on 20 December, he was about to be associated with the ecclesiastical establishment more closely than ever before.[2] The archbishopric of St Andrews, when it came, brought him not only increased revenues but a new area of personal initiative. To the weight of his influence with the king in political affairs was added the prestige of head of the first estate, enhanced by the international character of the cardinalate, and a greater opportunity than had hitherto been his of steering the combined policy of church and state into decidedly orthodox, pro-French channels. Two important areas of control remained to be worked for and were eventually won after the king's death, the faculty of legate _a latere_ in the ecclesiastical sphere and the chancellorship of the realm.

To be archbishop of St Andrews was to rule a kingdom within a kingdom, which stretched from Kincardine to the Lothians. Writs might be addressed to ' our subjects ' and the king's capital referred to as ' the toun of Edinburgh within our diocese of St Andrews.' The archbishop had control over the spiritual and material aspects of many lives and his representatives, professionally qualified and non-hereditary, were more closely supervised by him than were some royal officers by the king. He was at the head of two distinct but related administrative systems, each with its own courts, procedures and staff; one, ecclesiastical, operating through the diocesan machinery, the other, temporal, through which, as a landed magnate, he administered those lands which had accrued to the see over the centuries. There were areas of involvement with other authorities; the priory of St Andrews the canons of which formed the archbishop's chapter, the suffragan bishops of his province, the university of St Andrews of which he was chancellor. As primate of Scotland he had the opportunity to mould and lead the church's corporate attitude to public questions of religion and politics and to establish a _modus vivendi_ with the archbishop of Glasgow who claimed certain exemptions from the primatial see.

Because David Beaton is remembered as a prince of the church and a politician, his rôle as archbishop of St Andrews has tended to be overlooked. Since, on the whole, historians are still using a working interpretation of him largely created in the nineteenth and early twentieth centuries, it has been usual to consider his career against the panoramic background of big issues and not to look for echoes of his public policy in the details of his daily administration. Moreover, the traditional image of him as an almost apocalyptic figure, a tradition which began in near-contemporary writing, has tended to place him in notorious isolation so that so far no attempt has been made to analyse the composition of his household and administrative staff although such an analysis might be expected to throw light on his motives and methods where he had opportunity to choose his associates or was required to get on with those

2. J. Dowden, _The Bishops of Scotland_, 41

who were part of the machinery when he took it over. The present necessarily limited discussion is mainly concerned with his *familia* and circle of closest associates.

*   *   *   *

As an unusually preoccupied archbishop and because of the frequently crucial state of public affairs, he needed men whom he knew well and could trust in charge of his business. These facts, as much as the customary exercise of patronage, may help to explain the presence on his staff of so many relatives and men from east Fife families whom he had probably known all his life. It is significant, too, that he occasionally employed and, in some cases, appropriated the services of one or two royal clerks, not simply because he was the kind of master who liked his servants to be ' out of the top drawer ' but because these men formed a useful channel of information on what was going on behind the royal scenes.

The key diocesan posts, the two archdeaconries of St Andrews principal and Lothian, with their respective judicial deputies, the Officials, were either held or gradually filled by men with long-standing connections with David Beaton; his cousin, George Durie, abbot of Dunfermline; his brother, Mr Walter Beaton, canon of Glasgow; Mr Martin Balfour and Mr Abraham Crichton. While abbot of Arbroath, David had worked closely with his cousin George Durie, making him ' conservator ' of the abbey's privileges and once sharing with him the distinction of being ' cursed ' by their uncle for non-payment of certain fruits of their respective abbacies to which they had been appointed through the archbishop's classic nepotism.[3] George held the archdeaconry of St Andrews by the time of David's promotion, became one of the most frequent witnesses of his writs, was constantly in his company and, apparently, in his political counsels, a recognised member of ' the French party.'[4] He became an extraordinary lord of session and privy councillor and seems to have had a measure of personal influence over the governor, Arran. Mr Walter Beaton, who spent a commendable amount of time at the cathedral of Glasgow, where he was canon of Govan, became archdeacon of Lothian in 1545 after the death of Patrick Stewart.[5] Overshadowed by his younger, more famous brother, Walter had had an early career of ecclesiastical preferment and had preceded David to the university of Orleans, the great school of civil law.[6] After the latter's promotion to St Andrews, the brothers were more together, Walter receiving a pension of £100 from the archbishopric.[7] It was probably Walter, with his cousin, Andrew

3. British Museum, Additional MSS, 33245, fo 105r. S[cottish] R[ecord] O[ffice], Acta dominorum concilii et sessionis [Hereafter ADCS], ix, fo 142r.
4. J. Knox, *History of the Reformation in Scotland*, ed. W. C. Dickinson. [Hereafter Knox, *History*], i, 80, 99, 347.
5. Vatican transcripts, Reg. Supp., 2543, fo 234r; 2555, fo 135r.
6. *Miscellany of the Scottish History Society*, vol. 11 (1904), 84.
7. *Rentale Sancti Andree*, ed. R. K. Hannay (Scottish History Society), 1913 [Hereafter *Rentale*], 126.

Durie, whom the Cardinal detailed to look after the elderly papal legate, Marco Grimani, who arrived in Scotland in 1543. Andrew Durie, the only monk in his generation of Beatons, had a reputation for riotous living and versifying but Walter, who played the lute, had had a continental education and was to turn academic in later life, may have been good company.[8]

In 1540 the posts of Official of St Andrews and of Lothian required to be filled. Mr Martin Balfour, canon and later provost of St Salvator's, professor of theology, had served his apprenticeship for the post of Official of St Andrews by witnessing the acts of the then Official in the 1520s and by acting as commissary from 1528 to 1530 and in 1535.[9] Now and then he was appointed procurator for David Beaton as abbot of Arbroath, once in partnership with the rising young lawyer, Henry Balnaves.[10] In 1526 he witnessed a charter by the abbot's brother and became vicar of Monimail in the patronage of his uncle, the archbishop.[11] After 1539 he occasionally witnessed the Cardinal's charters and a charter *to* him in 1542.[12] Mr Abraham Crichton, who became Official of Lothian in 1540, had had sufficiently close connections with the Beaton family to be made joint-curator with the abbot of the latter's brother-in-law, John Wardlaw of Torry who, in 1532, was pronounced *non compos mentis*.[13] Although in the same year Mr Abraham appeared in the civil court on behalf of archbishop James Beaton in his case against his nephew over the revenues of Arbroath, and was at that time attached to the archbishop's household,[14] he seems to have worked well enough with David Beaton after the latter's promotion, being associated with him both at Edinburgh, where the Official held his consistorial court in St. Giles' church, and at St Andrews.[15]

During David Beaton's six years as archbishop, the other diocesan clergy, rural deans, commissaries and their deputies and the clerks of their courts moved around these posts a good deal.[16] While it is difficult to prove that the archbishop engineered these changes, he sometimes filled a vacancy with his own man. When the important rural deanery of Linlithgow, which held the rich mensal church and episcopal barony of Kirkliston, was resigned in 1539 by John Williamson who had held it since 1523, it was successively administered by the archbishop's two

8. Letters of the papal legate in *Scottish Historical Review*, vol. xi (1914), 21. SRO, Glasgow register of testaments, CC9/7/1, fos 95v-96r. *Muniments of the university of Glasgow* (Maitland Club, 1854), i, 57; ii, 172.
9. *Register of Crail collegiate church* (Grampian Club, 1877), 47. SRO, Crawford priory muniments, GD 20/73. *Fasti Ecclesiae Scoticanae Medii Aevi* (Scottish Record Society, 1969) [Hereafter *Fasti*], 328-29.
10. *Liber S. Thome de Aberbrothoc* (Bannatyne Club, 1848-56), ii, 588, 643, 750, 758, 836. [Hereafter *Liber Aberbrothoc*].
11. Ibid., ii, 588. *RMS*, iii, 897.
12. Ibid., iii, 2788.
13. *RSS*, ii, 1388.
14. SRO, ADCS, i, fos 119v-120r. *RMS*, iii, 1017.
15. SRO, Dick Lauder Papers, GD 41/375. *Rentale*, 184.
16. *Fasti*, 314-22, 328-32.

secretaries, Mr George Cook and Mr Andrew Oliphant. In fact, Cook held the rural deaneries of Haddington and Linlithgow concurrently from 1541 to 1543. Linlithgow may indeed be a case of deliberate replacement. So may Kinghorn and Fothrif of which Mr Andrew Oliphant was rural dean in 1539, lack of earlier records making it impossible as yet to determine when and from whom he took over. Mr John Brown, commissary of St Andrews and clerk of the Official's court, was demoted to deputy-clerk under the archbishop's chief secretary, Mr John Lauder, but thereafter acted as a notary in connection with the episcopal chancery.[17]

The man to whom David Beaton entrusted most non-diocesan business was a layman, his cousin, Archibald Beaton of Capildrae, who was his senior, being the oldest nephew and heir of archbishop James in whose household he had begun his career and for whom he became chamberlain of Dunfermline abbey in the 1530s.[18] Archibald became his cousin's right-hand man, auditor of the accounts, graniter from 1540, chamberlain from 1541 to 1542, in an experiment which temporarily united both offices in his hands, and bailie and steward of the regality from about 1541 to 1544. He was clearly a capable person who did not turn his offices into sinecures. The signature which he appended to documents, if somewhat unsophisticated, was more literate than that of the Cardinal's oldest brother, the laird of Balfour. In 1541, with Mr Henry Lumsden, a cleric, Archibald was appointed commissioner and 'place-holder' in regality business for the Cardinal, then going abroad, and was also entrusted with a list of presentees to benefices in the Cardinal's patronage to which the secretary, John Lauder, was empowered to grant collation, this in spite of the fact that a suffragan had been appointed.[19] Archibald witnessed many documents, was made one of the Cardinal's testamentary executors and a curator of his oldest natural son, David Beaton of Melgund.[20] Archibald Beaton's appointment as graniter displaced a cleric, Mr Alan Lamont, who is found in that capacity in 1535 and as chamberlain of the priory in 1528, an office which he continued to hold.[21]

The chamberlainry of the archbishopric passed through the hands of five men in David Beaton's time;[22] Mr Henry Lumsden, who had been James Beaton's chamberlain, Archibald Beaton, who was graniter at the same time, Mr Alexander Kinmond, appointed regent in arts in the New College, who was chamberlain in 1543, Mr Bernard Bailie, one of David Beaton's closest friends, of whom more will be said later, who held office

17. *Rentale*, 120, 135.
18. SRO, Acta dominorum concilii [Hereafter ADC], xxxviii, fo 62r *Exchequer Rolls*, xvi, 232, xvii, 52.
19. SRO, Protocol book of James Androsoun, NP 1/5a, fo 14. *Rentale*, liv, 117; Archibald Beaton became chamberlain on 12 April 1541, the Cardinal left for France in the following July.
20. *St Andrews Formulare*, ed. G. Donaldson (Stair Society, 1942-44) [Hereafter *Formulare*], 624.
21. SRO, Register House charters, RH 6/114a. *Lamont Papers* (Scottish Record Society, 1914), 37, 68.
22. *Rentale, passim*.

in 1544, and Mr Alexander Crichton, a relative of Mr Abraham Crichton, the Official of Lothian, who became chamberlain in 1545. There would almost seem to have been a definite policy of changing the holder of this office. Mr Henry Lumsden, James Beaton's chamberlain since at least 1527, who, as a chaplain in the abbey church of Dunfermline had been dispensed from making residence in order to attend on the archbishop, had been presented in 1534 to the vicarage of Tarves by David Beaton, as abbot of Arbroath, in whose patronage it lay.[23] Although replaced as chamberlain by Archibald Beaton, he continued in the Cardinal's household, acted as his commissioner during his absences abroad, witnessed many charters and audited the chamberlains' and graniter's accounts. Like the two Crichtons he belonged to Fife, a relative of Lumsden of Pitello.[24] As in the case of the chamberlainry, the jointly-held offices of steward and bailie of the regality passed through several hands, those of Archibald Beaton (1542-4), George Winchester, another layman, during whose short term of office a valuation of the regality was made for the purpose of taxation (1544-5),[25] and Robert Beaton of Creich, the Cardinal's second-cousin, who combined his office with that of steward of Fife for the king, which had been in his family for at least three generations.[26]

Apart from his near relatives, David Beaton's closest friend, to judge by the fact that he was constantly with him and was entrusted with much private and personal business, was Mr Bernard Bailie, parson of his home parish kirk of Lamington in the upper ward of Lanarkshire. David and he were distantly related[27] and their families may have been in touch in earlier years for Bernard's father, Mr Cuthbert Bailie, brother of the laird of Lamington, parson of Sanquhar and commendator of Glenluce, followed archbishop James Beaton as treasurer of the realm and sat with him as an auditor of the exchequer in 1511.[28] Bernard's younger brother, Richard, became one of the Cardinal's servants while he was still abbot of Arbroath.[29] There are no contemporary comments on Bernard Bailie as there are in the case of George Durie, but he seems to have been entirely in David Beaton's confidence and a regular member of his household. He was chamberlain of Arbroath by 1528 and held office for ten years after which he and sir James Auchmowty held the office alternately. He regularly witnessed the Cardinal's documents, audited his accounts and acted as chamberlain in 1544. With Archibald Beaton he became one of the Cardinal's testamentary executors and curator of the young laird of Melgund.

23. *RMS*, iii, 482. *RSS*, ii, 796. *Liber Aberbrothoc*, ii, 798.
24. SRO, Register of deeds, old series, vi, fo 334r. Alexander Crichton was brother of Crichton of Camnay; *RSS*, iii, 1335.
25. SRO, Miscellaneous collections, GD 1/54/2.
26. SRO, Clerk of Penicuik Muniments, GD 18/461.
27. Bernard's cousin, William Bailie of Bakky, married Janet, daughter of James, 1st earl of Arran, and the Cardinal's cousin, Janet Beaton of Creich.
28. *Exchequer Rolls*, xiii, 448, 606. *Transactions of the Dumfries and Galloway Natural History and Antiquarian Society*, 3rd series, vol. xii (1926), 72.
29. *RSS*, ii, 2166. *Rentale*, 140, 167

Sir James Auchmowty, a priest who served David Beaton for over sixteen years, probably belonged to the family of Auchmowty of that Ilk in the Cardinal's home parish of Markinch and may, therefore, have known him all his life. From 1530 onwards he handled the fees derived from David Beaton's keepership of the privy seal and from 1538 acted periodically as chamberlain of Arbroath abbey.[30] In 1540 he was a steward and provisor of the archbishop's household and is often found transacting business for him, ranging from the distribution of alms to the sale of the victual rents at Dunbar harbour.[31] In 1543 his brother, Mr Robert Auchmowty, acted temporarily as graniter for Archibald Beaton.[32] Sir David Christison, to whom the Cardinal gave considerable responsibility, also came from east Fife.[33] He was for a time in the royal household but at the same time was presented to several vicarages in the patronage of the abbot of Arbroath, including that of Lunan (traditionally associated with Walter Mill, the priest whom David Beaton is said to have early suspected of heresy) and was not the only royal clerk to go over to the abbot's service. In April 1536 he was still a steward in the royal household, but in the autumn of that year he acted as procurator for the abbot and was soon afterwards numbered among his servants.[34] He witnessed several of the Cardinal's writs and travelled far on his business, making two journeys to France in 1542.[35]

The sprinkling of chaplains in the archbishop's household included Mr John Methven and Mr William Young, who had charge of the private chapel in St Andrews castle, the two almoners, one of whom, Gilbert McMath, was a priest of Glasgow diocese, sir Walter Mar, son of a St Andrews baker, who was master of work at the New College as well as of the parish kirk of Holy Trinity, and sir John Simpson, the sub-graniter.[36] A priest who left the royal household under suspicion to enter David Beaton's service was sir Henry Balfour, royal chaplain and almoner, whom the Cardinal was accused of having bribed to draw up an instrument purporting to contain the dying king's will. If he can be identified with the priest of that name, who in February 1538-9 was accused of having torn a summons from the hands of a messenger, saying, 'and he had wantin his armis he suld stow his luggis,' he sounds just the man for such a job.[37] After the king's death Balfour joined the Cardinal's household and became a master of work at the castle.[38]

30. *RSS*, ii, pp. 766-67. SRO, ADCS, ix, fo 91v. *Rentale*, 120, 135.
31. Ibid., 92, 109, 142, 186.
32. Ibid., 166.
33. Chaplain at Crail in 1512; *Register of Crail*, 21. May have belonged to Dysart; *Notices of Local Records of Dysart* (Maitland Club, 1853), 24; *Rentale*, 126.
34. SRO, Royal Household Books, E 32/8, fo 130v. *RSS*, ii, 2166.
35. *Rentale*, 126, 139.
36. (McMath) St Andrews university muniments, SM 110 B1 P1 9. (Mar) W. Rankin, *Holy Trinity Church, St Andrews*, 87. *Rentale*, 83.
37. *Sheriff court book of Fife*, ed. W. C. Dickinson (Scottish History Society, 1928), 244. SRO, ADCS, xi, fo 134r. Vatican transcripts, Reg. Supp., 2435, fo 8v. *HMC Report*, xi, pt. vi, 219-30.
38. *Rentale*, 177, 179.

The archbishop's writing office was under the direction of his chief secretary, Mr John Lauder, a dominating personality with a finely-polished brain inside a rough exterior, a loud voice, a sense of drama and a tremendous capacity for work.[39] The pages of the great account book of the archbishopric, of the book of styles which he compiled during a busy working life and an impressive pile of extant charters, are covered with his bold handwriting. He and David Beaton got on well, for two such positive characters, although John had failed to see eye to eye with his uncle. He had a vast regard for his master's importance—' is not my lord cardinal the second person within this realm?' he demanded of George Wishart, a rhetorical question which would have made the governor wince had he heard it—and loved to roll his titles off his tongue, and pen. In addition to being chief secretary and notary, he kept the final accounts, all but one of which he audited, witnessed many documents and was chief clerk of the Official of St Andrews, with custody of the court registers and the Official's seal. He conducted several heresy trials at which he was a thorough interrogator, if a bit inclined to go beyond his terms of reference and argue with the accused, a fault for which he was reprimanded at Wishart's trial.[40] Lauder's senior colleague was Mr Andrew Oliphant, another Fife man and probable graduate of St Andrews, who had served archbishop James Beaton.[41] As the new archbishop's ' Weel belovit clerk ' he was secretary and notary, mainly in diocesan as distinct from regality business, his representative at Rome over the thorny question of the Glasgow exemption and rural dean of Kinghorn and Fothrif (1539-40) and Linlithgow (1544-5).[42] He was a considerable pluralist, holding the vicarages of Foulis, Ballantrae in Ayrshire and Carnbee in Fife, probably his home parish, as well as chaplainries in St Salvator's and St Andrews parish church.[43] Compared with his rumbustious colleague, Oliphant appears as an efficient, professional curial official, writing in a neat, almost impersonal notarial hand, who could keep his temper, something which long diplomatic experience had failed to teach his master. Even at the farcical trial of Sandy Furrour he refused to be provoked beyond giving the accused a terse initial warning.[44] When serving under his third archbishop he was described by Randolph as ' a faithfull chaplain and a paynefull . . .'[45]

Mr George Hay who at one time acted as secretary to both king and cardinal, in taking their petitions for the legateship to Rome, was dis-

---

39. *Formulare*, ii, Introduction, for biographical details.
40. Knox, *History*, ii, 233-43.
41. Probably an Oliphant of Kellie, Carnbee parish. Made oversman of his sister's testament in 1550; SRO, St Andrews register of testaments. CC20/4/1, fo 162v. *Acta Facultatis Artium Universitatis Sancti Andree*, ed. A. I. Dunlop (Scottish History Society, 1964), ii, 350. SRO, Justiciary Records, JC1/5, 6 May 1532. *RMS*, iii, 1017. *HMC Report*, vii, 306.
42. *Papers of Sir Ralph Sadler*, ed. A. Clifford (1809), ii, 239-40.
43. *RMS*, v, 1050. *RSS*, vi, 1402. Rankin, *Holy Trinity*, 98. SRO, register of presentations to benefices, CH 4/1/2, fo 79.
44. Knox, *History*, i, 18-19.
45. *Sadler Papers*, ii, 239-40.

FOURTEENTH-CENTURY TOMBSTONE: ST ANDREWS CATHEDRAL

This fourteenth-century tombstone in the south choir aisle of St Andrews cathedral probably marks the grave of William Bell, bishop-elect of St Andrews, 1332-1342. See page 86.

PLATE X. COAT OF ARMS OF THE ISLE OF MAN: ST ANDREWS CATHEDRAL.

In the Cathedral Museum there is a fragment of a late Gothic pier, on which is carved in high relief a shield bearing the coat of arms of the Isle of Man. This is probably from one of the nine pillars of the south arcade of the nave, reconstructed after the fire of 1378. The coat of arms would be that of John Dunbar, earl of Moray (1372-1391), whose grandfather Thomas Randolph had been granted Man, with Moray, in 1312.

tantly related to the latter.[46] In March 1538-9 he received a pension of £100 from David Beaton as the new archbishop and was sent to Rome in the following year.[47] He obtained the Aberdeen canonry of Rathven and the Glasgow one of Eddleston on the resignation of his brother, Mr Thomas Hay, who had been a royal secretary in the 1520s under the Albany regime.[48] George Hay wrote some of the formal documents issued from the episcopal chancery and witnessed many others. Mr George Cook, brother of an Edinburgh burgess, had served archbishop James Beaton till the end of his life. Six days before the archbishop's death he subscribed the charter in favour of the New College on behalf of the sick primate.[49] His earlier contacts with David Beaton arose from the fact that he had been made clerk of the privy seal for life in 1535, and it is from his memoranda scribbled in the register that we learn something of the administration of the office under David Beaton's keepership, and even information for his itinerary.[50] On one occasion Mr Bernard Bailie annoyed Cook by walking into the office and personally sealing a document, the contents of which he refused to divulge.[51] George Cook wrote the earliest extant document running in the Cardinal's name as archbishop of St Andrews, letters of collation to a prebend in Bothans collegiate church on behalf of the brother of Mr George Hay, dated 16 February 1538-9, two days after the death of James Beaton.[52]

Sir Thomas Knox, ' writer to the cardinal,' was an acquisition from Glasgow in which archdiocese he had been ordained and to which he returned after the Cardinal's death.[53] His beautiful, controlled handwriting was a gift to any chancery and is mainly to be found on the large prestige documents issued under the Cardinal's authority as legate *a latere* after 1544, although an early example is a decreet by the suffragan dated 15 June 1542 in which Knox is designated ' clerk of the city of Glasgow and notary public.'[54] Later that year, after the Cardinal's return from France, he was paid £5 for writing some of the archbishop's accounts and by 1545 he was permanently on the chancery staff. He and John Lauder wrote all the extant legatine writs, which were endorsed by Knox and entered by him in the appropriate register. In most cases Mr George Cook signed as *datarius*, dating and authenticating them, his subscription appearing on the front under the fold made to take the seal. In one case authentication was done by Andrew Oliphant. The margins of these documents are generous and the initial word is ornamented in clumsy imitation of the papal chancery style, a refinement used—rather better—

46. His mother was Janet Beaton, his father Mr George Hay of Minzean, second son of lord Hay of Yester; *Scots Peerage;* SRO, Yester Writs, GD 28/653, 656, 657.
47. *Rentale*, 94, 107. *Letters of James V*, ed. D. Hay (1954), 402, 405.
48. *RSS*, ii, 493. Vatican transcripts, Reg. Supp., 2485, fo 148v. SRO, ADC, xxxiii, fo 31r.
49. SRO, register of deeds, old series, xi, fos 23v-24r. St A. Univ. Mun. SM 110 B15 2.
50. *RSS*, ii, Appendix.
51. Ibid., ii, p. 772.
52. SRO, Yester Writs, GD 28/541.
53. *Thirds of Benefices*, ed. G. Donaldson (Scottish History Society, 1949), 164.
54. SRO, Yester Writs, GD 28/596.

E

by one of David Beaton's writers at Arbroath as early as 1529 when not only the initial word but the whole document was set out in the style of the papal chancery.[55] This practice continued at Arbroath, occurring on documents of 1533 and 1543, the latter a very ornate example although simply a piece of routine regality business.[56]

Some of the extant Arbroath charters dating from 1539 onwards were written in the episcopal chancery by Lauder and Knox and then sent to the monastery to be subscribed by the convent, sometimes *before* and at other times *after* subscription by the Cardinal as commendator. Another element of centralisation lay in the fact that Mr Bernard Bailie and sir James Auchmowty, who alternated as the abbey chamberlain, were regular members of the archbishop's household, although the graniter and sacrist of Arbroath, sir John Arnot and sir William Ford, the latter having charge of the great barn, seem to have been based at the abbey.

The Cardinal's French secretary, simply called 'Peter' in the accounts, may perhaps be identified with Francis Petrus, Frenchman, who was 'writer of letters and provisions' in archbishop John Hamilton's chancery in the 1550s and who used the italic hand.[57] Neither Knox nor Lauder wrote in italic but it may have been used by their French colleague in documents intended for the continent. A handful of notaries are known to have worked for the Cardinal and examples of their writing survive: Mr John Ballantyne, Mr John Chapman, Mr John Brown and Mr Henry Methven, layman and bailie of St Andrews, who lived in South Street and was clerk of the regality court.[58]

David Beaton's professional *familia* would appear to have been a group of experienced and versatile administrators and clerks. With the exception of Martin Balfour, none were academics, let alone scholars, although ten of those whom we have considered were at least Masters of Arts. His secretaries and clerks worked against a background of the coming and going of men about their worldly business, in St Andrews, Edinburgh, Linlithgow, Stirling or wherever their master happened to be, sometimes in the midst of a political crisis. The *familia*, in fact, took its character from the archbishop himself who was politician first and churchman afterwards, for whom the integrity of ecclesiastical authority was vital for the maintenance of the political order in which he believed and the survival of his family's fortunes which had been built upon it. The spirit of dynasticism which he had inherited from his uncle caused him to place much of his business in the hands of relatives and friends since these were the only men whom he could trust. Those closest to him were careerists like himself, if on a lesser scale, who relied on his patronage and shared his outlook and priorities. Some of them, including

55. SRO, Benhom Writs, GD 4/243.
56. SRO, Airlie Muniments, GD 16/25/81.
57. Protocol book of Gilbert Grote, ed. W. Angus (Scottish Record Society, 1914), no. 129.
58. SRO, St Andrews charters, B65/22/227, 253, 261. *Rentale*, 81, 115.

George Durie and Bernard Bailie, lived, like himself, in open concubin-
age, churchmen in no more than the letter of the law. It is significant,
incidentally, that while he was continually surrounded by relatives on
his father's side of the family, he seems to have had little contact with
his maternal relatives, the Moneypennys, who in the end threw in their
lot with his assassins.[59]

His household was that of a great lord: ' the cardinal keeps a great
house and gives great fees, such a house as was never under a king.' Those
who captured his castle of St. Andrews were astounded at its princely
furnishings. His household moved with him, wholly or in part, from one
residence to another, the castle towering above the sea at St Andrews,
the manor at Monimail, the abbot's house at Arbroath, where the king
was entertained on occasion, and the lodging in Edinburgh, on the corner
of the Blackfriars' Wynd and Cowgate. Arrangements were in the hands
of numerous officials and servants:[60] the captain of St Andrews castle
with his guards, men-at-arms, porter, engineer and gunners; the masters
of work who supplied and paid the masons, barrowmen, smiths and
wrights who were engaged during much of David Beaton's term of office
in strengthening the castle's fortifications; the provisors of the castle and
those of the household who bought food and fuel or received victual
directly from the graniter; the master of the household, cooks and kitchen
staff, from Gabriel the French cook who had his own servant to the
keeper of the pewter and the scullions; the master of the horse, muleteer
and stable servants; the upholsterers, baker, brewer and gardeners; the
Cardinal's personal attendants, pages, lackey, barber, tailors and apothecary. There were also about twenty other ' servants ' including William
Blair who ' played on the tabor ' and John Lowys, the fool, who had the
most dangerous occupation of them all! One group who may have tended
to keep themselves apart were the French servants, some of whom were
the Cardinal's personal attendants; Claud, the barber, Baugé, the lackey,
another Claud, a page, who may be synonymous with a singing boy of
that name, Stephen, the tailor, who, having taken steady delivery of red
cloth of all kinds, must have cut enthusiastically into the ' violet colored
camelot ' which cost £16 from an Edinburgh merchant, Gabriel, the
cook, already mentioned, John, the upholsterer, to whose young assistant
the Cardinal gave 22s to spend at his sister's wedding, Francis, deputy
master of the horse and Michael the muleteer. Amand Guthrie, the
Cardinal's chief page, listed among the French servants in the accounts,
may have belonged to an expatriate Scottish family. He accompanied the
Cardinal to France in 1541, receiving new clothes for the occasion costing
over £10.[61] In a graphic way the archbishopric accounts occasionally give
an identity to those servants who appear anonymously on the stage of

59. George Moneypenny was a servant of Henry Balnaves in 1544; *Rentale*, 194.
60. *Rentale, passim*. When in Edinburgh the Cardinal regularly patronised ' by appointment '
craftsmen, the king's baker, apothecary, goldsmith, tailor, embroiderer and shoemaker, and
borrowed money from leading merchants who also loaned to the king and nobility.
61. Ibid., 125, 141

recorded history; sir John Simpson, probably the priest who, in the uproar surrounding the Cardinal's arrest in January 1542-3, was seen scuttling out of the gateway at Holyrood, impeded by his master's processional cross, on his way to warn the captain of St Andrews castle,[62] and poor Ambrose Stirling, the castle porter, whose body Norman Leslie and his accomplices threw into the ditch on the morning of the Cardinal's assassination. Ironically, when so much of the castle that knew David Beaton has disappeared, one perfectly preserved feature is the slop-sink out of which Rutledge and Troillus, the scullions, cast the kitchen refuse. Troillus, who may, like some infinitely more exalted members of the staff, have been purloined from the royal household, must be one of few named medieval menials the scene of whose labours can be pointed out.[63]

The posts of provisor of the castle and household changed hands from time to time as did more important offices. Alan Coutts, chief provisor of the household, worked in turn with Mr William Young, sir James Auchmowty and sir Alexander Kerse, the last-named a former member of archbishop James Beaton's household. Coutts, a layman, was as versatile as any of the archbishop's clerks, not only supervising the provision of the household and keeping the diet books, but furnishing the ship, *Unicorn*, in which the Cardinal sailed to France in 1541, riding as far as Argyll on his master's business, confirming testaments in the Cardinal's name in absence of the chamberlain and receiving the victual rents from Stow from the officer there, Henry Knox. David Rutherford, master of the stable from 1539 to 1542, belonged to the Arbroath district and was probably a relative of the abbey's subprior, Thomas Rutherford, who, in 1549, witnessed a charter to David and his wife of the lands of Murehouse granted to them by James Beaton, the Cardinal's nephew, then abbot, ' in return for his long service to the late Cardinal in Scotland and France.'[64] Rutherford was succeeded as master of the stable by Robert Lindsay who may have set up as a stabler in Edinburgh after the Cardinal's death.[65]

John Beaton of Balfour, the Cardinal's nephew, as captain of St Andrews castle, was probably the most trusted relative of all. In addition to this responsible job he audited the accounts and was made one of his uncle's testamentary executors in 1544. Both Buchanan and Spottiswood in their *Histories* narrate, without naming John Beaton, how the captain of the castle invited George Wishart to have breakfast with him on the morning of the latter's death, receiving the complimentary reply, ' very willingly, and so much the rather because I perceive you to be a good

62. Ibid., 142.
63. Reference to ' Troillous the groom who keeps the dishes ' in the royal household books, in 1541; SRO, E34/5/2. First mentioned at St Andrews, in 1543; *Rentale*, 178.
64. SRO, Northesk Muniments, GD 130 Box 19. Rutherford was enough of a personal friend to be made curator of the Cardinal's daughter, Elizabeth; SRO, Dalhousie Muniments, GD 45/16/620.
65. SRO, Edinburgh testaments, CC8/8/1, fo 221.

Christian and a man fearing God.'[66] John must have been confident in handling his uncle to suggest any such thing although he may have broken into a cold sweat as the heretic turned breakfast into a protestant communion service. Even this, however, did not prevent his giving Wishart a final word of encouragement at the place of execution. It may have been a streak of charity in him which helped him to cope with his uncle's masterful personality.

Like the household of many great lords, that of David Beaton had its company of noblemen's and gentlemen's sons. Some were there simply to learn the arts of living in a great household. Young Thomas Maule, son of the laird of Panmure, who had been brought up in a lawyer's household in Edinburgh before joining that of David Beaton, went with him to France in 1541 and remained with him till his death, although he was fortunately out of the castle at the time of the assassination.[67] The barony of the young laird of Kellie, who was also a member of the household and for whom the Cardinal bought clothes, was in the regality of Arbroath, making it likely that he was the Cardinal's ward in the 1540s.[68] The sons of the ' baron of Dalzeil ' attended St. Andrews university on his expenses.[69] Other young men were with him as pledges of their own or their fathers' political support. The Governor's oldest son joined the household after his father's capitulation in the autumn of 1543 and the young lord Gray himself in terms of a bond of manrent between him and the Cardinal in 1544.[70] Alexander Crichton of Brunston and Norman Leslie were both in his following before disillusionment and king Henry's money encouraged them to work for his downfall. George Ramsay of Clatty was a personal friend and distant relative who, in the 1520s, had become security for David Beaton when the latter borrowed money to pay his uncle's share of the fruits of Arbroath and to redeem the earl of Moray's pension which was charged on the abbacy.[71]

The Cardinal had a wider circle of friends, including the cultivated lord Seton and the earl of Moray, the king's natural brother, to consider all of whom would lead to a discussion of politics which is not the purpose of this paper. An important personal friend was sir Adam Otterburn, professional lawyer, ambassador and provost of Edinburgh, whose efforts to promote good relations with England during James V's lifetime never lost him David Beaton's confidence. Basically, an orthodox Catholic and patriot, Otterburn withdrew his support from the pro-English party as soon as the extent of Henry VIII's designs on Scotland became clear. He

66. J. Spottiswood, *History of the church of Scotland* (London, 1851), i, 160. G. Buchanan, *History of Scotland* (Aberdeen, 1799), 149.
67. *Registrum de Panmure*, ed. J. Stuart (1874), i, xxxi. Robert Leslie, the ' man of law ' with whom Thomas Maule had lived, may have been Robert Leslie of Innerpeffar who handled David Beaton's legal business as abbot of Arbroath; *Liber Aberbrothoc*, ii, 675.
68. *Rentale*, 224.
69. Ibid., 198.
70. *Spalding Club Miscellany*, v. 295-96.
71. SRO, ADC, xxxv, fo 20r-v.

told Sadler shrewdly, when plans for the marriage of the infant queen and prince Edward failed to mature, that if England had had ' the lass ' and Scotland ' the lad ' Henry would not have been so anxious for the union.[72] On 8 April 1546 Otterburn wrote to the Cardinal refuting allegations of ' scharpeness ' laid against him by Oliver Sinclair whom he had ' assolzeit ' of a standing debt for months on end, adding, ' I have na gude to pay my dettis and my dochteris tocher quham I have marrit laitlie except that det.'[73] Since David Beaton may well have received his friend's letter on the day on which he settled 4,000 merks on his own daughter, about to marry the master of Crawford, the side-shaft was extremely pertinent if not actually intentional.[74] Another civil lawyer in David Beaton's circle was Mr Thomas Marjoribanks, advocate, provost of Edinburgh in 1540 and eventually clerk register. Marjoribanks, who may still have been at Orleans university when David arrived in 1519, loaned him money on several occasions to meet his diplomatic expenses in France and was his regular advocate in the civil court.[75] He witnessed his charter to lord Borthwick on 22 March 1543-4 in company with a number of those closest to him.[76] The Cardinal seems to have put his faith in the civil lawyers rather than the canonists.

Unreflective activist though he was, he did have some contacts with a more scholarly circle. Mr Adam Mure, a Paris graduate, who taught in Edinburgh grammar school in the 1530s, became his servant at a fee of £40 a year and acted as pedagogue to his young relatives, taking his great-nephews to Crail grammar school and buying books for his son, Alexander, whom Mure may have tutored.[77] In a letter to the pope in 1544 the Cardinal referred to him as his secretary. Mr William Manderston, student and friend of John Major, philosopher and doctor of medicine, gave both archbishop James Beaton and the Cardinal the benefit of his medical advice, receiving an annual fee of £40 and his travelling expenses. In the late autumn of 1542 he and the apothecary rode to Arbroath, in company with John Beaton, presumably to attend on the Cardinal.[78] In January 1539-40, in association with John Major, Manderston founded a bursary in theology in St Salvator's, the Cardinal being among those for whom it was laid down the holder should say mass.[79] He witnessed a charter by the Cardinal in October 1542.[80] The

---

72. J. A. Inglis, *Sir Adam Otterburn* (1935), 74-75.
73. *Scottish Correspondence of Mary of Lorraine*, ed. A. I. Cameron (Scottish History Society, 1927), 161-62.
74. Otterburn wrote his letter on 8 April, Margaret Beaton's marriage contract was drawn up on 10 April; SRO, Dalhousie Muniments, GD45/17/9. Sir Adam had loaned the Cardinal's cousin, Andrew Durie, 1,800 merks towards the expenses of his provision to Melrose abbey in 1527. SRO, Morton Papers, GD 150/1449.
75. *Miscellany of the Scottish History Society*, vol. 11 (1904), 98. *Rentale*, 93, 125. SRO, ADC, *passim*.
76. SRO, Stair muniments, GD 135/78.
77. *Rentale*, 95, 107, 199. Presented to the vicarage of Kinearny by the Cardinal as commendator of Arbroath, c January 1540-1; *Formulare*, ii, 426.
78. With archbishop James Beaton six days before latter's death; St A. Univ. Mun. SM 110 B1 P2 4. *Rentale*, 94, 101, 107, 115, 131, 141.
79. St A. Univ. Mun. B, fos 108r-09v.
80. *RMS*, iii, 2662.

latter's choice of a suffragan fell on Mr William Gibson, an academic with practical experience of the civil law, who was a native of Scoonie parish, Fife. His vicars-general, first appointed in 1539, were Alexander Myln, abbot of Cambuskenneth, president of the court of session, and Robert Reid, abbot of Kinloss and, from 1541, bishop of Orkney. Reid, sincere in his religion and conservative in his churchmanship, concerned for the intellectual revival of the church, probably hoped for a lead from the new primate in restoring ecclesiastical prestige. In the spring and summer of 1543 when the Cardinal was working to regain political control, the bishop of Orkney contacted Sadler on his behalf and was his spokesman, with lord Fleming, with the Governor's party.[81] He was with the Cardinal at Dundee in 1544 and at Arbroath in 1545.[82]

David Beaton seems to have had a fairly good working relationship with his eight suffragans some of whom, including the reactionary John Hepburn of Brechin, George Crichton of Dunkeld and William Chisholm of Dunblane, were prepared to back him fully in his repressive campaign against heresy. The unsettled state of affairs in the 1540s threw the prelates in upon themselves, giving them a cohesion as a party which they might not have had in quieter times. Five of the suffragan sees fell vacant during David Beaton's primacy and while further research will be necessary to determine the extent of his influence in the new appointments, it can at least be said that the results suited him very well.[83] Aberdeen and Caithness eventually went to the uncle and brother of his ally, Huntly. After the death of George Crichton of Dunkeld and litigation with his kinsman, Robert Crichton, that see came into the hands of the Governor's natural brother, John Hamilton, while that of Ross was given to his secretary, David Paniter, giving the Cardinal important footholds in Arran's circle. Orkney, of course, went to Robert Reid. He could always count on support from the dissolute Patrick Hepburn, the bishop of Brechin's nephew, former prior of St Andrews, who was promoted to Moray in 1538, whom he had once personally prevented from assaulting an outspoken canon of the priory.

While we cannot take time here to discuss the Cardinal's persistent attempts to win from Gavin Dunbar, archbishop of Glasgow, recognition of his ultimate jurisdiction—the extent of Glasgow's exemption had defied definition since 1492—it is worth noting that Dunbar must have been irritated by the fact that his rival had pockets of personal influence within the province of Glasgow. His brother, Walter Beaton, as canon of Govan, attended a fair number of chapter meetings at Glasgow cathedral and would no doubt keep him informed of what happened there. His chief secretary, John Lauder, was archdeacon of Teviotdale, with supervisory powers over the clergy of that detached but extensive

81. *Sadler Papers*, i, 167 *LP Henry VIII*, xviii, pt. ii, 9.
82. SRO, Crawford priory muniments, GD 20/107. *The Burnets of Leys* (New Spalding Club 1901), 171-75.
83. *Fasti, passim*.

portion of Glasgow archdiocese. In 1541 his cousin, Andrew Durie, became bishop of Galloway, a suffragan see of Glasgow, an appointment which spread the Cardinal's personal contacts right across country.[84] In November 1544, in the involved litigation over the vacancy in the bishopric of the Isles, another of Dunbar's suffragans, the Cardinal reinforced the Governor's letters of nomination by writing himself to the Cardinal of Carpi on behalf of the Crown nominee, Roderick McLean.[85]

His circle of contacts had an international dimension created through his own diplomatic activities until the autumn of 1542, by his correspondents and spies who carried his letters to and from France and the Low Countries and kept him informed of English manoeuvres, by his representatives at the Roman court and by those servants who administered his French bishopric, about whom we know, unfortunately, very little. There are glimpses here and there of his agents, including William Rattray, Alexander Crichton and sir David Christison, who crossed and recrossed to the continent on his affairs. Anthony Westputyws, born in the diocese of Mirepoix, on whose behalf his brother-in-law, M. de Moulins, wrote a begging letter to the Cardinal in April 1545, probably asking for a benefice for him, was called ' the cardinal's spy ' by the English authorities.[86] M. de Moulins himself operated between the Low Countries and the French court where he obtained a royal audience, at the Cardinal's request, for Dr Richard Hilliard, the bishop of Durham's fugitive chaplain, whom the Cardinal had sheltered in Scotland for over three years.[87] If de Moulins can be identified with the lieutenant of that name who came to Scotland with the Sieur de Lorges in the spring of 1545, his letter on behalf of Westputyws shows him to have been in touch with David Beaton before coming to Scotland in May of that year to intimate de Lorge's approach. De Moulins' letter was written by a Scottish amanuensis known to the Cardinal, who apologised jocularly for his bad writing: ' Zowris Grace in the hald fassone scraton . . . My Lord ye knaw this plesand hand.' William Thomson, a Minorite in Antwerp, born there of Scottish parents, corresponded with both Beaton and Pole. In May 1545 he was closely questioned by the English agents after a packet of letters addressed to the Scottish Cardinal had been confiscated from among his belongings on board a Scottish ship. He was said to have twice passed letters to the Cardinal from an English priest working in his interests at Rome, sending them by the ship of a Scottish merchant, John Cockburn.[88] At the Curia itself the Cardinal used the good offices of Cardinals S. Crucis, Ancona and Carpi. He also commissioned his secretaries, Mr Andrew Oliphant and Mr George Hay to undertake business there and in May 1543 sent Mr David Bonar to explain his

84. Ibid., 132.
85. SRO, State Papers, SP1/2/107.
86. LP Henry VIII, xx, pt. i, 608.
87. Ibid., xx, pt. i, 508-09.
88. Ibid., xx, pt. i, 696.

inability to attend the council of Trent.[89] Bonar, described as ' a person of intelligence and experience at Rome,' was the brother of William Bonar of Rossie, in Collessie parish, Fife.[90] Once prosecuted for barratry, he can be found in the papal register of supplications petitioning for something like fifteen benefices in all parts of the country.[91]

For a short time the Cardinal employed the services of the Italian, Alessandro Thealdini, previously secretary to the papal legate, Marco Grimani, with whom he came to Scotland in October 1543. On 2 April 1544, in the legate's house in Edinburgh and on his behalf, Thealdini confirmed a deed of excambion involving a piece of land in St Andrews set aside for part of the New College.[92] He is mentioned in the archbishopric accounts as having been with the Cardinal at Castle Campbell early in May 1544, just after the invasion by the earl of Hertford, from whence he was conducted to Lindores.[93] On leaving Scotland he was offered the post of vicar-general for the Cardinal in connection with Mirepoix, but declined at that time. Towards the end of 1545, after the legate's death, Thealdini was captured by the English on a return journey to France at which time the Cardinal wrote to the pope on his behalf.[94] On 8 January 1545-6, freed from his English prison but penniless, he wrote to Andrew Oliphant asking him to find out if the Cardinal's offer of a post and salary still held good.[95] No clear evidence has come to light of his connection with the Cardinal in the subsequent months, but he is known to have worked at Rome for Scottish patrons in later years.

*   *   *   *

No doubt David Beaton was an exacting master, increasingly difficult to work with as the debonair confidence of his early career hardened into the aggressiveness of his later years. Involved in so many great issues, his ruthlessness is, perhaps, the measure of his involvement. Much of his power over the wills of men, which enabled him to reconcile enemies and hold together a reasonably workable coalition of factious magnates, must have been due to sheer force of personality, an elusive element in written records but an important one in real-life situations. His urbanity and open-handedness contrasted with his determination to win and the vindictiveness that was the weakness of his strength. In spite of a diplomatic training, he was quick-tempered, resorted to bullying when thwarted and got flustered when taken off his guard. He had a streak of impulsiveness for all his astuteness—dropping a remark that almost provoked a duel and telling an English agent that Henry VIII would not have the honour to begin the war.[96] His contemporaries, aware

89. Ibid., xviii, pt. i, 494
90. SRO, ADCS, xiii, fo 249v.
91. Vatican transcripts, Reg. Supp., 2162-2553, *passim*.
92. St A. Univ. Mun. SM 110 B16 6.
93. *Rentale*, 179.
94. SRO, State Papers, SP 1/2/138.
95. *Scottish Correspondence of Mary of Lorraine*, 154-55.
96. *Hamilton Papers*, ii, 161-62.

of the essential layman in him, treated him accordingly—Arran drawing his sword on him in the royal presence and de Lorges cuffing him on the cheek, although on this occasion it may well have looked as if the Cardinal had intended to hit first.[97] Unlike some great men, he never moved away entirely from the environment of his early years and resentment of his success was an important element in the opposition that formed against him. Nor did he always get his own way. On the tense day of George Wishart's trial, when his historic reputation was largely made, there were indications of the restraining hands of his episcopal colleagues. Even the elderly provincial of the Carmelites, whom he personally threatened with ' perpetual prison ' if he refused to resign his office, managed to stagger off afterwards to the nearest notary's booth where he took an instrument that the whole thing had been done against his will and the resignation was, therefore, invalid.[98]

Yet, on the whole he was well served and seems to have been capable of delegating responsibility, a vital element in good master-and-servant relations. Understandably, his chosen servants shared his own background and outlook and while he appears to have known where to lay his hand on a rascal when he wanted one, he could also work with a man like Robert Reid or win the goodwill of the blind scholar, Robert Wauchope. In his lifetime he was a figurehead who meant different things to different people. Reaction to him ranged from that of ' those who live under Monsieur d'Albrot and love him wonderfully '[99] to that of Angus's servant, Sandy Jardane, who swore that he would cheerfully boil seven years in hell if only he could get the better of him.[100] How men regarded what he stood for determined their attitude to him at the time and their interpretation of him afterwards. It is a pity that we do not have the ' Memoirs ' of Andrew Oliphant to set alongside the *History* of George Buchanan.

---

97. Ibid., i, 267.
98. SRO, ADCS, xiv, fos 190r-94r; Ibid., xv, fo 2r.
99. *LP Henry VIII*, xii, pt. i, 647.
100. Ibid., xix, pt. i, 326.

'THE GLORIOUS HOUSE OF ST ANDREW'

by

DAVID MCROBERTS

Surprisingly little has been written about the medieval cathedral of St Andrews considering that, until our Victorian grandfathers began building enormous railway stations, hotels and hospitals, it was the largest building ever erected in Scotland. Not only was it the largest edifice in the kingdom, it was also, ecclesiastically, the most important and it probably contained a substantial part of the medieval artistic heritage of the nation.

Those modern writers who have dealt with the cathedral have been almost exclusively concerned with the architectural history of the fabric as evidenced in its scanty remains. Little has been written, describing the building, its furnishing or its daily use, because no medieval inventories or descriptions have survived. However, scattered in late medieval chronicles and other documents, a few precious details can be found, and these incidental pieces of information must be accepted as first-hand evidence because in many cases the writers, men like Walter Bower,[1] Andrew Wyntoun[2] or John Law,[3] were canons of the cathedral. One detects a note of pride when these men have occasion to mention the high kirk of St Andrews: their attitude is summed up in the phrase used by Prior James Haldenstone in his letter of 1418, announcing to the community at St Andrews his appointment as their prior. He speaks of the church as *gloriosa domus Sancti Andree*—the glorious house of St Andrew.[4] In these pages, we shall attempt to gather together the scattered references so as to form some idea of the appearance and daily life of the cathedral in late medieval times.

THE CATHEDRAL CHURCH

The medieval visitor to St Andrews would be impressed at once by the great size of the cathedral, especially of its nave. The aristocratic prelates, who were appointed to bishoprics in England after the Norman Conquest, were energetic builders. During the eleventh and twelfth centuries, they built vast romanesque cathedral and monastic churches, often with abnormally long processional naves, to replace earlier churches in the south and east of England.[5] St Andrews cathedral, begun under

1. *Joannis de Fordun Scotichronicon cum Supplementis et Continuatione Walteri Boweri*, ed. W. Goodall (Edinburgh, 1759): hereafter *Chron. Bower*.
2. *The Original Chronicle of Andrew of Wyntoun* (STS, 1903-14): hereafter *Chron. Wyntoun*.
3. Chronicle of John Law, Edinburgh University Library, MS DC. 7. 63: hereafter *Law MS*. The St Andrews cathedral information from this MS is printed in John Durkan, ' St Andrews in the John Law Chronicle ' below, pp. 137-150.
4. *St Andrews Copiale*, 16.
5. Francis Bond, *Gothic Architecture in England* (London, 1912), 15. Kenneth John Conant, *Carolingian and Romanesque Architecture, 800-1200* (London, 1959), 286.

Bishop Arnold (1160-62), should probably be regarded as the most northerly (and the only Scottish) example of this Norman megalomania.

The building was, of course, divided by screens of stone, wood or metal into separate sections. There was the nave, which originally extended from the west door to the eastern piers of the crossing but, after the reconstruction completed by Prior Haldenstone in the early fifteenth century, it terminated at the new rood screen which crossed the church in the easternmost bay of the nave. There were the northern and southern transepts, each with its group of three chapels. The eastern arm of the cruciform building contained the choir of the canons, and the sanctuary with the high altar. The north and south aisles terminated in chapels and, east of the sanctuary, was the important chapel where the relics of St Andrew were enshrined. The year 1378 is an important date in the history of the church. In that year the cathedral was extensively damaged by fire.[6] The subsequent reconstruction, which continued throughout the priorships of Stephen Pay (1363-85), Robert Montrose (1385-93), James Bisset (1393-1417), and James Haldenstone (1417-43), brought about an enlargement of the monastic choir and considerable replanning of the whole eastern arm of the church. The various parts of the cathedral will be discussed separately.

THE CHOIR

The most important and most sacred areas of the cathedral were located in the eastern arm of the cruciform building. Up to the time of the extensive reconstruction of the church (c 1378 to 1443), the choir screen crossed the church on the line of the eastern piers of the crossing. Eastwards from this was the canons' choir, occupying three bays of the chancel: the sanctuary, containing the high altar, being located in the fourth bay from the choir screen or pulpitum. The high altar would be set against a screen, which extended between the north-east and south-east pillars of that bay. The north and south aisles and the passage behind the high altar formed a continuous ambulatory round the choir and sanctuary. Opening off the eastern section of this ambulatory, and no doubt separated from it by screens, were three chapels, two small chapels which were the eastern ends of the north and south chancel aisles and a central chapel, the unaisled eastern section of the chancel, in which were enshrined the famous relics of the apostle. The evidence for the original position of the choir screen and for the original arrangement of the eastern area of the building is to be found in incidental remarks of the chroniclers who unfortunately did not consider it necessary to describe the building systematically. Wyntoun, writing in the early years of the fifteenth century, indicates the position of the early ' chaunscellar dur,' or door in the choir screen, when he speaks of the building work

---

6. *Chron. Bower,* i, 364: *Chron. Pluscarden,* i, 313: *Chron. Wyntoun,* vi, 309-11. Apart from the destruction detailed by the chroniclers, excavation has yielded a great deal of burnt glass and lead especially from the windows in the north-east corner of the nave and the middle chapel of the north transept. (David Hay Fleming, *St Andrews Cathedral Museum,* Edinburgh, 1931, 191, 196)

done by Bishop William Wishart. There was some obvious change in the masonry of the south arcade of the nave which showed where the earlier builders had finished off and a new type of masonry took over. There were twelve pillars (including the south-west pier of the crossing) in the south arcade and Wyntoun seems to indicate that the change occurred in the bay between the third pillar (including the south-west pier of the crossing) from the east and the ninth pillar from the west.[7] He measures this structural change

' Fra the chaunscellar dur sen thar '[8]

and this would place the choir screen, in the early fifteenth century, on the line of the eastern piers of the crossing. Wyntoun confirms this same position, viewing it from the east side, when he speaks of the three bishops' tombs in the north choir aisle, with Bishop Walter Trail's tomb standing next to the pulpitum or choir screen.[9] Wyntoun had been a canon at St Andrews towards the end of the fourteenth century, so his testimony is that of an eye-witness. He finished his chronicle somewhere about 1420 to 1424 and, by that time, a thorough replanning of the chancel of the cathedral was in progress to provide a much enlarged choir for the canons and a more spacious sanctuary for liturgical cere-monial. Possibly the prime mover in this project was Bishop Henry Wardlaw (1403-1440) because the new arrangement created an ideal position for Wardlaw's tomb and one may suspect that this was envisaged from the start and was one of the motives in the replanning. Dates are not easy to ascertain, but we do know that, in May 1406, Wardlaw sent off two ships to Prussia, carrying an expedition led by John Galichtli to purchase timber for church-building purposes.[10]

Hector Boece states that liturgical ceremonial was greatly increased, new forms of music were introduced and a more modern type of organ began to be used during the reign of King James I (1406-1437).[11] This expansion of liturgical worship was widespread in Christendom and we can see evidence of it in the reconstruction of choirs at Glasgow, Aberdeen, Kinloss, Dunkeld, Melrose and other churches in fifteenth-century Scotland. The bishops of St Andrews, taking advantage of the reconstruction made necessary by the fire of 1378, enlarged the choir and sanctuary to make their church more suitable for the increased magnificence of the liturgy and so led off the fashion for fifteenth-century Scottish churches.

---

7. The transition appears in the surviving south wall between the eighth and ninth bays from the west but, in the vanished arcade, it was apparently in the tenth bay from the west.
8. *Chron. Wyntoun*, v, 127.
9. *Chron. Wyntoun*, v, 381.
10. *Rotuli Scotiae*, ii, 178. In Longforgan church, which belonged to the priory of St Andrews, there was discovered in 1899 the tombstone of a John de Galychtly of Ebruks and his spouse. The dates of demise of the couple have not been completed in the inscription but the evidence points to the first half of the fifteenth century. John de Galychtly and his wife are depicted on the tombstone as devout clients of St Andrew and this may well be the tomb of the man who led the expedition sent by Wardlaw to Prussia in May 1406 (*Proc. Soc. Antiq. Scot.*, xxxiv (1899-1900), 463-75).
11. Boece, *Historiae*, fos 348v-349.

During his priorship, the excellent James Bisset fitted the choir with new stalls—*chorum installavit.*[12] The next prior, James Haldenstone, extended the choir westwards under the crossing and the new choir screen was constructed (and probably designed) by William Bower, one of the canons, in the easternmost bay of the nave. The stalls were moved westwards and Haldenstone had them enriched with carving and painted imagery—*tam in sculpturis stallorum quam picturis imaginum decoravit.*[13] The floor of the choir was paved with large tiles, black and brown, yellow and green, ten inches square and laid diagonally: some of these were dug up in September 1887,[14] others in 1903,[15] the few which remain *in situ*, until recently, retained some of their yellow glaze. The next prior, William Bonar, continued the work of furnishing the choir. He provided new choir books—*chorum libris necessariis decenter ornauit,* probably the large graduals and antiphonals which would rest on the big wooden lectern in the midst of the choir. He provided the large organ, which probably stood on the pulpitum, and the smaller organ, which would stand alongside the stalls. He also provided the chiming clock, the *horecudium,* which stood in the choir.[16]

THE LADY CHAPEL

Not only was the choir extended westward but the sanctuary with the high altar was moved one bay eastward. The ambulatory, which occupied the bay behind the high altar and gave access to the three eastern chapels was eliminated. Moved one bay eastward, the high altar was set against a screen, which now enclosed the chapel of the relics. This replanning doubled the size of the chapels which stood at the eastern end of the north and south choir-aisles. The southern chapel was probably a chapel of St Andrew. The northern chapel was the chapel of Our Lady. The enlargement of the Lady chapel made available an ideal position for Bishop Wardlaw's tomb, where he was buried in 1440, just north of the new site of the high altar and, opposite Wardlaw's tomb, in the north wall of the Lady chapel, in 1443, was buried Prior James Haldenstone. Haldenstone ensured the importance of the Lady chapel in the liturgical life of the community by founding at its altar a solemn mass of Our Lady, at which the prior used the newly conceded *pontificalia,* mitre, crosier and ring— *servitium divinum in solennizatione missae nostrae Dominae in capella eius, ad ipsorum laudem, insigniter ampliavit.*[17] The new importance of

---

12. *Chron. Bower,* i, 372.
13. Ibid., 375.
14. *Proc. Soc. Antiq. Scot.,* x (1887-8), 148.
15. *Scot. Hist. Rev.,* i (1904), 108. Tiles required for the cathedral church and the dependent churches would be manufactured at St Andrews (see *PSAS,* 104 (1971-2), 252-6). The *ustrinae* which Prior James Bisset repaired (*Chron. Bower,* i, 372) were kilns of various kinds and would include a tile-kiln. An earlier *ustrina* had been provided by Prior William Loudon about the year 1350 (*Chron. Bower,* i, 370). Luxury articles would, of course, be imported from Flanders like the thousand tiles that Archdeacon Robert Wells imported in 1499 to renew the floor of his chamber at St Andrews (*Halyburton's Ledger,* 162, 251).
16. Law MS, fo 20v.
17. *Chron. Bower,* i, 375.

the Lady chapel is apparent in the following episcopate when Bishop James Kennedy, on 6 May 1465, founded there a daily mass for his own soul and for the soul of his mother, Mariota Stewart.[18] Nothing remains to indicate the medieval appearance of the Lady chapel but, during some excavations here in 1904, fragments of 'very dark green' flooring tiles were unearthed.[19]

THE CHAPEL OF THE RELICS

Beyond the screen which formed the reredos of the high altar lay the chapel in which the relics of St Andrew were enshrined. After Halden-stone's reconstruction, the chapel of the relics could only be entered by the doors in the screen on either side of the high altar. From the brief notice in the Scotichronicon and from the surviving remains, it is evident that the appearance of the chapel was completely changed by Halden-stone. The fenestration of the east gable was altered to give more light. The engaged columns of the twelfth-century wall-arcading were removed. The floor level was raised by about four feet, presumably by an infilling of rubble, covered with a floor of stone slabs or encaustic tiles. The huge tombstone which remains *in situ* indicates the late medieval floor level. The reliquary containing the bones of St Andrew would be in an architec-tural shrine, 'the relict almrie,' in the centre of the chapel, built high enough to be seen over the reredos of the high altar by those in the choir. In front of this 'relict almrie' would be an altar. Around the walls, con-cealing the remains of the twelfth-century arcading, Haldenstone placed the pleasantly designed and costly aumbries to hold relics and other treasures of the church—*Revestiarium cum reliquiis et earum reparationi-bus et clausuris, non sine magnis impendiis, placenter perornavit.*[20] It was a normal arrangement which could be seen at Durham, at Canterbury and at many medieval shrines. Strong screens of stone or wood separated the chapel of the relics from the Lady chapel to the north and from the corresponding chapel to the south. The security of the apostolic relics and of the other treasures of the church would be much in Haldenstone's thoughts as he replanned this part of the cathedral and we shall return to this question of security when we discuss the choir screen. Only very privileged persons would be admitted to the chapel of the relics to see the treasures of the cathedral. No medieval inventory of these relics and treasures has survived, but we do know that, in addition to the Morbrac, the ancient reliquary containing the bones of St Andrew, there were other 'fayr iowelis' to interest the visitor. When King Alexander I, in the year 1121, granted the territory, known as the Boar's Raik, the *Cursus Apri*, to the church of St Andrews, he made the donation symbolically by having

> 'His cumly steid of Araby,
> Sadillit and bridlyt costly,'

18. Sir William Fraser, *Memorials of the Family of Wemyss of Wemyss* (Edinburgh, 1888), ii, 88-9.
19. *Scot. Hist. Rev.*, i (1904), 243
20. *Chron. Bower*, i, 375.

led to the altar of the old cathedral and given over to the church.[21] The shaft of the king's spear, his ' speire of siluer quhite,' was later made into the shaft of a processional cross and was preserved among the treasures of the church.[22] Also, in memory of that ancient endowment, there were preserved the tusks of the monstrous boar which gave the Boar's Raik its name. These tusks, sixteen inches long, Boece tells us, were fixed by small chains to the choir stalls of the cathedral.[23] Among the church's treasures would be kept also the crystal cross from the field of Bannockburn of which we shall speak later and, among the reliquaries, there were two presented by Archbishop James Stewart,[24] and John Law, who had been sacrist of the cathedral, particularly admired the fine reliquary—perpulchrum jocale—of St Margaret which the ill-fated Archbishop Patrick Graham got made for his metropolitan church.[25]

THE HIGH ALTAR

The focal point of the whole church was, of course, the sanctuary and the high altar. Set against the screen, which enclosed the chapel of the relics, the high altar had a mid-fifteenth-century altarpiece, provided by Prior David Ramsay (1462-1469). John Law's phrase: asportauit tabernaculum magni altaris,[26] gives no indication as to whether this altarpiece was of native artistry or imported from one of those ateliers which David Ramsay would see on his journey to Florence and Rome in 1440. The statues of Our Lady and of St Andrew, which stood to the north and south of the high altar, will be discussed in a moment, as will the Anglo-Saxon rood which seems to have stood on the beam over the altar.

Lacking any detailed medieval inventories, we can mention only a few ornaments of the high altar. The one item of which the metropolitan cathedral was especially proud was the textus, or gospel-book, presented to the church by Bishop Fothad which, in late medieval times, stood on the gospel side of the high altar and still retained its ancient silver cover with the inscription:

> ' Hanc Ewangelii tecam construxit [aviti]
> Fodauch, qui Scotis primus episcopus est.'[27]

As feastday succeeded feastday throughout the year, the liturgy at the high altar would be adorned by the accumulated ornaments, vestments and furnishings given by pious laymen and successive bishops. There were the sets of vestments, presented by former bishops such as William de Landallis or Walter Trail; the mitre, crosier and precious red vestment, imaginibus contextum, given by William Lamberton;[28] the set of white

---

21. Chron. Wyntoun, iv, 375.
22. Law MS, fos 13-13v.
23. Boece, Historiae, fo 263.
24. Law MS, fo 17.
25. Law MS, fo 16v.
26. Law MS, fo 20v.
27. Chron. Wyntoun, iv, 193.
28. Law MS, fo 15v. The donors of the various sets of vestments would be known (as the Glasgow cathedral inventory of 1432 makes clear) from the coats of arms embroidered on them. The coat of arms carved on the chasuble of Bishop Wardlaw's effigy illustrates this practice .

PLATE XI. TOMBSTONE OF JOHN GALYCHTLY OF EBRUKS.

This tombstone was discovered in 1899 in Longforgan church, which
belonged to St Andrews priory. John Galychtly and his wife are
depicted in prayer to St Andrew. The dates have not been completed
in the inscription but this appears to be the man who led the expedition to Prussia in May 1406 to bring back timber for Bishop Wardlaw's building work.

PLATE XII.   HENRY WARDLAW, BISHOP OF ST ANDREWS, 1403-1440.

The mutilated head of the bishop from the recumbent effigy which lay on his tomb in the Lady chapel of the cathedral.

vestments, used at high mass on the feasts of Our Lady, gifted by Bishop James Kennedy, who also gave the great red carpet—*mattam magnam rubram bisso intextam*—which covered the sanctuary floor on the principal feastdays.[29] The velvet cushions, which lay on the altar as book rests, the silver gilt cruets and the silver *aspersarium* were all gifts of Walter Trail.[30] As at Glasgow, the missals and the other altar books would be the gifts of benefactors, laymen and ecclesiastics, accumulated over many generations. William de Landallis and William Lamberton are both remembered as having bequeathed excellent books—*libros valde bonos*.[31] The great Lenten veil, which was conspicuous in the chancel at Passiontide, was quite evidently an impressive object, exquisitely embroidered with beasts and divers figures; it had been commissioned by Prior William Loudon in the mid-fourteenth century.[32] The brief allusions in the chronicles to the painted and gilded imagery of the choir stalls and to the embroidered vestments, the broken bits of multi-coloured floor tiles, stray pieces of painted window glass, fragments of carved tombs with traces of vivid colouring—red, yellow, black—all conjure up the picture of a sumptuous and resplendent interior, which would reach its climax in the chancel around the high altar.

In addition to its liturgical function, the high altar was occasionally the place where important legal matters were transacted so that the sacred character of the place would add its own sanction. On Easter Sunday, 29 March 1304, King Edward I of England, endeavouring vainly to procure an oath of fealty that would bind the bishop of Glasgow, caused Robert Wishart to swear allegiance in presence of his parliament —*en presence des Countes, Barouns et des autres gantz Seigneurs d Engleterre et d Escoce*—for the sixth time—*la sisme fois*—on the Blessed Sacrament, on the Holy Gospels, on the Cross of Neyth, and on the Black Rood of Scotland, at the high altar of St Andrews cathedral.[33]

In the year 1284, King Alexander III confirmed the privilege that the bishops of St Andrews had long enjoyed of minting coins and this was done solemnly at the high altar in the cathedral:

> 'And in the kyrk standande thar
> Dewotly befor the hey altar
> In wytnes of al that thar was by
> Gadryt and standande, than frely
> Til God and til Sancte Androis he
> Grantyt the strak of the monei.'[34]

Again, in 1342, when Patrick, earl of March, founded the collegiate church of Dunbar, he pledged at the high altar in St Andrews that the

---

29. Law MS, fo 16v.
30. *Chron. Wyntoun*, vi, 311-13.
31. *Chron. Wyntoun*, vi, 311, and Law MS, fo 16.
32. *Chron. Bower*, i, 369-70.
33. Palgrave, *Docs. Hist. Scot.*, 345-6.
34. *Chron. Wyntoun*, v. 137.

F

new foundation would not infringe the rights of the diocese—*Patricius de Dunbar, comes Marchie, pro se et suis successoribus, tactis Dei evangeliis, super magnum altare ecclesie beati santiandree in presentia multorum, corporale prestitit iuramentum.*[35]

Two important features of the chancel which demand some detailed consideration are the statues of the Blessed Virgin and of St Andrew which stood respectively to the north and south of the high altar. Information concerning these statues comes from a document of about the year 1425, in which Archibald, duke of Touraine, earl of Douglas, lord of Galloway and Annandale, friend and correspondent of Prior James Haldenstone, renews an annual grant of two merks from the lands of Wester Collessie to maintain a light before the statue of St Andrew at the high altar. The document links the statue of St Andrew with a statue of Our Lady, called ' le Douglas Lady ': *ad sustentacionem luminaris coram ymagine sancti andree in cathedrali ecclesia eiusdem ad magnum altare ubi collocatur ymago illa quae wlgariter nuncupatur le douglas lady, quam quidem elemosinam antecessores nostri fundaverunt, concesserunt et donaverunt deo et sancto Andree apostolo inperpetuum ab antico prout nos longeuus vsus et auctentica scripta plene informarunt—* for the maintenance of a lamp before the statue of St Andrew in his cathedral church alongside the high altar where stands the statue commonly called ' le Douglas Lady ' and, as immemorial usage and authentic documents clearly declare, our forefathers, in olden times, founded, gave and granted forever this benefaction to God and St Andrew the apostle.[36]

This document tells us a great deal. There were two notable statues alongside the high altar, one of Our Lady, the other of St Andrew. These two statues were associated with the family of Douglas, the statue of Our Lady was commonly called ' le Douglas Lady ' and, at the statue of St Andrew, a light had been maintained by the Douglas family from time immemorial. One can only conclude that these were the principal images— *imagines principales*—of the cathedral and had been part of the furnishing of the church from an early date and certainly from the consecration of the building. Prior to the War of Independence, ecclesiastical usages in Scotland were largely identical with the liturgy and canon law of the church in England and much of this traditional usage survived, along with the Sarum Use, into later times. It was customary in England to have in every church, near the high altar, a statue of the saint, in whose name the church was dedicated. By the constitution of Archbishop Robert Winchelsey, published in 1305 at the synod of Merton, the provision of the ' principal image ' of the titular saint in the chancel was the respon-

---

35. *Scot. Hist. Soc., Miscel.* vi, 96.
36. *St Andrews Liber*, 406.

sibility of the laity of each parish.[37] In most cases there were two images, one of Our Lady on the north side of the high altar, and another of the titular saint of the church at the south side of the high altar. It was not unusual for people to seek burial near one or other of these statues in the chancel. Bishop Mayo of Hereford, for example, who died in 1516, asked to be buried near the statue of St Ethelbert, patron of the cathedral and, near Bishop Mayo's tomb on the south side of the high altar in Hereford cathedral, can still be seen the fourteenth-century statue of the patron saint standing on its original corbel to the south of the high altar.[38] This custom was maintained in Scotland even after the War of Independence. In the year 1340, the high altar of St Nicholas' church, Aberdeen, was presented with a new ' principal image ' of the patron saint to be set in a central position at the altar—*principaliore et maiore ymagine sancti Nicholai in medio magni altaris situata*, but they still retained the original statue of St Nicholas at the south end of the high altar, where it had stood since the building of the church.[39] In a refurbishing of the high altar in St Machar's cathedral in Aberdeen, in the fifteenth century, the principal images of St Mary and St Machar were presented by Dean Richard Forbes.[40] We can be sure that the Augustinian canons followed the general custom of having *imagines principales* on either side of their high altar since the first item in the dissolution inventory, made in 1538, at Barnwell Priory, reads: ' Fyrst at the hygh alter ij images of wood, ij lampes of laten . . .'[41]

As principal images, the statues of ' le Douglas Lady ' and of St Andrew would be located to the north and to the south of the high altar in the cathedral of St Andrews. If, as we suspect, Haldenstone moved the high altar one bay eastwards, these principal images would be moved correspondingly and this would possibly be the occasion for the renewal of the Douglas benefaction regarding the lamp at the statue of St Andrew. Like other carved work in the cathedral, these statues would be brightly coloured and they would be adorned with precious *ex voto* offerings, as witness Haldenstone's denunciation of the thieves whose burglary in the vicinity of the high altar had included part of a very valuable jewel from a ring of St Andrew.[42]

ST. MARGARET'S ROOD

Prior Haldenstone's denunciation of the robbers, who violated the sanctuary area of the cathedral, contains another extremely interesting clue to one of the valuable ornaments of the high altar. Amongst their other depredations, he charges the thieves with stripping off and laying

37. D. Wilkins, *Concilia Magnae Britanniae*, ii, 280.
38. F. T. Havergal, *Fasti Herefordenses* (1869), 110 and plate II.
39. *Aberdeen St Nicholas Cartularium*, i, 14-6.
40. *Aberdeen Registrum*, ii, 137.
41. John Willis Clark, *The Observances in use at the Augustinian Priory of S. Giles and S. Andrew at Barnwell* (Cambridge, 1897), xxiii.
42. *St Andrews Copiale*, 138.

bare the feet of Christ crucified above the high altar—*cum excoriacione sive denudacione pedum christi crucifixi supra magnum altare.*[43] Clearly he is referring to a large rood which stood on the beam over the high altar. The figure of Christ on the cross and, no doubt, the cross also was encased in plates of precious metal. The rood was too high up for the thieves to reach and they succeeded only in ripping off some of the precious metal from the feet of the figure.

The crucifix above the high altar at St Andrews seems to have been one of those precious roods which were fashionable in cathedral and monastic churches in Anglo-Saxon England. St Aldhelm describes such a rood in the lines:

' Hic crucis ex auro splendescit lamina fulvo
Argentique simul gemmis ornata metalla.'[44]

The best description of a Scottish example is Turgot's description of the rich cross, plated with gold and silver and encrusted with jewels, which was presented by St Margaret to the abbey church at Dunfermline: *Crucem quoque incomparabilis pretii imaginem Salvatoris habentem quam auro purissimo et argento intercurrentibus gemmis vestiri fecerat ibidem collocavit,* and Turgot adds that, among other proofs of St Margaret's piety, was a similar cross of surpassing beauty which the queen gave to the church of St Andrews and which was still there when Turgot wrote the saint's biography.[45] It is not at all unlikely that the precious rood which the fifteenth-century thieves tried to despoil was the actual gift of Malcolm Canmore's queen to the shrine of the apostle which, like Bishop Fothad's silver-encased gospel-book, King Alexander I's silver lance and the tusks of the Great Boar, had been brought from the old cathedral to adorn the sanctuary of the new church.

THE CHOIR SCREEN

The security of a large medieval church, especially of a pilgrimage church which had accumulated, over the centuries, objects of great value and important works of art, was a source of constant concern for its guardians. The two great dangers were fire and burglary. The constitutions of the Augustinian Canons place firmly on the sacrist and subsacrist the duty of supervising the vestments, books and treasures of the church, making sure that lights are properly maintained and all doors properly locked. The sacrist and his assistant are to sleep in the church at night to ensure its safety.[46] Among the precautions used were screens of stone, timber or metal, with locked gates, which controlled access to the more important parts of the church. At St Andrews, access to the

---

43. Ibid.
44. Migne, *Patres Latini,* ci, 1311.
45. *Acta Sanctorum Junii,* ii, 329
46. John Willis Clark, *op. cit.,* 69-79. Like other large churches the cathedral would have stone cresset lamps placed at strategic points to facilitate movement about the building after dark. A small stone lamp of this kind has survived and is in the cathedral museum (David Hay Fleming, *Museum,* 205 and fig. 122).

chancel, and especially to the chapel of the relics with its collection of treasures, would be restricted to the clergy of the cathedral, their most trusted servants and to specially privileged visitors. The procedure is illustrated clearly in the early sixteenth-century visit of Erasmus and John Colet to Canterbury. Within the iron railings, which protected the eastern section of the cathedral, they were shown, in a conducted tour, the rich vestments of the sacristy and the relics and treasures kept in the wall-cupboards surrounding the choir and finally the prior came and uncovered the shrine of St Thomas and all of this was done because Erasmus had a letter of introduction from Archbishop William Warham.[47]

The main protection for the treasures of St Andrews lay in the solid stone screen which, in the early fifteenth century, was built across the easternmost bay of the nave. The new screen was apparently designed by one of the canons, William Bower, whom his namesake, the author of the Scotichronicon, describes as a very praiseworthy man, a good religious and kindly—vir multum laudabilis, religiosus et benignus.[48] The brief description of this screen and its scanty remains give us some idea of what it was like. The actual wall of the choir screen, with the entrance to the choir, was built between the two western piers of the crossing. Then from each pier, running westwards, were solid walls filling up the space between the piers and the adjacent pillars. Springing from these side walls, a vault was constructed across the central space of the nave. The open west side of this vaulted area was enclosed with a screen which was probably of wood. The whole design formed an enclosed vestibule, or entrance, to the choir. On either side of the doorway leading into the choir were altars. In the surviving stone floor there is the large tombstone of a cleric who has been buried in front of the southern altar. Above this enclosed vestibule, the solid surface of the vault provided the platform on which was erected the altar of the Holy Cross, behind which rose the Great Rood and the figures of Our Lady and St John, sumptuous figures which dominated the nave of the cathedral—altare crucifixi in nave ecclesiae, cum solio ejus solido et imaginibus sumptuosis adornatum.[49] The parapet across the front of the gallery may have been adorned with figures of Christ and the twelve apostles which was a fairly usual adornment of rood screens on the Continent and in Scotland, where it occurred at Dunkeld, Foulis Easter and elsewhere. The access stair up to the Holy

47. Peregrinatio Religionis ergo in J. Le Clerc (ed.) Opera Omnia Erasmi (Leiden, 1703), i, cols. 774-87.
48. Chron. Bower, ii, 447. The small external door in the south aisle of the choir would seem to be a weak point in the security of the chancel. This door was possibly in use when the parish church existed some yards to the east of the cathedral up to the year 1412. When Haldenstone was tightening up the security of the chancel in the early fifteenth century, this door was probably built up. This must, however, remain a matter for conjecture because the evidence was destroyed, in July 1915, when the infilling was removed (David Hay Fleming, Museum, 193).
49. Chron. Bower, i, 375-6. Solium here, as in other Scottish documents of this period, means the gallery on which the rood altar stood. It does not mean a throne. Accordingly, Lord Bute's suggestion of a parallel between the arrangement at St Andrews and the imperial thrones at Frankfort and Aachen is pointless (D. MacGibbon and T. Ross, Ecclesiastical Architecture of Scotland, ii, xvi-xvii).

Cross altar in the rood loft was in the easternmost bay of the north aisle of the nave and the choir screen would be extended northwards across that part of the north aisle, ensuring that access to the north transept and choir could be gained only through a door which could be securely locked. Similarly, the choir screen would enclose the easternmost bay of the south aisle of the nave with lockfast screens on either side so that processions entering the church from the sacristy in the cloister could make their way either into the monastic church to the east or into the nave to the west. This east door from the cloister has been widened and heightened in the later medieval period by the insertion of an elliptical arch to facilitate the movement of processions. Probably somewhere in the upper part of the choir screen, over the north or south aisles, would be located the watch-chambers where the sacrist and sub-sacrist would spend the night to ensure the safety of the church from fire and robbery.

In the later Middle Ages, in northern Europe, devotion to the Blessed Sacrament found expression in continuous exposition of the Holy Eucharist either in a monstrance or in a Sacrament House with a latticed door. This exposition was sometimes maintained at the Holy Cross altar on the rood loft where the Holy Eucharist would be visible to all in the nave of the church. This apparently was the case in the abbey church of Kelso in the year 1517: *In medio ecclesie super illo pariete qui distinguit monachos a parrochianis est solum quoddam lignum ubi est Venerabilis ara Crucis super qua diligentissime asservatur et colitur Corpus Christi et ibi est magna religio et devotio parrochianorum.*[50] It is not at all unlikely that the Holy Cross altar on the rood loft at St Andrews was a similar centre for eucharistic devotion.

It was traditional practice that lay people should not normally enter the choir of a church. This is clearly stated in the Kelso document just quoted. The general principle is enunciated by a Scottish provincial council in the thirteenth century,[51] but the construction of massive choir screens in the later Middle Ages must have emphasised a growing alienation between laic and cleric. In this connection Walter Bower quotes a puerile macaronic verse which, he says, was written by someone on the choir screen of a church:

> ' *Ite foras laici, vester non est locus ici:*
> *Sed sedent ici, qui sunt altaris amici.*'[52]

and one wonders if this might not have been a graffito which he found scribbled on William Bower's screen at St Andrews.

There was, on the other hand, much to be said in favour of choir screens. The later Middle Ages had their share of violence and even the peaceful cloister of St Andrews could feel its threat. Apart from the

50. Theiner, *Monumenta*, 527.
51. Robertson, *Concilia*, ii, 46.
52. *Chron. Bower*, i, 394.

murder of Prior Robert Montrose, which took place in the priory in 1393,[53] there was the scandalous affair of Richard of North Berwick. Richard, a chaplain, had been appointed rector of Essy.[54] Contumaciously, he had refused to pay the fees due to the Apostolic Camera and his sentence of excommunication had been duly posted up, in the usual fashion on the doors of the cathedral. The details of the case have long since been lost but Richard, on the 15 March 1421, forced his way into the metropolitan church at the hour of vespers (Haldenstone adds the aggravating circumstance that it was a Sunday and a feastday)[55] when all the canons were in their stalls ready to begin the divine office. It was not lawful to say the office with an excommunicated person present. The subprior, William de Balbuthy, tried to persuade Richard to leave but unavailingly, so he rang a bell and sent Canon William Stury to the choir screen—*ad pulpitum chori*, to explain to the assembled congregation why vespers were being delayed. Some members of the congregation volunteered to remove Richard from the sacred building—*absque violentia*—but these were prevented by some clerics who supported Richard. As the situation grew more confused and menacing, the canons had to leave the choir without singing vespers.

Of great interest is the document in which Prior James Haldenstone denounces some persons unknown who had committed acts of robbery in the church.[56] There had been the sacrilegious theft, in broad daylight, of a silver gilt chalice and paten from the altar of Our Lady, a theft which, Haldenstone feels certain, could only have been carried out by some servant of the community, who had access to that part of the church. This reminds him of an earlier incident when thieves stole the community's most precious gold chalice, encrusted with gems and the gold paten of a lesser chalice. They stole a valuable jewel from a ring on the statue of St Andrew, despoiled a *textus* and tore off some of the precious metal from the feet of the figure of Christ crucified which was over the altar. Occurrences such as these, together with the disastrous fire of 1378, must have made the canons alert to the dangers which constantly beset their magnificent church.

THE NAVE

West of the choir screen was the nave, the only public part of the church. The nave had suffered extensive damage in the fire of 1378 and much of its furnishing probably belonged to the subsequent reconstruction. Prior James Bisset had organised the structural repairs to pillars, walls and roof. Bower gives an impressive list of work accomplished by him for the material and spiritual wellbeing of the church; the resplendent altars,

---

53. *Chron. Bower*, i, 371-2.
54. *St Andrews Copiale*, 33-8.
55. It was in fact a Saturday evening, but the canons were preparing to sing First Vespers of Palm Sunday.
56. *St Andrews Copiale*, 138.

the glowing lights, the spotless altar vessels, fine vestments, worthy clerics, the orderly singing of the divine office, the devotion of the people; all showed the results of his careful administration. The chronicler waxes lyrical in Bisset's praise: St Andrews was a monastic paradise—*claustralis paradisus*, in his day.[57] Bisset's restoration of the nave was completed by Prior James Haldenstone. Bower's description says that, while Bisset had restored the nave with great magnificence—*sumptuose*—it was unfurnished and resembled a vast, empty synagogue. Haldenstone proceeded to furnish it with altars, statues and other ornaments and he laid the floor of smooth stone slabs, some vestiges of which remain to this day.[58] One item of Bower's description calls for special comment because it has been consistently mistranslated. Bower says that Haldenstone provided ' *luminaria vitrea* ' throughout the nave. C. J. Lyon, in his *History of St Andrews* translates this as glass windows and in this he has been followed by more recent writers. Bower is using ' *luminaria* ' in its normal meaning of ' lamps ' and, to prove the point one need only look at the preceding page of his chronicle where he distinguishes between ' *fenestrae*,' windows, and ' *luminaria*,' lamps.[59] In other words Haldenstone provided glass lamps throughout the nave, probably some kind of glass bowls suspended from the roof which were furnished with oil and a wick. A central keystone from the vault of one of the bays of an aisle of the nave is in the cathedral museum: it has an iron hook inserted in it for suspending such a lamp. Glass lamps were not unusual: as early as 1260, we find the register of St Andrews speaking of the glass lamp in the church of Ceres and the oil required annually for its maintenance.[60]

The dominating feature of the nave, as we have seen, would be the choir screen and altar of the Holy Cross. The bays of the north and south aisles would be enclosed with screens to form individual chapels, each with its own altar, ornaments and furnishing. Fragments of foundation at the sixth bay from the west in the north aisle seem to indicate that the chapel in that bay had some kind of external annexe built on to it: this was possibly a consistory house or other office because the chapels of that aisle, called the Archdeacon's Aisle, were normally used for diocesan courts and other administrative purposes. A fragment of foundation at the third bay from the west probably indicates the site of the porch of the north door, the ' northe dure ' mentioned by Wyntoun.[61]

The chapel of St John the Baptist was in the north-west corner of the nave,[62] so it is likely that the baptismal font stood somewhere in that part of the church. Probably in the south-west corner stood the holy water

57. *Chron. Bower*, i, 373.
58. Between the pillars of the third bay from the west on the north side of the nave and in the easternmost bay of the nave in front of the site of the choir screen.
59. *Chron. Bower*, i, 375 and 372.
60. *St Andrews Liber*, 384.
61. *Chron. Wyntoun*, v, 127.
62. A. I. Dunlop, *Acta Facultatis Artium Universitatis Sanctiandree*, 1413-1588 (Edinburgh, 1964), 248.

stoup, the *aspersorium*, near which Prior William Bonar was buried in 1462.[63] Against one of the pillars on the south side of the nave, probably halfway along the nave, would be the pulpit, which is mentioned in a document of 1484—*in polpito cathedralis ecclesie sanctiandree.*[64] A large, colourful medieval clock would be conspicuous somewhere, possibly in the triforium gallery: no record of such a clock has survived but these were common in lesser churches in Scotland in the fifteenth and sixteenth centuries and St Andrews cathedral would not lack one of these.[65] The chiming clock—*horecudium*, supplied by Prior William Bonar was intended for the use of the choir.[66]

The people of the town gathered in the nave for the singing of the divine office as the case against Richard of North Berwick clearly shows. The people gathered there also for high mass at 10 a.m. on Sunday mornings.[67] The nave would be crowded also on special occasions and particularly during the pardons celebrated in the cathedral. At other times it seems to have been used as a promenade by the townsfolk. In the statutes of St Leonard's college the students are warned that, if they go to the cathedral (for which they must seek permission) they must not strut about blethering in the nave of the church or in the neighbourhood of the choir but rather go and say their prayers in some secluded corner— *in navi ecclesie seu versus chorum tempore divini officii confabulando seu procaciter incedendo non deambulent, sed potius in locis privatis devotioni . . . religiose se disponant.*[68]

THE GALILEE PORCH AND WEST DOOR

When Bishop William Wishart (1271-1279) reconstructed the west gable of the cathedral, he constructed a large vaulted galilee porch on the site of the two westernmost bays of the nave. It has been asserted that this galilee porch was removed after only being in existence about a century.[69] The architectural evidence for this statement possibly needs further consideration because there is no obvious reason why a useful porch like this should be removed when such features were retained by other large churches in Europe. It seems strange that, if the galilee was removed in the fourteenth century, that such unsightly vestiges of it should be allowed to remain in the facade of the church and in the south wall during the two centuries that the cathedral remained in use and that nothing was done, in the fifteenth-century reconstruction, to make the

63. Law MS, fo 20v.
64. Fraser, *Wemyss*, ii, 101.
65. Church clocks are mentioned, for example, at the Holy Trinity parish church, St Andrews, in 1449 (W. E. K. Rankin, *The Parish Church of the Holy Trinity, St Andrews*, Edinburgh, 1955, 28) and in St. Mary's parish church, Dundee, on 10 March 1442 (*Hist. MSS Comm.*, *4th Report*, 1874, 507).
66. Law MS, fo 20v.
67. Fraser, *Wemyss*, ii, 101.
68. John Herkless and Robert Kerr Hannay, *The College of St Leonard* (Edinburgh, 1905), 153.
69. *Hist. Mon. Comm. (Fife)*, 234.

disproportionately small west door a little more imposing. Also, during the whole medieval period the west door of the church was used as a public notice board on which were fixed announcements, broadsheets, decrees, and one would expect these official notices to have some protection from the weather.

Affixed to the west door of the cathedral could be found sentences of courts such as excommunication,[70] the regulations made by synods,[71] notices which reflected the academic and civic life of the town and, much appreciated by the general reader, were the lampoons surreptitiously posted up on the doors. There seems to be a long history of such pasquils on the west door of the metropolitan church from the rather silly exchange chalked up on the door by Bishop Abel de Gullane and the canons in 1254[72] to the pasquils which appeared on the door during the equally foolish Pater Noster controversy of 1551.[73]

THE CATHEDRAL WELL

It is strange that no one seems ever to have commented on the well in the nave of the cathedral. Wells, of course, are commonplace in large churches where they supplied water for the liturgical ceremonies, for scouring floors and other purposes. The remarkable and possibly unique feature of the well in St Andrews cathedral is its position. In other churches the well is located in some corner where it can be useful without being obtrusive. St Mungo's well, in Glasgow cathedral, is in the southeast corner of the lower church. At Rheims, the well, known as Les Puits de St Rigobert, is conveniently placed in the passage-way to the sacristy. Wells are normally tucked away in some convenient corner but not so at St Andrews.[74] The cathedral well at St Andrews must have been planned and dug by the twelfth-century architect, originally to supply water for the construction of the building: it lies exactly on the central axis of the church and exactly halfway between the east gable and the original western facade. After the building was completed, although two wells were dug to supply the domestic needs of the priory, no attempt seems to have been made to provide a well in a less conspicuous part of the cathedral. Cathedral wells were often given an appropriate architectural setting as at Strassburg or Freiburg im Breisgau, or at Regensburg where the canopy over the well bears the figures of Christ and the Samaritan woman. We know nothing about the ornamentation of the St Andrews well but, in such a prominent position, it must have had some kind of monumental well-head, if not an architectural canopy. The ecclesiastics who retained this well in this prominent central position, standing before

---

70. *St Andrews Formulare*, i, no. 93: *St Andrews Copiale*, 34.
71. Robertson, *Concilia*, i, cclxx.
72. *Chron. Bower*, i, 360.
73. *The Acts and Monuments of John Foxe*, ed. S. R. Cattley (London, 1838), v, 642-3.
74. The well in Dunfermline abbey church is also conspicuous, being in the middle of the south aisle of the nave (*Hist. Mon. Comm. (Fife)*, 113).

the rood screen with its altar of the Crucified must have felt something of that same awareness of its profound symbolism which induced the Van Eyck brothers to place the fountain of grace in front of the altar of the Lamb in the very centre of their great altarpiece at Ghent.

SACRISTIES AND OTHER OFFICES

In many of the larger churches of late medieval Scotland there was a two-storied annexe built on to the north or south side of the chancel. Of these two stories, the chamber which was on a level with the chancel was the sacristy and the other storey (the upper storey at Dunkeld or the lower storey at Glasgow) was the treasury of the church. This was not the case at St Andrews. Being a monastic church, some of the ancillary offices were incorporated in the complex of monastic buildings attached to the cloister. No reference has survived in the medieval writers or in George Martine's *Reliquiae Divi Andreae* to any treasury at St Andrews. From the description of Haldenstone's reconstruction of the chapel of the relics with its lockfast cupboards, it would seem that that chapel was regarded as the cathedral treasury. The muniment room, or ' the charter-house, a close stone room,' was alongside the Senzie Hall in the west wing of the cloister.[75] Marcus Wagner speaks of the library but he does not indicate its whereabouts in the monastery.[76] The chapter house was, of course, as much a monastic place as an adjunct to the cathedral. Enough survives of the early chapter house and the new chapter house built by Bishop Lamberton just south of the south transept to indicate its former splendour. The three-bayed apartment in the east range of the cloister, immediately south of the chapter house, was the sacristy, the ' vestiarie ' as Martine calls it.[77] The wall cupboards for altar vessels still exist in its west wall. The proportions of the room have been destroyed by a stair intruded in post-Reformation times to adapt the building to domestic purposes. There was a second sacristy, according to Martine, in the south wing of the cloister in the corner to the east of the refectory. It was ' a faire four square rowme for copes and albs, etc. beside (i.e. in addition to) the common vestiarie.'[78] Here would be kept the huge semi-circular or quadrant-shaped cope-chests on whose ornamental ironwork the medieval blacksmith expended much skill and artistry.

ALTAR DEDICATIONS

Lack of information, through destruction of records, becomes painfully evident when we seek to identify the site and dedication of the numerous altars which once stood in the medieval cathedral. We have already discussed the site and the appearance of the high altar. In addition to the high altar, there were three other altars in the east end of the

75. George Martine, *Reliquiae Divi Andreae* (St Andrews, 1797), 188.
76. *St Andrews Copiale*, xxvii.
77. Martine, *op. cit.*, 189.
78. Ibid.

cathedral. In the chapel or aisle to the north of the sanctuary was the altar of Our Blessed Lady. Its location is clearly stated by the chroniclers in relation to the tombs of Bishop Wardlaw and Prior Haldenstone.[79] The altar and chapel to the south of the sanctuary was probably dedicated to St Andrew. A chapel of St Andrew is mentioned when an appeal, about the year 1540, from a chaplain of Dunkeld was to be heard: *in insula sancti A[ndree]*—in the chapel of St A[ndrew] in the metropolitan and primatial church.[80] In the chapel of the relics there would be an altar of St Andrew, or ' of the relics ' on the west side of ' the relict almrie,' the structure in the centre of the chapel in which the relics of St Andrew were enshrined.

In the north transept there were three chapels ranged along the east wall but no information concerning the titular saints of their altars has survived. There were three chapels in the corresponding position in the south transept; two of these were dedicated to St Michael and to St Lawrence[81] but we do not know their exact positions. It may be significant that in the corresponding area of Salisbury cathedral there were altars of these two saints and there the altar of St Lawrence occupied the central bay and the altar of St Michael was in the south-east corner.[82] St Lawrence's altar is mentioned on one occasion as a meeting place of the official's court.[83]

There seem to have been three altars in the choir screen complex. The altar in the gallery over the screen was, as we have seen, dedicated to the Holy Cross. We have no documentary evidence concerning the altars on either side of the entrance to the choir, but there is one slight clue which is perhaps worth mentioning briefly. Bishop de Landallis was buried in the pavement of the church, according to Bower, at the east processional door from the cloister—*coram ostio vestibuli*,[84] and, according to Spottiswood, the tomb was near the choir screen door—' at the Chancery door.'[85] The general location indicated is close to the altar standing to the south of the entrance to the choir. Now, Sir James Balfour (1600-1657), in his lives of the bishops of St Andrews, says that Bishop de Landallis was buried: *coram ostio vestibuli, Divi Pauli*,[86] which suggests that the nearby altar was dedicated to St Paul. One might speculate further that if there was an altar of St Paul on the south of the entrance door to the choir, the corresponding altar to the north is likely to have been dedicated to St Peter. Such a pair of dedications would fit neatly into the historical context. The altar dedications in the cathedral would no doubt emphasise

---

79. *Chron. Bower*, i, 366, 375.
80. *St Andrews Formulare*, ii, 109.
81. *Chron. Bower*, i, 371.
82. C. Wordsworth. *Ceremonies and Processions of the Cathedral Church of Salisbury* (Cambridge, 1901), 77.
83. SRO, Liber Sententiarum Officialis S. Andree principalis, fo 68v.
84. *Chron. Bower*, i, 364.
85. John Spotswood, *The History of the Church of Scotland* (London, 1666), 55.
86. Sir James Balfour, ' Lives of the bishops of St Andrews,' NLS, Adv. MS, 33.2.8. fo 27.

the apostolic character of the titular saint of the church and St Peter and St Paul would be prominent among these dedications. Incidentally, the cathedral had a much frequented indulgence for the feast of Saints Peter and Paul (and in 1418, about the time the new choir screen was built, a supplication was made to have that indulgence extended).[87] It was under Prior Haldenstone that the new choir screen was erected and he would influence the choice of the titular saints for the new altars. Haldenstone was a man who incurred criticism from his contemporaries for his excessive enthusiasm in returning Scotland to the obedience of the Roman popes[88] and it would not be surprising if he dedicated the two new altars in his choir screen to the two patron saints of the Roman papacy.

The nave west of the choir screen had altars, apparently erected at various periods. Some may have dated to an early period in the history of the building: others were provided by Prior James Bisset after the fire of 1378: others again were set up by Prior Haldenstone. Scarcely any information has survived concerning these altars in the nave of the cathedral. Nave altars were erected either in front of pillars (as in Glasgow cathedral)[89] or in the bays of the aisles which were surrounded by screens to form separate chapels (as in Dunblane cathedral).[90] From the remaining grooves, cut in the south wall of the nave, it is evident that the general arrangement in the medieval nave of St Andrews was that the bays of the aisles were screened off to form chapels, but we can only conjecture the number of chapels thus formed. It is not unlikely that, apart from the bays immediately in front of the choir screen[91] and the bays which formed the vestibules of the north and south doors, all of the bays were separate chapels. This would give eighteen chapels and altars in the nave. This is not an excessive number for a large Scottish church. While English cathedrals had a limited number of altars, the number of altars in Scottish cathedrals and large burgh churches, following the Continental fashion, was generally large.[92] Nothing whatever seems to be known about the individual dedications of altars in the south aisle of the nave. The north aisle of the nave was known as the Archdeacon's Aisle, probably because some chapels there were founded by archdeacons or were used for administrative offices and courts of the diocese. The names of two separate chapels in the Archdeacon's Aisle have survived.

---

87. *Cal. Scot. Supp.*, i, 10.
88. *St Andrews Copiale*, 7-16.
89. John Durkan, ' Notes on Glasgow Cathedral ' in *Innes Review*, xxi (1970), 46-76.
90. David McRoberts, ' Dunblane Cathedral under the Chisholms ' in *Society of Friends of Dunblane Cathedral*, xi (1971), 37-52.
91. The remains of a piscina can be seen in the second bay from the east of the south nave aisle. This piscina possibly survived from an altar which once stood here before the fifteenth-century choir screen was built across this part of the church. The piscina may have been kept to serve the new altars on either side of the choir screen entrance.
92. In the later Middle Ages, altars proliferated in larger Scottish churches. The cathedrals of St Andrews and of Glasgow had about thirty altars each, while the devout citizens of Edinburgh crowded over forty altars into their church of St Giles. This pious congestion was made worse by having several chaplainries founded at certain altars. In comparison large English churches had remarkably few altars (York, 24; Durham, 20; Wells, 18; Exeter, 16; Salisbury, 12) according to Peter B. G. Binnall, ' Notes on the medieval altars and chapels in Lincoln Cathedral,' in *The Antiquaries Journal*, xlii (1962), 68.

On 5 May 1494, Master Alexander Inglis, archdeacon of St Andrews, founded a chaplainry of the Annunciation and All Saints at the already existing altar of St John the Baptist and the charter indicates the position of that altar.[93] It stood in the nave of the metropolitan church in what is commonly called the Archdeacon's Aisle on the north side of the church and at the west end. This chapel then occupied one of the bays in the north-west corner of the nave and probably it was one of the earliest chapels founded in the nave. Since the cathedral was a thank-offering for the victory at Bannockburn, it would have, from the beginning, an altar dedicated to the saint on whose feast day the battle was won. It seems likely also that the baptismal font of the cathedral would be located somewhere near this chapel. The name of this chapel appears in various legal and administrative acts of the fifteenth and sixteenth centuries. It was here on 23 May 1459, after a two-day hearing of the case, that the decree arbitral was pronounced on the marriage of the earl of Rothes ' read and pronounced in the presence of the said earl of Rothes, in the cathedral church of St Andrews, in the aisle of St John the Baptist.'[94] It was here that the appointment of Sir Gilbert Barde to the vicarage of Alvah was signed and sealed, on 23 December 1520: *apud ecclesiam metropolitanam sanctiandree in sacello archidiaconi principalis eiusdem hora quasi decima ante meridiem.*[95]

The successor of Alexander Inglis, Archdeacon Robert Wells, on 7 May 1501, founded another chaplainry in honour of Our Lady and St John the Evangelist at the altar in the chapel, or *insula*, of St John the Evangelist in the metropolitan church.[96] This chapel was regularly used for meetings of the official's court: there was a case concerning the validity of a charter heard here on 27 May 1551[97] and several cases from Archbishop Forman's time are known to have been heard in this chapel.[98] A charter of 1573 tells us that this chapel was in the Archdeacon's Aisle, or the north aisle and possibly it was in the sixth bay from the west where there are some vestiges of an annexe, built on to the chapel, which may have been a consistory house or repository for court records. We catch a glimpse of Archdeacon Robert Wells refurnishing the chapel in connection with his new chaplainry, in 1499, when he bought through Andrew Halyburton, twenty-four pillars of brass, four of which would be the fashionable brass riddel-posts of the period and the remainder may have formed a new screen round the chapel. He bought also two candlesticks at £19, a silver chalice, double gilt, at £6 9s. and an embroidered altar frontal of red silk, which cost him eighteen shillings.[99] One of the people

---

93. *Evidence . . . taken and received by the Commissioners . . . for visiting the Universities of Scotland* (1837), iii, 353.
94. *Hist. MSS Comm. 4th Report* (1874), 507.
95. *Coupar Angus Chrs.,* ii, 127.
96. *Evidence . . . ,* iii, 354.
97. *Laing Chrs.,* no. 582.
98. *St Andrews Formulare,* i, 11, 26, 74, 387.
99. *Halyburton's Ledger,* 159-60.

for whose soul the chaplainry was founded was Elizabeth, countess of Ross, so presumably the tomb which Wells bought for Lady Ross was destined for this chapel.[100]

An altar of St Catherine is mentioned in various documents but this appears to have been, in fact, a chaplainry of St Catherine at the altar of St John the Evangelist in the Archdeacon's Aisle. This is made clear in a charter of 1573, in which Master William Murray, treasurer of Dunblane, is described as perpetual chaplain of the altar, or rather chaplainry of St Catherine, in the metropolitan church of St Andrews, within the aisle of St John the Evangelist, called the Archdeacon's Aisle.[101] The chaplainry provided an alternative name for the altar. Under the title of St Catherine's, this altar is mentioned regularly in connection with court proceedings and the repayment of debts. The official's decision, for example, on the right of patronage of St Bothan's was pronounced at St Catherine's altar on 4 March 1470.[102] It was at this altar that Sir John Wemyss had to pay the redemption of the lands of Methil in 1465, 1470 and on Sunday, 21 March 1484, when at ten o'clock in the morning, the time of the Sunday high mass, Master Thomas Tod read out from the pulpit in a loud and intelligible voice, the summons to the subpriors of St Andrews and Lindores to repair to the altar of St Catherine for the payment of the redemption money.[103] On 18 April 1572, redemption money was still being paid at the place where the altar of St Catherine was formerly situated in the cathedral.[104]

In all, there were probably about thirty separate altars in the cathedral with numerous chaplainries. Most of these were founded, maintained and served by the Augustinian community. Details of their foundation, furnishing and personnel would be preserved among the domestic records of the priory and the wholesale destruction of these monastic records would account for our dearth of information.

THE TOMBS IN THE CATHEDRAL

The most striking feature of the cathedral after the altars would be the numerous tombs. The stone pavements on all sides were bestrewn with ' throwchts ' or flat tombstones of ecclesiastics and layfolk, nobles and commoners, famous and unknown, displaying heraldry, or calvary crosses, or the tools of various trades. Fine examples of these stones are the tombstone of Patrick Ogilvie, a priest who died on 5 April 1350; his tombstone has a floriated cross, a chalice, and an open missal inscribed

100. *Evidence* . . . , iii, 354, and *Halyburton's Ledger*, 160.
101. *Reg. Mag. Sig.*, iv, no. 2153. A difficulty arises from the fact that the word *insula* has two meanings in late medieval Scottish documents. It can mean the aisle of a church but its more usual meaning is a section of a church screened off to form a separate chapel.
102. *Yester Writs*, no. 161.
103. Fraser, *Wemyss*, i, 87, ii, 87, 94, 101.
104. SRO, Prot. Bk. of James Nicolson, fo 103r.

with the Holy Name, Ihesus;[105] or the massive slab, with its finely cut heraldry, which once covered the tomb of Archdeacon Alexander Inglis near the altar of St John the Baptist.[106] Set in the walls would be inscriptions and epitaphs and monuments, such as the well-known effigy of a fourteenth-century stonemason with the mell and square of his trade.[107] The cathedral had no royal tombs[108] and the most prominent monuments were the splendid altar-tombs of the prelates of St Andrews, ornately carved and resplendent with vivid colouring, and equally bright were the incised brass lairs which were fashionable throughout the whole medieval period.

The motive underlying these elaborate monuments and inscriptions was to ask for prayers for the souls of the departed. This purpose could more effectively be achieved if the tomb was situated in a frequented part of the church, if possible near some favourite altar or statue. This accounts for the large tombstone of a layman (possibly someone of the Douglas family) inserted in the pavement to the north of the high altar where it would lie just in front of the statue called ' le Douglas Lady.' This was the reason also for Prior William Bonar placing his brass lair at the holy water stoup where people, entering the church, would say a prayer as they paused to bless themselves with holy water—ad aspersorium ubi aqua benedicta aspergitur.[109]

Some detailed examination of the burials of the bishops of St Andrews seems necessary since the subject has never had the attention that it merits. A convenient starting point is the burial of Bishop David de Bernham, who died in 1253. The chance survival of Bernham's Pontificale, with its impressive list of the churches he consecrated, has posthumously enhanced his reputation as a conscientious pastoral bishop.[110] The medieval canons of St Andrews remembered him with somewhat less enthusiasm. The Scotichronicon describes him in one place as ' altogether praiseworthy '—vir per omnia commendabilis,[111] but elsewhere it speaks of him as harsh and exacting towards his community of canons and recalls how he deprived them for a time of their church of Inchture,[112] but what was quite unforgivable was that Bernham, to these injuries, added the ultimate insult that he chose to be buried in Kelso and not in his own cathedral. This was equivalent to a public declaration that he placed more reliance on the prayers of the Kelso Benedictines than on those of his own Augustinian canons at St Andrews. Naturally such conduct did not go unchallenged and the burial took place only in the

---

105. David Hay Fleming, Museum, 59. This tombstone was found at the Kirkhill in 1860 (op. cit., 238), but it illustrates the type of monument to be found in the cathedral.
106. Broken in two, this fine monument now serves as window sills in Queen Mary's house.
107. Proc. Soc. Antiq. Scot., xlix (1914-5), 221-3.
108. The tomb of Archbishop James Stewart might be regarded as a royal tomb.
109. Law MS, fo 20v.
110. W. Lockhart, The Church of Scotland in the Thirteenth Century (Edinburgh, 1892).
111. Chron. Bower, ii, 89.
112. Chron. Bower, i, 359. The divergent estimates of character are due to the composite nature of the Scotichronicon

PLATE XIII. WILLIAM SCHEVEZ, ARCHBISHOP OF ST ANDREWS, 1476-1497.

Archbishop William Schevez celebrated the bull of Pope Innocent VIII (27 March 1487), which made the archbishops of St Andrews primates of the Scottish Church and *legati nati* of the Apostolic See, by commissioning this fine medal from the Flemish artist Quentin Matsys in 1491.

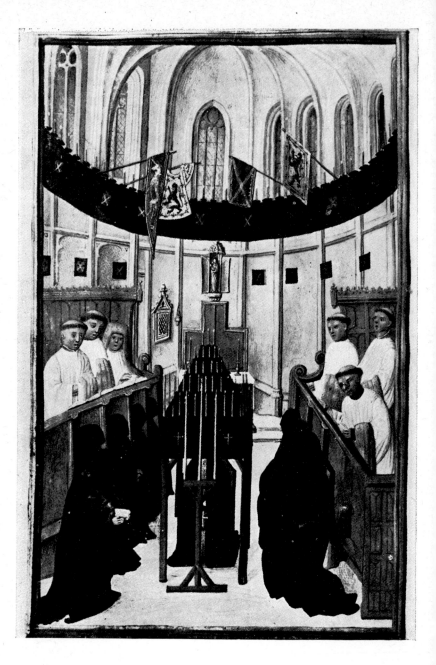

PLATE XIV. A ROYAL DIRGE.

This miniature in the Book of Hours of King James IV (Ost. Nationalbibliothek Wien, C 1897, fo 141v) shows a church decorated with candles and hatchments for a royal dirge illustrates how St Andrews cathedral would be decorated with the enormous number of can and hatchments that were supplied for the obsequies of Archbishop James Stewart, brot of King James IV, in 1504.

face of the protest and prohibition of the church of St Andrews.[113] There is more than a touch of acidity in Wyntoun's reference to Bishop David de Bernham:

'The bischope Dauid of Bername
Past of this warlde til his lange hame.
As he did here sa fande he thar;
Off hym I bid to spek na mare.
He cheyssit his layr in to Kelsow,
Noucht in the kyrk of Sancte Androw.'[114]

And Wyntoun omits to commend David de Bernham's soul 'in to Paradys.' The important point is that the chancel of the cathedral was regarded as the only proper place where bishops of St Andrews should be buried. Bower speaks of the chancel of the metropolitan church as the official burial place of the bishops—*in sepulchro pontificum*,[115] and four centuries later, John Law describes Bernham's action as *contra morem*, contrary to the tradition of the diocese.[116] The antiquity of this tradition is illustrated by the tombs of twelfth-century bishops who were buried in the old cathedral, where their epitaphs provided chronological data for fifteenth-century chroniclers.

Bishop Roger, who died in 1202, was the last bishop to be buried in the old cathedral. His successor, Bishop William Malvoisin, was buried in the new cathedral—*in nova ecclesia Sancti Andree*—in 1238.[117] The exact position of Malvoisin's tomb is not recorded but it seems most likely that his would be one of the three monuments which stood between the pillars on the south side of the original choir. After Malvoisin came Bernham who, as we have seen, was buried in Kelso. The next bishop was Abel de Gullane, who died in 1254 and, like Bernham, was unpopular with the canons. Bower states that Gullane was buried in the new cathedral[118] and the Wodrow manuscript adds that he was buried 'before the hei altar,'[119] so he also was buried in one of the three tombs between the pillars in the south choir aisle. Bishop Gamelin came next but we shall discuss his place of burial in a moment. Gamelin's successor, Bishop William Wishart, was interred, according to Bower, on 2 June 1279, in the new church in front of the high altar—*in nova ecclesia ante altare*,[120] so he too occupied one of the three tombs between the pillars of the south choir aisle.

---

113. Ibid.
114. *Chron. Wyntoun*, v, 119.
115. *Chron. Bower*, i, 365.
116. Law MS, fo 15.
117. *Chron. Bower*, i, 359.
118. *Chron. Bower*, i, 360.
119. NLS Wodrow MSS Qto. XX, fo 7. This Wodrow MS 'The Bishops of St Andrewes after the extermination of the Pechtes' was written during the episcopate of George Gledstanes (1610-15). The author has made use of traditional information (not always accurate) concerning the place of burial of the bishops. The manuscript was published in *Analecta Scotica* (Second Series) (Edinburgh, 1837), 4-10.
120. *Chron. Bower*, i, 361.

G

Omitting Bishop William Fraser and Bishop William Lamberton for the moment, we go on to deal with the fourteenth-century bishops. Bishop James Ben died in 1332 at Bruges and was buried in the Augustinian church at Eeckhout.[121] After Ben's death the see remained vacant for fully ten years. William Bell, dean of Dunkeld, who was elected, failed to get papal confirmation of his election. He resided with the canons, fell into ill health, became blind and finally resigned his right in order to facilitate the election of Bishop William de Landallis in 1342 and died in 1343.[122] The unfortunate career of this bishop-elect probably explains a tombstone in the south choir aisle which has been something of a puzzle. Between the pillars of the south choir aisle, in the fourth bay from the crossing, there is a large tombstone, still *in situ*, inserted in the paved floor of the aisle. The incised figure shows an ecclesiastic in mass vestments, the face, the hands, the chalice and the scroll which carried the inscription round the border of the stone, were all brass inserts of which only the empty matrices now remain. There are no episcopal insignia and the figure is not dressed in the habit of an Augustinian canon so this ecclesiastic is neither bishop nor prior. Some explanation is necessary for the burial of this ecclesiastic in the place reserved for the bishops of St Andrews. The stone is very similar to an example at Ashby Puerorum in Lincolnshire, which can be dated to the early fourteenth century.[123] If we accept that this St Andrews tombstone is mid-fourteenth century in date, then it seems reasonable to suggest that this stone marks the grave of William Bell, bishop-elect of St Andrews from 1332 to 1342. This tombstone seems never to have been disturbed so that excavation might reveal the remains of this bishop-elect.

The next bishop, Bishop William de Landallis, died in 1385. The Scotichronicon states that he was buried in the paved floor in front of the door to the sacristy in the high kirk under a finely carved stone—*in pavimento, coram ostio vestibuli, in magna ecclesia, sub artificioso lapide.*[124] The door in question must be the east processional door to the cloister which led directly from the church to the sacristy in the east range of the cloister. Sir James Balfour, as we have seen, adds the words: *Divi Pauli*, which suggests that there may have been an altar of St Paul near this door. Archbishop Spottiswood, in his history, states that Landallis ' was buried in the cathedral church at the Chancery Door.'[125] This area was incorporated in the new choir screen built by Prior James Haldenstone so that the tomb of Landallis could easily be described as being near the

---

121. *Chron. Bower*, i, 363.
122. Ibid.
123. Illustrated in Rev. Herbert Haines, *A Manual of Monumental Brasses* (Bath, 1970), 256.
124. *Chron. Bower*, i, 364
125. See note 85 above. Richard Augustine Hay states that William Bell ' was buried att the chancery door in the cathedral church ' (Scotia Sacra, NLS, Adv. MS, 34.1.8. fo 95), but clearly Hay has been using Archbishop Spottiswoode's *History* and has telescoped the episcopates of Bell and Landallis

door of the choir screen—' at the Chancery Door.' There is a slight discrepancy in the descriptions of Landallis's tomb. Bower says that it was a finely carved stone—*artificioso lapide*,[126] while John Law says that it was a brass—*in tumba ex aere fabricata*.[127] The possible explanation is that, like the contemporary tombstone that we have assigned to the bishop-elect, William Bell, the tombstone of Landallis was cut in stone with brass inserts for various features of the design. The burial of Bishop William de Landallis at a distance from his predecessors may be due to the work of reconstruction which followed the catastrophic fire of 1378.

Landallis's successor, Stephen Pay, died among his English captors in 1386 and was buried in exile and so we come to the burial of Bishop Walter Trail, who died in 1401. Trail's tomb was one of a group of three which occupied the spaces between the pillars in the north choir aisle and some documentary evidence concerning this group of tombs has survived. The three tombs were those of Bishop Gamelin (who died in 1271), Bishop William Lamberton (who died in 1328) and Bishop Walter Trail (who died in 1401). Of Bishop Gamelin, Bower says that he was buried in the new church alongside the high altar—*iuxta magnum altare*,[128] while John Law says that he was buried in front of the high altar—*ante magnum altare*.[129] Bishop William Lamberton is said by Bower to have been buried on the north side of the high altar—*ad borealem partem magni altaris*,[130] and John Law repeats that information.[131] Bower says of Bishop Walter Trail that he was interred honourably in the burial place of the bishops near the high altar, on the north side, within the choir screen—*sepultus est honorifice in sepulchro pontificum iuxta magnum altare ecclesie Sancti Andree ad aquilonem intra pulpitum*, and he quotes the simple epitaph that was written on his tomb:

> ' *Hic fuit ecclesiae directa columna, fenestra*
> *Lucida, thuribulum redolens, campana sonora.*'[132]

John Law simply says that he was buried on the north side of the church —*in parte aquilonali sanctiandree*.[133] Andrew Wyntoun, the chronicler, however, who had been a canon of St Andrews and who, almost certainly, had assisted at the burial of Bishop Walter Trail, describes the row of three tombs in the north choir aisle. He describes how Bishop William

---

126. *Chron. Bower, loc cit.*
127. Law MS, fo 16.
128. *Chron. Bower*, i, 360.
129. Law MS, fo 15v. The change in the preposition is due to the altar having been moved eastwards between the dates of the two chronicles.
130. *Chron. Bower*, i, 362.
131. Law MS, fo 16.
132. *Chron. Bower*, i, 365.
133. Law MS, fo 16. Law makes no reference to the pulpitum which, by his day, had been moved westwards away from Trail's tomb.

87

Lamberton, like other bishops before him, prepared his own tomb in advance:

> ' On the northe half of the new kyrk
> Cathedrale, he gert ane arche wyrk,
> Now seyne betweyn the tombis twa,
> Off Gamyl the estmost was of tha.
> And the space that was lewide
> Betwix the pulpit and his hewide,
> Ane arche of fayr werk and fyne
> The bischop Waltyr gert mak syne,
> Vndyr that now lyis he.
> Thus lyande ar tha bischopis thre
> On northe half the Hie Kyrk
> In tombis that thaim self gert wyrk.'[134]

Between the pillars of the north choir arcade and against the wall enclosing the choir, the three bishops had their tombs constructed in contemporary style. The pulpitum, or choir screen, still crossed the church on the line of the eastern piers of the crossing. Immediately east of the pulpitum was the tomb of Trail, then that of Lamberton and, in the third bay, stood the earlier tomb of Gamelin. A further bishop was commemorated here. Bishop William Fraser, who had sought refuge in Paris from King Edward I, and who died there in 1297, had asked that his heart be buried in his own cathedral church at St Andrews. This was done and Bishop Fraser's heart was buried by Bishop Lamberton in the choir wall alongside the tomb of Bishop Gamelin—*in pariete ecclesie Sancti Andree iuxta tumbam episcopi Gamelini.*[135] It was a solemn occasion, as Wyntoun recalls:

> ' Bot his hart ordanyt he
> Broucht in Scotlande for to be;
> And swa it was withe honoure
> And laid in halowyt sepulture.
> In til Sancte Androwis Cathedralle
> Kyrk, the conwentualle
> Chanownys to gedyr gadryt al
> And laid that hart withein the wal,
> Cloyssit and laid richt suttelly
> In that plasse and honorably,
> Qwhar now ar towmbis twa
> Off Gamyl and Lambartone ar tha.
> Wilyame Freseris hart was laide
> Betweyn tha towmbis twa forsaide.'[136]

And the chronicler's statement that this was done ' richt suttelly ' suggests that the heart-burial monument, in which Fraser's heart was entombed, was a notable piece of craftsmanship.

---

134. *Chron. Wyntoun*, v, 381.
135. *Chron. Bower*, i, 361.
136. *Chron. Wyntoun*, v, 311-3.

The episcopate of Bishop Henry Wardlaw and the priorship of James Haldenstone ran contemporaneously and were marked by the reorganisation and enlargement of the choir of the cathedral. In this reconstruction, the ambulatory behind the high altar disappeared and the high altar and sanctuary were moved one bay eastwards. One of the effects of this rearrangement (if indeed it was not its prime motive) was that the enlarged Lady chapel now provided very desirable locations for the tombs of Bishop Wardlaw and Prior Haldenstone. Bishop Wardlaw's tomb was set against the wall between the extended Lady chapel and the new sanctuary. Perhaps remembering all the work that went into preparing this site, Bower says that Wardlaw was buried with greater fuss than any of his predecessors—*honorificentius antecessoribus suis.*[137] Bower quotes Bishop Wardlaw's epitaph, which is an acrostic based on the letters of the bishop's name:

> ' *Si quis quaesierit, de quo sunt haec, reperire,*
> *Versibus hic poterit mox per capitalia scire,'*[138]

and when it was written, in 1440, Wardlaw's university of St Andrews was still the sole university in Scotland:

> ' *Ad rivuli laticem bibit huius Scotia tota.'*

Bower states that Wardlaw was interred in the wall separating the choir from the Lady chapel.[139] John Law, however, gives a clearer indication of the position of the tomb. Looking at the monument from the front, he says that Wardlaw was buried at the entrance to the Lady chapel—*in ostio capelle nostre domine.*[140] The entrance to the newly enlarged Lady chapel would be through a screen and, on entering, Bishop Wardlaw's tomb stood on the right and Prior Haldenstone's tomb was in the north wall to the left. Bower quotes the epitaph inscribed on Haldenstone's monument:

> ' *Qui docui mores, mundi vitare favores,*
> *Inter doctores sacros sortitus honores,*
> *Vermibus hic donor: et sic ostendere conor,*
> *Quod sicut ponor, ponitur omnis honor.'*[141]

Bishop Wardlaw's tomb, and other tombs in the Lady chapel, were uncovered in one of Dr David Hay Fleming's ' howkings ' in 1903 and the carved fragments of the superstructure of the tomb, still showing traces of colouring and gilding, were discovered at that time.[142] Fragments of the recumbent effigy of the bishop have also been recovered from different sites. The broken figure carved finely in local stone wears a full chasuble, embellished with the bishop's coat of arms. The crosier has been of metal and dowelled into the stone figure.[143] The mutilated head

137. *Chron. Bower*, i, 366.
138. Ibid.
139. Ibid.
140. Law MS, fo 16v.
141. *Chron. Bower*, i, 375.
142. *Scot. Hist. Rev.*, i (1904), 243.
143. W. Norman Robertson, ' Fragments of Sculptured Stone-work from the Tomb of Henry Wardlaw, Bishop of St Andrews ' in *Proc. Soc. Antiq. Scot.*, 101 (1968-9), 146-9.

wearing a splendid fifteenth-century mitre is that of a young man and shows that the bishop must have commissioned this tomb in the early years of his long episcopate.[144]

Wardlaw's successor, Bishop James Kennedy, probably commissioned his elaborate tomb early in his episcopate. The dimensions of Kennedy's tomb show that it was originally intended to stand between two of the pillars in the chancel arcade in the cathedral, probably the position in the southern arcade corresponding to the Wardlaw tomb in the northern aisle. However, Kennedy later founded St Salvator's college and his tomb was eventually erected in the chapel of that college. The passage of time has reduced Kennedy's tomb to a shadow of that original magnificence of which John Major disapproved — *nec sepulchri sumptuositatem approbo*,[145] but enough remains to indicate something of the splendour of the monuments which once adorned the cathedral.

Next came the unfortunate Patrick Graham, the first archbishop. He died in the priory of Lochleven and was buried in that priory church. His successor, Archbishop William Schevez, the first effective archbishop, chose as his place of burial the centre of the chancel directly in front of the high altar. John Law, a contemporary, states that he was buried in the paved floor, in front of the high altar under a worthy tomb—*in pavimento ante magnum altare sub decenti tumba.*[146] The Wodrow manuscript adds: ' and a lair of brass laid on him.'[147] The archbishop's tombstone, or ' throwcht,' was bought in Bruges in February 1495; it is entered in Andrew Halyburton's account book as: ' Item Fewirzer, anno 95: bocht a throwcht in Brugis for my Lord, price 22 li. gl. of the quhilk paid in arllis . . . 1 li.'[148] The matrix stone of the archbishop's monument has been shattered by falling masonry: the grooves cut in the stone (which is ten feet by five feet, five inches) shows the size of the plate of brass, which once displayed the incised figure of the archbishop. At each corner of the stone can be seen the lead-filled sockets which held the pins, securing the brass to the matrix stone. This tombstone is still *in situ* and has never been disturbed so that excavation would probably reveal the remains of the learned Archbishop Schevez.

To succeed Schevez, King James IV procured the appointment of his younger brother, Archbishop James Stewart, duke of Ross. Ill health or a premonition of his early demise caused the young prelate to have his tomb prepared at the very outset of his career. Thanks to the survival of Andrew Halyburton's accounts for this period, we know more about Stewart's tomb than about any other at St Andrews. Various expenses are

---

144. See Plate XII.
145. Joannes Major, *Historia Majoris Britanniae* (Edimburgi, MDCCXL), 328
146. Law MS, fo 17v. In selecting this central position for his tomb, Schevez did precisely what the first archbishop of Glasgow planned to do in Glasgow cathedral a decade later. See John Durkan, ' Archbishop Robert Blackadder's Will ' in *Innes Review*, xxiii (1972), 138-148.
147. Wodrow MS, fo 10.
148. *Halyburton's Ledger*, 7.

listed in the accounts between 1497 and 1499.[149] The stone cost £25: the 'patron,' or design for it, cost twenty-eight shillings. The sum of eight shillings and fourpence were paid in toll at Bruges. It took sixteen ' pynoris,' or porters, three days apparently to stow it safely aboard ship at a cost of twenty-four shillings. The whole cost of the monument seems to have been thirty-one pounds, eight shillings and two guldins, but extra expenses of six pounds, sixteen shillings and three pounds, sixteen shillings are mentioned. Halyburton refers to this tombstone as ' the gret stan ' and in spite of the collapse of the cathedral of St Andrews and its exposure to the elements, it still remains ' the great stone,' lying practically in its original position in the cathedral. The stone is 11 feet 4 inches by 7 feet 7½ inches and it is about 6 inches in thickness. From the hollow cut in the stone to take the brass, we can see that the brass plate, which displayed the incised figure of the archbishop, was approximately 10 feet 9 inches by 7 feet 1½inches, which means that it was one of the biggest monumental brasses in Europe.[150]

The young archbishop, still unconsecrated, died unexpectedly on 13 January 1504. The royal accounts record the enormous expenses of his obsequies in the metropolitan cathedral. Candles and tapers—' torches and prekatis,' to the value of £69 - 7 - 6 were supplied by William Foular of Edinburgh and sent to St Andrews for ' the Archbeschopes tyrment.' No less than 303 dozen ' armes for the said tyrment ' were supplied, at a cost of £28 - 2 - 0, to be used in the adornment of the cathedral for the solemn requiem and funeral.[151] One can see how these candles and hatchments were arranged in the church from the miniature of a dirge for a king of Scots which was painted just about this time in the Book of Hours of King James IV.

The young archbishop had shown his love for his cathedral church both by his gifts and by his desire to be buried in front of the relics of the apostle—*sepultus ante reliquias*.[152] The Wodrow manuscript is more explicit and says that ' he was bureit befoir the relict almrie in the abbay kirk.'[153] The great stone, which has not moved since the rubble which covered it was removed in 1826,[154] helps us to identify the exact place where the famous relics of St Andrew were enshrined. The ' relict almrie ' stood in the centre of the eastern chapel. In front of it, on its western side, would be an altar, with its footpace, and inserted in the pavement between this and the screen, which formed the reredos of the high altar, was the tombstone of Archbishop James Stewart. The surface of Archbishop Stewart's tombstone is now four feet above the ground level but this

149. *Halyburton's Ledger*, 160, 161, 215, 250, 251.
150. W. F. Creeney, *A Book of Monumental Brasses* (London, 1884), lists some of the biggest European brasses: the brass of Pieter Claesson Palink (1546) in the church of St Lawrence, Alkmaar, is 95 x 52 inches (pp. 72-3): the brass of Bishop John Tydeman (1561) in Lubeck is 123 x 90 inches (pp. 66-7): the brass of Cardinal Cazimiri (1510) in Cracow is 111 x 62 inches (pp. 60-1): and the brass of Gerart, duke of Julich (1475) in Altenberg abbey church is 134 x 68 inches (pp. 38-9).
151. *Treasurer Accts.*, ii, 257, 415-7, 268.
152. Law MS, fo 17.
153. Wodrow MS, fo 10.
154. Rev. C. J. Lyon, *History of St Andrews* (Edinburgh, 1843), ii, 156.

represents the height to which the floor level of the relic chapel was raised by Prior Haldenstone. As with all relic shrines of this kind, there were numerous burials in the vicinity of the relics of St Andrew and some rearrangement of coffins had evidently to be made to clear a space for Archbishop Stewart's burial. The great stone rests on three stone coffins of an earlier period. The central coffin was probably emptied in 1504 to take the remains of the archbishop. In 1826, the impartial Barons of the Exchequer cleared out the bones from all three coffins and buried them in an unrecorded grave.[155]

The next archbishop, Alexander Stewart, nephew of his predecessor, died on the field of Flodden and the silence of all the sources suggests that his body was never brought back to St Andrews for burial. Andrew Forman, the next archbishop, died in 1521. The Wodrow manuscript says that he was buried in Dunfermline, but much more reliable is the testimony of John Law who was a canon of St Andrews during the whole of Forman's episcopate and Law states that Forman was buried in the paved floor of the chancel in front of the high altar alongside his predecessor Schevez—*sepultus in pavimento ante magnum altare iuxta predicessorem suum Willelmum scheweze.*[156] What was probably part of the skeleton of Archbishop Forman, or of his successor, Archbishop James Beaton, was disturbed in the course of one of Dr David Hay Fleming's ' howkings ' in August 1903.[157] The small lead weight which is now in the museum was found here and probably came from an archbishop's pallium.[158]

Forman's successor, Archbishop James Beaton, died in 1539 and, according to the Wodrow manuscript, ' was burriet befoir the hey alter in the Abbay Kirk.'[159] His nephew and successor, Cardinal David Beaton, dutifully attended to his uncle's obsequies and, in the cardinal's accounts, payment is made to ' John Eliot, bedellus of the church of St Andrews, and his servant, for lighting tapers on the late archbishop's tomb and keeping and covering it (*conservatione et coopertura*) at the time of service (*tempore divinorum*) from his death to March 8th, 1541, 45s.'[160] James Beaton's tomb was probably also in the floor alongside Archbishop Schevez.

The last two archbishops died violent deaths. Cardinal David Beaton was murdered in his castle at St Andrews and later buried at the Blackfriars church in the town.[161] Archbishop John Hamilton was hanged in Stirling and buried in the abbey church at Paisley in 1571, by which time, the metropolitan cathedral church of St Andrews was a desecrated ruin.[162]

---

155. Ibid.
156. Law MS, fo 17v.
157. *Scot. Hist. Rev.*, i (1904), 108.
158. David Hay Fleming, *Museum*, 204.
159. Wodrow MS, fo 10.
160. *St Andrews Rentale*, 126.
161. NLS, Adv. MS, fo 39.
162. NLS, Adv. MS, fo 40.

LITURGY AND FEASTDAYS

We have no detailed information about the liturgy used in St Andrews cathedral because no missal or breviary or calendar of the foundation has survived. The Arbuthnot missal illustrates the liturgy used in the diocese but, in the cathedral church itself, the basic Sarum Use was presumably adapted to the requirements and customs of the metropolitan church. There was, for example, at least one additional feastday related to the famous relics, the feast of the Coming of the Relics, which was celebrated on 6 February.[163] Richard Augustine Hay claimed to have seen a missal which had been used in St Andrews cathedral in pre-Reformation times[164] and he states that it was the custom at St Andrews that the holy water for the Asperges should be blessed every Sunday by the subprior at the altar of Our Lady and he also transcribes the form of blessing of candles used at Candlemas. In his letter, appealing for funds for the fabric, Prior James Haldenstone quotes several phrases from an office of St Andrew which seems to have been peculiar to the cathedral church.[165] The various gratuities to cathedral personnel, mentioned in Cardinal David Beaton's accounts are not very informative. The cardinal's gift of fourteen shillings to John Eliot, the bedellus of the cathedral, shows that he celebrated the Christmas mass in the cathedral in 1540.[166] One would like to know more about the gratuities bestowed, in 1541, to the incense-bearers at the feast of the Epiphany in St Andrews.[167] Was this simply a traditional reward for the assistants who carried out the solemn incensation of the altar and the chanting of the *Genealogia Christi*, which took place at the end of matins on that feastday or, as seems much more likely from a similar payment at St Giles, Edinburgh, in 1542,[168] did the cardinal make an offering of incense on that day in remembrance of the gifts offered by the Magi to the Infant Christ?

The few surviving references illustrate how the cathedral ceremonial must have been dependent on the help of other bishops because of the involvement of the archbishops of St Andrews in state affairs. Archbishop William Schevez had the assistance of a suffragan bishop, Bishop James Lindsay, appointed in 1483[169] and, about 1485, he had some assistance from the exotic George de Brana, bishop of Dromore, who describes himself as 'quondam dominus Athenarum.'[170] In his last years, Edward Stewart, the aged and infirm bishop of Orkney, seems to have resided in St Andrews. On Ember Saturday, 19 December 1521, we find him, acting

163. *Chron. Bower*, ii, 446.
164. Scotia Sacra, NLS, Adv. MS, 34.1.8. fo 152. This is by no means an unlikely claim since Richard Augustine Hay's maternal great grand uncle was John Spotiswood, archbishop of St Andrews (1615-38) (*Genealogie of the Hayes of Tweeddale*, Edinburgh, 1835, 47) and his own great grandfather. Sir John Hay, Lord Clerk Register had, in 1634, on the orders of King Charles I. taken delivery of various records of the cathedral of St Andrews in connection with the foundation of the new diocese of Edinburgh (Adv. MS. 34.1.8. fo 143).
165. *St Andrews Copiale*, 119-23.
166. *St Andrews Rentale*, 109.
167. *Op. cit.*, 109.
168. *Op. cit.*, 140.
169. C. Eubel, *Hierarchia Catholica Medii Aevi* (Monasterii, MDCCCCXIV), ii, 144.
170. *Arbroath Liber*, ii, 226-7.

on behalf of Archbishop Beaton, at an ordination ceremony in the old cathedral at St Andrews.[171] The short-lived suffragan of Cardinal David Beaton, William Gibson, bishop of Libaria, performed the holy week ceremonies in the cathedral in 1542 and consecrated the holy oils and, that same year, along with Abbot Milne of Cambuskenneth, he presided over the diocesan synod at St Andrews.[172]

In common with other churches, the cathedral of St Andrews had indulgences, or pardons, granted by papal authority, to the faithful who visited the church and received the sacraments on specified feastdays. Such indulgences were important elements in the pastoral work of the church and they were important also in the commercial and social life of medieval towns. At St Andrews, the indulgences of the Assumption, St Andrew's Day and the Dedication of the Cathedral had been granted by Pope Nicholas IV in 1290.[173] The importance of the Corpus Christi indulgence can be gauged from the space Abbot Bower devotes to it in his chronicle.[174] In 1418, the subprior, who acted as papal penitentiary for the indulgence of SS. Peter and Paul, petitioned the extension of that indulgence right up to the feast of the Assumption for the convenience of the faithful.[175]

In the later Middle Ages, the most important indulgence at St Andrews seems to have been the indulgence granted for the feast of St Michael (29 September) and its octave. The cultus of St Michael was ancient and widespread in Scotland.[176] St Andrews had one of the earliest recorded dedications to the archangel in Britain[177] and the foundation legend claims that the apostle's relics arrived at St Andrews on the eve of St Michael's feastday.[178] It was Archbishop Patrick Graham who obtained this efficacious indulgence for St Andrews—*hic indulgentias efficacissimas sancti michaelis sedi et ecclesie sanctiandree obtinere promeruit.*[179] It was a ' grant in perpetuity of plenary indulgence and remission of all their sins to all who, being truly penitent and having confessed, visit the church of St Andrews in Scotland (which the present pope lately erected into the metropolitan church of all Scotland) on the feast of St Michael the Archangel in September, from the first to the second vespers and throughout the octave, every year for the next seven years, and thereafter every three years, the Jubilee year always excepted, and give alms for the conservation, etc. of its buildings.'[180] From the time of Archbishop Graham until the Reformation this indulgence, or pardon,

---

171. *Wigtownshire Chrs.*, no. 232. Bishop Edward Stewart was buried in the parish church of St Andrews (*Laing Chrs.*, 368).
172. Eubel, iii, 224: *St Andrews Rentale*, 130-1.
173. *Cal. Papal Letters*, i, 520.
174. *Chron. Bower*, ii, 93-6.
175. *Cai. Scot. Supp.*, i, 10.
176. David McRoberts, ' The Cult of St Michael in Scotland ' in *Millénaire Monastique du Mont Saint-Michel* (Paris, 1971), iii, 471-9.
177. *Chron. Picts-Scots*, 10.
178. *Op. cit.*, 185.
179. Law MS, fo 16v.
180. *Cal. Papal Letters*, xiii, 203, and xiv, 178-9.

was celebrated on every third year (except as in 1525 when it coincided with the Roman Jubilee year). This triennial indulgence occurred in 1495, when we find King James IV making an offering of eighteen shillings 'vpone Sanct Michaelis day in Sanctandrois.'[181] The extant royal accounts show that King James IV returned to St Andrews for the Michaelmas Pardon again in 1504: 'Item, the penult day of September, Sanct Micheles day, to the Kingis offerand at the hie mes in Sanctandrois . . . xxviij s.'[182] The document in the *Formulare* by which Archbishop Forman appoints commissaries to select suitable confessors to hear the confessions of the men and women, who will soon be flocking to the metropolitan church for the indulgence of St Michael, must be dated either in 1516 or 1519, which were indulgence years.[183] In 1519 the Faculty of Arts postponed their statutory meeting till after the octave of St Michael because the indulgences fell that year.[184] The difficult passage in Pitscottie, where he says that King James V, accompanied by the queen mother and 'ane ambassadour of the Paipis wha was in Scotland for the tym . . . past to St Andros and thair remained till the Michaelmas pardon' would have to be dated either in 1528, 1531 or 1534.[185] James V was certainly at the Michaelmas Pardon in 1531, when he sent to Stirling for one of the Greyfriars to ride to St Andrews to hear his confession.[186] Cardinal Beaton is recorded as having made an offering of £3 6s. at the Michaelmas Pardon of 1540.[187] It was possibly in 1525, though in that year the Michaelmas Pardon was impeded by the Roman Jubilee year, that Patrick Hamilton, abbot of Fearn, conducted the nine-part mass of his own composition for the feast of St Michael.[188]

THE CATHEDRAL MUSIC

Patrick Hamilton's nine-part mass of St Michael is a reminder of the splendid musical tradition of the metropolitan cathedral. It is indicative of this interest in the cathedral music that, fifty years after his death, John Law's chronicle recalls that Prior David Ramsay was an outstanding singer—*cantor egregius.*[189] Boece, writing in 1522, speaks of this tradition when he mentions Prior John Hepburn's anxiety to provide the cathedral with men skilled in music, 'an art which has always had its excellent and famous exponents there'—*qua semper ibi excellentes et clari fuere.*[190] Boece's assertion of a fine musical tradition at St Andrews is borne out

181. *Treasurer Accts.*, i, 242.
182. *Op. cit.*, ii, 264.
183. *St Andrews Formulare*, i, 65-6.
184. A. I. Dunlop, *Acta Facultatis Artium Universitatis Sanctiandree*, 1413-1588 (Edinburgh, 1964), 329.
185. Pitscottie, *Historie*, i, 339.
186. *Treasurer Accts.*, vi, 32 and 48.
187. *St Andrews Rentale*, 107.
188. The reference to Patrick Hamilton's nine-part mass for St Michael's feastday occurs in the commentary on the third verse of Psalm xxxvii in *Primus Liber Psalmorum iuxta Hebraeorum et Divi Hieronymi supputationem; Expositus ab Alexandro Alesio, D. in celebri Academia Lipsensi*, 1554, 'Missam ut vocant musici, novem vocum figurali cantu composuit in honorem angelorum, super tenore vel plano cantu officii missae Benedicant Dominum omnes angeli eius, etc. Hanc cantionem in ecclesia metropolitana S. Andreae curavit cani, et ipse precentorem egit.' Quoted in Rev. Peter Lorimer, *Patrick Hamilton* (Edinburgh, 1857), 238.
189. Law MS, fo 132v.
190. Boece, *Vitae*, 87.

by the survival of two manuscripts of liturgical music which had belonged to the cathedral. Stolen from St Andrews cathedral in 1553 by Marcus Wagner, an agent of Flacius Illyricus, these volumes are now in the Herzog August Bibliothek at Wolfenbüttel.[191] The high musical aspirations of St Andrews cathedral in the early Middle Ages are revealed by these two thirteenth-century collections of masses and other liturgical compositions, of which some were probably written at St Andrews, some are of English origin and many were written by the celebrated composers of the cathedral of Notre Dame in Paris, which was the foremost school of liturgical music of its day.[192]

The last outstanding name in the St Andrews musical tradition is that of Canon David Peebles, ' ane of the principall mussitians in all this land in his tyme.'[193] There has survived a four-part arrangement of the Magnificat antiphon for first vespers of Whitsunday, *Si quis diligit me*. This was composed by David Peebles in 1530 and presented to the music-loving King James V and we are told that one of the novices, a pupil of David Peebles, called Francis Heggie, set a fifth part for it ' a lyttil before Pinky [1547] and that uerray weell.'[194] The final eclipse of the centuries-old musical tradition of St Andrews can be seen in the life of David Peebles. Peebles was well advanced in years when the medieval faith and liturgy were overturned at St Andrews. We do not know how willingly or unwillingly he accepted the Reformation and went through a form of marriage with Katherine Kinneir. In 1571, he still continued to occupy a house and garden within the priory[195] but we are told that ' the said Dauid he wes not earnest ' in executing the commission given him by the prior, Lord James Stewart, to harmonise the psalm tunes of the Geneva Psalter and the editor of that psalter, Thomas Wood, ' was euer requesting and solisting till thay wer all set.'[196] The ' Sang Scole in the Abbay ' was obviously an important institution but no information has survived concerning it until the Reformation when it was under the charge of Alexander Smyth who, James Melville tells us, ' haid been treaned upe amangis the mounks in the Abbay.'[197] In no sphere was the senseless destruction of manuscripts more regrettable than in the records of the St Andrews 'Sang Scole' and of the other cathedral and monastic schools. The musical achievement of medieval Scotland seems to have been notable, but practically all trace of it has been obliterated.

THE MORBRAC AND THE PILGRIMAGE

At some unknown date in the Dark Ages, the church of Kinrimund came into possession of some bones which were claimed, on what evidence or authority we do not know, to be relics of the apostle St

191. J. H. Baxter, *An Old St Andrews Music Book* (London, 1931), iii-xix.
192. Gilbert Reaney (ed.), *Manuscripts of Polyphonic Music* (Munchen-Duisburg, 1965), 97-205.
193. David Laing, ' An account of the Scottish Psalter of A.D. 1566 ' in *Proc. Soc. Antiq. Scot.*, vii (1866-7), 445-458.
194. Ibid.
195. David Hay Fleming, *The Reformation in Scotland* (London, 1910), 613-4.
196. *Proc. Soc. Antiq. Scot.*, vii, 449.
197. *Autobiography and Diary of Mr James Melvill* (Wodrow Society, 1842), 29.

Andrew. William F. Skene conjectured that these relics might have been brought to Kinrimund, in the year 732, by Acca, bishop of Hexham, when he was forced to leave his see and live in exile among the Picts.[198] Possibly this conjecture is as near the truth as we shall ever get. To satisfy popular interest in these relics, a *legenda* was compiled from a variety of sources to explain how they came to Kinrimund. The Dark Ages have scores of such foundation-legends, in which local pride and imagination try to outdo all rivals by attributing fictitious antiquity to a local church or by alleging its foundation by some important personage from the pages of the New Testament. Byzantium claimed St Andrew as its founder in its efforts to challenge the apostolic see of Rome. The church of Marseille was founded by Lazarus and his sisters. Mantua was founded by Longinus, the soldier who pierced Christ's side on Calvary. Glastonbury was founded by Joseph of Arimathea. Paris was founded by Dionysius the Areopagite. In the Dark Ages the romantic tales of the legend-makers knew no bounds and suffered from no historical criticism. The audacity of the St Andrews foundation-legend lies in the fact that, apart from Compostela, it is the only church outside of Italy and the Levant which claims possession of important corporeal relics of an apostle and it seems possible that its legend is at least as old as that of Santiago.

As the church of Kinrimund emerges into the light of documented history, some few facts appear. The eleventh-century poem, called the Prophecy of Berchan, speaks of several kings and princes ending their days as pilgrims or religious at ' the house of the apostle ' on the edge of the wave.[199] King Constantine, son of Aed, retired to the monastic life at St Andrews in 947, where he died as abbot in 952.[200] His son, Indulf, died ' in the house of the same holy apostle ' in the year 962.[201] An Irish royal prince Aed, son of Maelmithid, is said to have ' died in pilgrimage ' at St Andrews in the year 965.[202] In the late tenth-century life of St Catroë, Rigmonath, or St Andrews, is spoken of as a place of importance.[203] By the eleventh century the older place-name was being superseded by the name of the apostle. At the end of that century a frequent pilgrim was St Godric of Finchale, for whom it was the far-famed house of St Andrew —*quam maxime famosum illud domicilium Sancti Apostoli Andreae*[204] and, for his contemporary, the author of the life of St Cadoc, it seemed reasonable for his sixth-century saint to round off his pilgrimages to Jerusalem and Rome with a visit to the ' much longed for basilica of St Andrew '—*surgens igitur vir Dei cum tribus discipulis suis in Albaniam perrexit, prelibateque basilice beati Andree limina adivit.*[205]

198. William F. Skene, 'Notice of the Early Ecclesiastical Settlements at St Andrews' in *Proc. Soc. Antiq. Scot.*, iv (1860-62), 300-321.
199. Anderson, *Early Sources*, 448.
200. *Early Sources*, 447.
201. *Early Sources*, 471.
202. *Early Sources*, 472.
203. *Chron. Picts-Scots*, 108.
204. *Libellus de Vita et Miraculis S. Godrici* (Surtees Soc., 1847), 31.
205. Rev. W. J. Rees, *The Lives of the Cambro British Saints* (Llandovery, 1853), 56.

Pilgrimages to St Andrews from the south were sufficiently numerous in the eleventh and twelfth centuries to merit the institution of two ferries across the Firth of Forth, equipped with pilgrim hostels on the northern and southern shores. The longer ferry, plying between North Berwick and Ardross, known as the Earl's Ferry—*passagium comitis*—with its hostels for pilgrims at North Berwick and Ardross, was founded in the mid-twelfth century by Duncan, fourth earl of Fife, and it was granted by his son and heir to the nuns of North Berwick.[206] Some seventy years ago, a thirteenth-century stone mould for the manufacture of pilgrim's signs was unearthed at North Berwick.[207] Its design shows St Andrew on his cross, and it is obviously the *signaculum* used by pilgrims who crossed by the Earl's Ferry to St Andrews. Further west was the older and better known Queen's Ferry—*passagium reginae*—founded by St Margaret, with its hostels on either shore.[208] Pilgrims from the south, crossing by the Queen's Ferry, would make their way north-east to the ancient pilgrim hostel, which was refounded by Bishop Malvoisin in the early thirteenth century 'beside the bridge of Lochleven.'[209] Continuing eastward, these pilgrims would travel through Cupar by the king's highway to St Andrews—*viam regis que ducit ad villam Sancti Andree*.[210] Travellers, coming from the north-east of Scotland would cross the Firth of Tay in '*lie ferribott extra Taum*,' which was managed by the priory of St Andrews.[211] In the city of St Andrews, the ancient pilgrim hostel of St Leonard was given a fresh endowment by Bishop Robert in 1144 and placed under the care of the canons of the priory.[212]

The fragmentary records suggest that there was an adequate provision of ferries, bridges, hostels and roads for the needs of the pilgrims journeying to St Andrews. This obvious care for the welfare of pilgrims would have been especially evident in the city of St Andrews and its immediate neighbourhood and, in view of this, it might be useful to take a fresh look at the derivation of the name of the bridge which spans the River Eden some four miles north of St Andrews. Its present name, Guardbridge, represents a medieval form, written as 'le gairbrig' or 'le garbrig.'[213] In this connection, one might consider the bridge over the River Bladnoch some eight miles to the north of St Ninian's shrine at Whithorn. In 1441, Margaret, countess of Douglas, replaced an earlier wooden structure with a stone bridge over the River Bladnoch and, petitioning the grant of an indulgence to secure alms for the work, she stated that the bridge was

---

206. *Scot. Hist. Soc. Miscell.*, iv, 308-9.
207. *Trans. Scot. Ecclesiol. Soc.*, i (1903-6), 189-200.
208. Free passage on the Queen's Ferry was given to pilgrims and it was also one of the privileges of the canons of St Andrews (*St Andrews Liber*, 57), but apparently bishops of St Andrews had to pay for their retinues. When Bishop William Lamberton died in 1328 he owed five shillings to the boatmen (*Exch. Rolls.*, i, 217).
209. *St Andrews Liber*, 175-6.
210. *Balmerino Liber*, 38.
211. *Reg. Mag. Sig.*, v, 2273.
212. *St Andrews Liber*, 123.
213. Law MS, fo 16v.

a place where 'pilgrims to St Ninian assemble.'[214] In other words, the Bladnoch bridge was a *statio* or halting place on the pilgrimage road into Whithorn. Similarly the bridge over the River Eden may have been a *statio* or assembly point for pilgrims coming into St Andrews. Presumably there was an early wooden bridge at this point which the Norman ecclesiastics referred to as a *gare* or *statio* for pilgrims. The wooden bridge had disappeared by the year 1419 when Bishop Wardlaw began to build the present stone structure which would inherit the name of the earlier wooden bridge.[215]

The relics which attracted the pilgrims to St Andrews were several bones: a detailed list of these is given by the late medieval writers. Prior James Haldenstone, for example, speaks of the right humerus, three finger-bones of the right hand, the right knee-cap, one tooth and a bone from the saint's head.[216] These bones were not enshrined in separate reliquaries but were all preserved in one single reliquary. The English chronicler, John Hardyng, who visited St Andrews in the early fifteenth century, mentions this single reliquary, when he speaks of King Hungus in his chronicle:

> 'He founded then a mynster of his fundacion
> Of saynt Andrewe, wher his bones shryned been,
> As there in dede I was and haue it seen.'[217]

The reliquary would have been fashioned by some craftsman of the Celtic era and, like other ancient reliquaries of that period, it seems to have had a traditional Celtic name. Just as the crosier-reliquary of St Fillan was called the Quigrich, or the enshrined psalter of St Columba was called the Cathach, so the importance of the reliquary of St Andrew was emphasised by its traditional name: it was called quite simply the Morbrac, the Great Reliquary.[218]

The name Morbrac occurs in an agreement, made about the year 1200 concerning the lands of Scoonie and Garriach, in which a certain Gellin, son of Gillecrist Maccusseger, is guaranteed by the canons of St Andrews that he will have the privilege of carrying the Morbrac just as Gillemur formerly did and will have the emoluments of food and clothing which his predecessor had enjoyed. This document may imply that, in the early Middle Ages, the office of dewar or keeper of the reliquary of St Andrew was in some way attached to the lands of Scoonie or Garriach and that it was not hereditary as in the case of other Celtic reliquaries.[219]

---

214. *Dumfriesshire Trans.*, xxvii (1948-9), 153.
215. *Cal. Scot. Supp.*, i, 109.
216. *St Andrews Copiale*, 120: *Chron. Bower*, i, 94: Boece, *Historiae*, 105: Joannes Major, *Historia Majoris Britanniae* (Edinburgi, 1740), 48.
217. *The Chronicle of John Hardyng*, ed. Henry Ellis (London, 1812), 188.
218. *Breac* is actually an adjective, usually translated as 'speckled.' It has the meaning of 'bright with various colours' and probably refers to the multi-coloured enamelling which decorated these examples of Celtic metalwork. The adjective appears to be used occasionally as a substantive to indicate a certain type of reliquary; it occurs, in this sense here in the name *Morbrac*, in the well-known Scottish *Brecbennoch* and in the Irish *Breac Moedoc* (cf. Joseph Anderson, *Scotland in Early Christian Times*, Edinburgh, 1881, 241-51).
219. *St Andrews Liber*, 329.

Gellin's claim to carry the Morbrac may have applied only to certain specific duties but, in any case, as the medieval period advanced, the Morbrac would be preserved carefully in the relic chapel of the cathedral and its principal public appearances would be when it was carried in solemn procession through the city. We have no information about these processions: there would be one on the principal feast of St Andrew, Andermess, the 30 November, and Bower tells us that there was a solemn procession on the 6 February, when the feast of the Coming of the Relics was celebrated, but there were probably other occasions in the course of the year. We can get some idea of what the procession was like from the evidence provided at other towns and especially at pilgrimage centres such as Dunfermline or Whithorn. In preparation, the streets would be cleaned at the public expense as the town of Ayr was wont to do for the annual Corpus Christi procession.[220] The trade guilds would provide religious tableaux, or pageants to walk in the procession as at Aberdeen, Lanark, Haddington and elsewhere.[221] The masters and scholars of the colleges would carry flowers and leafy branches as their counterparts of Glasgow did.[222] The Blackfriars and Greyfriars would take part, as would the canons of the chapel royal of St Mary of the Rock. The canons of the metropolitan church would take pride of place near the reliquary: they would wear the finest vestments from the cathedral sacristy and would wear garlands of flowers or jewelled fillets around their heads.[223] The Great Reliquary, the Morbrac, would be carried on a feretory, or bier, under a canopy, either by the canons of the cathedral or by prominent laymen. At Whithorn the task of carrying the reliquary of St Ninian in the solemn procession was a hereditary privilege, jealously passed on from father to son. There the procession took place on the Tuesday of Whitsun week and it went from the priory out to Chapel Outon and back, thus inaugurating the Great Pardon of Whithorn which lasted until the feast of St John the Baptist.

> ' The quhilk fertir mene beris ay
> Of witsone owke the twysday
> Vith festiuale processione
> Til a chepal be-owt the tone
> Nere the quartare of a myl
> &, as It thare has bene a quhile,
> Hame to the abbay thai it bere
> Vith gret solempnyte & fere;
> Bot one It lais na-mane hand
> Bot the maste vorthi of the land,

---

220. *Ayr Burgh Accts.*, 20.
221. *Aberdeen Council Register*, i, 450-1.
222. *Glasgow Univ. Munimenta*, ii, 39.
223. The Corpus Christi miniature in the mid-fifteenth-century missal of Jouvenel des Ursins (illustrated in *Histoire de Paris et des Parisiens*, in the series Panoramas d'Histoire, Paris, 1957, plate 126) shows participants in the procession wearing wreaths of roses. The Corpus Christi miniature of the Monypenny Breviary (illustrated in *Proc. Soc. Antiq. Scot.*, lvi (1921-2) 104), shows the procession at Bourges, where it was customary for the assistants to wear wreaths of gillyflowers and violets. The well-dressed canon in Van der Goes' picture of *St Victor and a Donor*, in Kelvingrove Art Gallery, Glasgow, wears a splendid cope and has a jewelled fillet on his head.

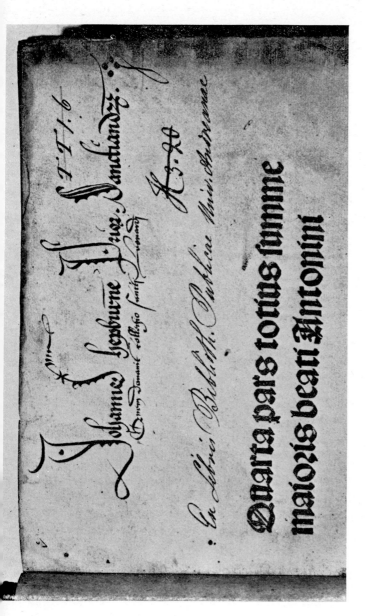

PLATE XV. SIGNATURE OF JOHN HEPBURN, PRIOR OF ST ANDREWS.

The ornate signature of John Hepburn, prior of St Andrews (1482-1522) on a copy of the *Summa Maior* of St Antoninus, presented to the college of St Leonard, which was Hepburn's own foundation. John Hepburn was an able administrator under whom the life of the priory at St Andrews flourished. It was he who built the great precinct wall which still displays his motto, *Ad vitam.*

PLATE XVI.

ALEXANDER STEWART, ARCHBISHOP OF ST ANDREWS, 1504-1513.

Drawing by Jacques Le Boucq of Valenciennes (fl.c.1559). From the collection of drawings, based on contemporary portraits, in the Bibliothèque municipale d'Arras, (R.C. Strong, *Catalogue of Tudor and Jacobean Portraits*, London, 1969). A legend under this portrait reads: ' L' archevescque de St Andrieu fils [bâtard] du roy de scoce quy fut occis a la bataille avec son pere contre les anglois.'

That be lyne of successione
Beris it in processione.'[224]

The bier, or stretcher, on which the reliquary was carried in the procession was called a 'table.'[225] This 'table' seems to have been placed in the midst of the chancel during the mass, in preparation for the procession,[226] and this may help to explain the curious sockets in the centre of the choir steps at St Andrews, which were discovered during some excavations in 1915.[227] These sockets were probably intended to secure some support on which the 'table' holding the reliquary could be placed until the bearers lifted it on to their shoulders for the procession.

The hymns sung in the procession and the joyful ringing of the bells of the cathedral and the other churches would make the whole city resound in a public act of praise and devotion to the apostle. We have no documentary evidence concerning the route followed by these processions but as one looks at the plan of the medieval city of St Andrews, with its North Street and South Street converging on the west door of the cathedral while, at the same time, its central thoroughfare is cut off from the cathedral, it seems specifically planned to provide a circular route for a grand procession around the town, leaving undisturbed the booths and stalls in the Market Street where, later in the day, the merchants and itinerant showmen would provide food, trade and entertainment for the concourse of pilgrims. So well adapted is the plan of the medieval city to a great procession that one is tempted to think that the layout of the streets might simply have developed out of an already traditional processional route. This would make St Andrews rather like some lovely old sea-shell, which still retains the shape of the living creature which originally formed it and dwelt within it.

The feasts of St Andrew with their indulgences and great processions would attract large numbers of pilgrims. The Scotichronicon quotes an *ex voto* inscription—*tabulariter scriptum*, which presumably was extant in the cathedral in the fifteenth century and which listed the nationalities who came to St Andrews in former times: the boastful Frank and bellicose Norman, the Flemish weaver, the uncouth Teuton, the Englishman, the German, the Hollander, strangers from Poitou and quarrelsome folk from Angers, men who drank the waters of the Rhine and the Rhone or the lordly Tiber, they all come here to seek the help of St Andrew:

' *Hic sinus iste maris, male fertile littus, opima*
Transcendit patriae fertilitate loca.
Hic regio prius orba viret; paupercula pridem,
Nunc dives; dudum foeda, decora modo.
Huc etenim veniunt orare remota tenentes
Castra viri; patrio turba profecta solo:

224. *Legends of the Saints* (STS, 1888), ii, 325.
225. C. Wordsworth, *Ceremonies and Processions of the Cathedral Church of Salisbury* (Cambridge, 1901), 163
226. *Glasgow St Mary Liber*, 50-2.
227. *Proc. Soc. Antiq. Scot.*, xlix (1914-5), 215-20.

101

H

Francus magniloquus, belli Normannus amator,
Textor Flandrensis, Teutonicusque rudis;
Anglicus, Almannus, Hollandus, Pictavus expers
Velleris, et caedis Andegavensis amans:
Qui Rhenum, Rhodanumque bibunt, Tiberimque
potentem,
Andreae veniunt huc adhibere preces.
Nos quoque, si tantos inter modo nomen habemus,
Venimus huc vecti prosperiore rota.' [228]

It is an interesting list of nationalities and one suspects that many of these pilgrims would be combining trade with piety as St Godric seems to have done in the twelfth century.

Records of individual medieval pilgrims have all but disappeared. In the mid-twelfth century a learned Englishman from Chester, John Scot, came on pilgrimage—*limina Sancti Andree apostoli disposuit visitare.* He decided to remain and eventually he became bishop of St Andrews.[229] At the end of that century Reginald of Coldingham and his group of Durham monks, questing for alms in Scotland, visited St Andrews as pilgrims.[230] In August 1273, King Edward I granted safe-conduct to three of his subjects, Richard, son of Philip, Lawrence Scot and Nicholas de Wygenhale, to make pilgrimage to St Andrews.[231] Thirty years later, King Edward himself is at St Andrews where he and his queen each offer a golden ouch at the relics—*ad brachium Sancti Andree.*[232] In the later Middle Ages occasional entries in the treasurer's accounts record the gifts of kings and queens at the shrine of the apostle. Queen Mary of Gueldres is there in 1461[233] and throughout his reign King James IV made frequent offerings at the relics.[234] Individual pilgrims seem still to have visited St Andrews in the mid-sixteenth century since, in 1553, Marcus Wagner, the Protestant agent of Flacius Illyricus, was able to get access to the priory as a Catholic pilgrim calling in at St Andrews on his way to Jerusalem.[235]

While individual pilgrims from afar might come occasionally, the St Andrews pilgrimage, like most other pilgrimages in Christendom, apart from Jerusalem, Rome and Compostela, was predominantly a local affair. Such pilgrimages are often referred to as ' pardons '; the Breton pardons are the best known examples of the type. All over Europe these local pilgrimages followed the traditional medieval pattern which, in most

---

228. Votive poems of this type were not uncommon in pilgrimage churches. The list of nationalities, which suggests that the poem is of early medieval date, might be compared with the much more curious list given in *Chron. Picts-Scots*, 140. The best known example of this type of *ex voto* is, of course, the Greek poem in honour of Our Lady that Erasmus set up in the church of Walsingham in the summer of 1512 (J. Le Clerc, *Opera Omnia D. Erasmi* (Leiden, 1703-6), v, 1325).
229. *Chron. Bower*, i, 350-1.
230. *Reginaldi Monachi Dunelmensis Libellus de Admirandis Beati Cuthberti Virtutibus* (Surtees Society, 1835), 219.
231. *Cal. Docs. Scot.*, ii, 2.
232. *Op. cit.*, iv, 486.
233. *Exch. Rolls*, vii, 79.
234. *Treasurer Accts.*, i, 290, 332, 371, 376: ii, 264: iii, 70, 71: iv, 40.
235. *St Andrews Copiale*, xxiii.

places, continued unaltered until after the Second World War, when many have been commercialized by modern tourism. Breton peasants, going to the pardon of St Anne d'Auray, or Italian contadini, making their way to the festa of the Madonna del Buon Consiglio at Genazzano, the popular Romerías of the Andalucian country folk, the Swiss, flocking to the shrine of Einsiedeln, or pious Rhinelanders, crowding into Aachen for the septennial exposition of the Great Relics of Charlemagne's basilica; all are following the pattern set by their medieval forbears. This same pattern was observed in Fife throughout the Middle Ages. In the twelfth century, Reginald of Coldingham speaks of great numbers of men and women hurrying to Dunfermline in groups —catervatim—to be present at the procession on the feast of St Margaret[236] and there is the amusing case of the English soldiers, under John de Strivelyn, in the year 1335, going off, in the midst of their siege of Lochleven castle, to join the crowds, thronging to St Margaret's feastday at Dunfermline, with disastrous results for their military plans.[237] The general pattern would be the same at St Andrews. The cathedral would be crowded for the high mass. Many would approach the sacraments to gain the indulgence. The streets would be thronged for the procession and, when that was over, the fair would absorb everyone's interest.

This traditional routine probably continued with little change throughout the medieval centuries. The routine would be repeated several times each year, with greater or less ceremonial, on the feasts for which a pardon or indulgence was granted, such as the feasts of St Andrew, Corpus Christi, the Assumption and, with especial solemnity, the triennial pardon held during the feast and octave of St Michael the Archangel. On some of these feasts, the ancient reliquary, the Morbrac, would be carried in the procession around the city. The only interruptions to this immemorial usage would be in times of pestilence or war. There must have been considerable dislocation of the customary ceremonial of St Andrews, for example, in the year 1350, when the Black Death carried off no fewer than twenty-four canons of the St Andrews community,[238] or in the second visitation of the pestilence, which lasted for the whole of 1362, from Candlemas to Christmas, during which time King David II and his court and Bishop William de Landallis took refuge in the province of Moray, which escaped the plague.[239] Similarly, in wartime, ceremonial would have to be curtailed. An undated document, surviving from the troubled years which followed the death of King James V, tells how the canons of St Andrews sent some of their relics and other valuables to Lochleven castle for safe keeping. This was probably in the year 1543, when Henry VIII was uttering dire threats 'to spoyle and turne upset downe the cardinalles town of St Andrews.'[240] To Lochleven were sent 'thre kystis

236. *Reginaldi Dunelmensis Libellus*, 218.
237. *Chron. Bower*, ii, 313-4.
238. *Chron. Bower*, ii, 347.
239. *Chron. Bower*, ii, 364-5. *Chron. Wyntoun*, vi, 249-51.
240. *Hamilton Papers*, ii, 326.

contening certane reliquis and claithis of silk and gold with divers geir pertening to our place [of Sanctandrois] quhilk we causit be put thair [Lochlewyne] to be suirlie kepit fra our enimeis handis of Ingland befoir the raid of Langhop.'[241]

Lastly, when speaking of pilgrims to St Andrews, we should remember that pilgrimage was a two-way traffic, which helped to spread information and ideas throughout Christendom. Bishops of St Andrews were not insular in their devotions. When Bishop James Kennedy sailed out of Pittenweem on 1 September 1459, on pilgrimage to St John the Baptist at Amiens,[242] he was possibly using devotion as a cover for diplomacy, but his pilgrimage to Rome, late in 1450, would be to gain the indulgences of that Holy Year[243] and when, on his return journey, he walked in the Holy Blood procession at Bruges on 3 May 1451,[244] he would no doubt note many things which might, with advantage, be introduced at St Andrews. One hundred years earlier, Bishop William de Landallis, with a company of twenty mounted companions, went on pilgrimage to St James for the Compostellan Holy Year of 1361.[245] He, no doubt, noticed with some satisfaction that the Galician cathedral was not quite so large as his own church at St Andrews. The following year, he was on pilgrimage, with twenty-eight fellow pilgrims to St Thomas at Canterbury cathedral,[246] where the dramatic rise in floor levels from the nave towards the eastern chapel which contained Becket's shrine may well have inspired the subsequent raising of the floor level in the relic chapel at St Andrews. He was off on his travels again in 1365 to visit various unspecified shrines overseas,[247] where possibly he purchased some of those vestments, books and ' fayre jowallis ' that he later bequeathed to his cathedral church.[248]

HISTORIC OCCASIONS

The ever-changing panorama of liturgical feasts by which the church taught the life of Christ and the basic truths of the Christian message, formed the background to many other great occasions, both joyful and sad, in the life of the cathedral. Perhaps the happiest event that the chroniclers recall in the cathedral was the reception of the privileges of the new university of St Andrews.[249] Granted in his remote stronghold of Peñiscola in Aragon, by the aged pope, Benedict XIII, the bulls of foundation were carried to St Andrews by Master Henry Ogilvie, reaching their destination on Saturday, 3 February 1414. Their *joyeuse entrée* into the city was signalled by the pealing of all the church bells in St Andrews.

241. *Morton Registrum*, i, 6.
242. *St Andrews Liber*, xx.
243. A. I. Dunlop, *James Kennedy* (Edinburgh, 1950), 115-7. Kennedy did not leave for Rome until the autumn of 1450. One of the reasons for this late departure would be the pestilence which raged in Rome throughout the summer (Herbert Thurston, *The Holy Year of Jubilee* (London, 1900), 67-9).
244 *Op. cit.*, 135.
245. *Rotuli Scotiae*, i, 854.
246. *Op. cit.*, i, 865.
247. *Op. cit.*, i, 893.
248. *Chron. Wyntoun*, vi, 311.
249. *Chron. Bower*, ii, 445-6.

The following day, which was Sunday, in presence of all the clergy, assembled at nine o'clock in the refectory of the priory, which had been splendidly arrayed for the occasion, the bulls were formally presented to Bishop Henry Wardlaw, chancellor of the new foundation. When the bulls had been duly promulgated, the diocesan clergy and the canons of the priory went in procession, singing the Te Deum, to the high altar of the cathedral church, where Alexander Waghorn, bishop of Ross, intoned the versicle and collect of the Holy Ghost: *Deus qui corda fidelium*. This ceremony was obviously timed to finish just before the conventual high mass which normally began at ten o'clock in the morning. Bower, who was, almost certainly, an eyewitness, adds that the rest of that day was passed in boundless joy, *bibentes vinum in laetitia*, and after nightfall, there were huge bonfires in the streets. A solemn procession was arranged for the following Tuesday so that the rejoicing for the reception of the privileges of the university might be celebrated along with the feast of the Coming of St Andrew's Relics, which fell on that day, 6 February. The chronicler finds it hard to describe the procession in words: the melodious singing of the clergy, the rapturous emotion of the people, the pealing of bells and the organ music: it began with the solemn mass of the Holy Ghost, celebrated by the prior, James Bisset, at which the bishop of Ross, Alexander Waghorn, preached the sermon and, in addition to a wondrous multitude of layfolk, the bedellus counted some four hundred priests, as well as many in minor orders and novices, who walked in that procession to give glory to God and to confer praise and honour on the new university.

More than a century later, there were similar rejoicings for the marriage at St Andrews, in June 1538, of King James V and his French bride, Marie de Lorraine. There were pageants, devised by Sir David Lindsay of the Mount, jousting and hunting, banquets and ' gritt mirriness.' Pitscottie describes how, on the morning after her arrival in St Andrews, the French princess went to the cathedral for the conventual high mass at ten o'clock: ' on the morne, at ten houres, shoe passed to the abbey kirk, quhair shoe saw manie lustie lordis and barrones, weale arrayed in thair abulyiementis againes hir cuming: also the bischopis, abbotis, monkis and channones maid regular and great solemnitie in the abbey with mess, songis and playing on the organes. Efter this the queine was ressaved be the king in the abbey to hir denner quhair thair was great mirth of shalmes, trumpettis and diverss vtheris instrumentis all that day.'[250]

It was at St Andrews in the following year, 1539, that the king's eldest son was born and, according to Pitscottie, ' was honorabilie baptized with great triumph, as was the wse of the countrie, and was stylled James Stewart, duik of Rothsay and prince of Scotland,'[251] but that joy was

---

250. Pitscottie, *Historie*, i, 379-80.
251. *Op. cit.*, i, 382.

short-lived. When Pitscottie speaks of 'the wse of the countrie,' he possibly means that it was customary that the heir to the crown should be baptized by the archbishop of St Andrews at the cathedral. Some such traditional usage seems to be implied by the fact that, whereas the future King James III was born at Stirling on 10 July 1451, the solemn ceremonies of his baptism and the proclamation of his princely style, took place at St Andrews in the presence of his father, King James II, only in January 1453.[252] This may well have been a long established custom, for Wyntoun tells us that it was Gamelin, bishop of St Andrews, who baptized, in 1264, the young prince of Scotland, Alexander, the son of King Alexander III.[253]

SYNODS

As the principal ecclesiastical building in Scotland, one might have expected that St Andrews cathedral would have been the scene of provincial and national councils of the Scottish Church. This was not the case. The scanty surviving records show that these councils were held in convenient localities such as Perth, Stirling, Linlithgow or Edinburgh and cathedral cities were carefully avoided, perhaps to safeguard the parity of individual bishops which was peculiar to the medieval Scottish hierarchy down to the year 1472.[254]

Diocesan synods were a different matter. Surviving records suggest that, at least in the later Middle Ages, these were held annually in each diocese. In the diocese of St Andrews, early synods were held in various towns, in Berwick-on-Tweed in 1150,[255] at St Cuthbert's church, Edinburgh, about the year 1170,[256] and at Musselburgh in 1200.[257] In some extant synodal decrees of the fourteenth century,[258] a bishop of St Andrews provides for the synod to be held each year after Easter in duplicate: the clergy of the archdeaconry of St Andrews assembling in the parish church of St Andrews and the clergy of the archdeaconry of Lothian assembling in the parish church of Edinburgh.[259] After the erection of the archbishopric, the diocesan synod seems to have been held normally in the cathedral at St Andrews and occasionally in the abbey church of Holyrood. Sometimes the archbishop presided over these synods in person and sometimes the vicar general or some commissary took his place. Archbishop Schevez presided personally at the synod held in the metropolitan cathedral on 24 April 1487,[260] and apparently at another held about the year 1479.[261] There are references to Archbishop

252. *Exch. Rolls*, v, lxxxvii-ix, 607.
253. *Chron. Wyntoun*, v, 125.
254. The city of St Andrews was suggested as an alternative venue for the provincial council planned to be held on Thursday, 14 August 1550, but by that date, of course, St Andrews had long since achieved metropolitan and primatial status (Robertson, *Concilia*, ii, 127).
255. Robertson, *Concilia*, i, clxxxiii.
256. *Op. cit.*, i, clxxxiii.
257. *Op. cit.*, i, clxxxiii-iv.
258. *Op. cit.*, ii, 64-73.
259. *Op. cit.*, ii, 70.
260. *Arbroath Liber*, ii, 254.
261. NLS, Adv. MS, 34.7.3, fo 28.

Forman presiding personally at synods held at St Andrews and at Holy-rood and some synodal constitutions, published by him, are still extant.[262] Alesius claims that, when he was a canon of St Andrews, he preached before ' a synod of bishops and priests ' in 1529 and, because of his out-spoken comments on clerical incontinence, he was imprisoned by Prior Patrick Hepburn, who considered the sermon to be a personal attack on himself.[263] In a monitorium, Cardinal David Beaton refers to a synod he held ' in his metropolitan and primatial church of St Andrews' on Tuesday, 22 April 1544, at which he had presided personally, and to ' his other general synods.'[264] One of these synods was held after Easter at St Andrews in 1542 and was presided over by the two vicars-general, the bishop of Libaria and the abbot of Cambuskenneth, the cardinal being at that time in France.[265] John Knox refers to the ' seinze,' or synod, held by the cardinal in 1546: 'After the Pasche, he came to Edinburgh to hold the seinze (as the Papists term their unhappy assembly of Baal's shaven sort).'[266]

The synod, comprising all the clergy of the archdiocese from arch-bishop, abbots and priors, down to curates and chaplains, must have been a very large gathering. The clergy assembled at eight o'clock in the morning at the cemetery (the old cathedral, the chapel of St Mary Mag-dalen and other buildings there would provide changing rooms where they could change into choir dress), wearing clean surplices and with their hair cut to an acceptable length—*crinibus decenter abbreuiatis.*[267] They went in procession, as directed by the deans, to the metropolitan cathe-dral, where they had to remain for mass, sermon and the deliberations of the synod. No one was allowed to leave, unless with permission from the archbishop or his commissary, until the synod was over. The legislation of the synod covered all aspects of ecclesiastical life in the archdiocese. Parish dues were paid and, of course, the reason for holding the synod immediately after Easter was to ensure that the new holy oils, consecrated on Maundy Thursday, were distributed to each parish in the archdio-cese.[268] A special hall, in the west range of the cloister at St Andrews, was set apart for the business of the synod and it was called the Senzie (or Synod) hall.[269]

Clergy coming to the synod, on horseback or on foot, would be carry-ing money to pay parochial dues and carrying some objects of value such as silver chrismatories for the holy oils. For mutual protection, they would

---

262. Robertson, *Concilia*, i, cclxx-ccxc
263. Patrick, *Statutes*, xlv-xlvi.
264. Robertson, *Concilia*, i, ccxci.
265. *St Andrews Rentale*, 130-1.
266. Knox, *History*, i, 75. There is no need for the suggestion that this may have been a mistake for the provincial council held earlier or for a privy council meeting held about that time (note 2).
267. Robertson, *Statuta*, i, cclxx. There was no excuse for being late because there was a large clock dial on the western side of the old cathedral tower.
268. *Instructions for Parish Priests by John Myrc*, ed. Edward Peacock (Early English Text Society, 1868), 20.
269. George Martine, *Reliquiae Divi Andreae*, 188.

travel in groups and this is probably the background to the tragedy during the episcopate of Bishop Henry Wardlaw, when in one accident a group of fifteen priests were drowned trying to ford the River Eden on their way into St Andrews.[270]

Such a large gathering of ecclesiastics, meeting regularly in St Andrews after Easter, naturally attracted commercial interests and gave rise to the city's most important fair, the Senzie, or Synod Fair, 'that renowned faire of St Andrews, called the Senzie Mercat, held and kept for fifteen dayes and beginning the second week after Easter, whereunto resorted merchants from most of the then trading kingdomes in Europe.'[271] The fair outlived the synod and, after the Reformation, its venue was transferred to the secularized cloister of the cathedral. The importance and the duration of the Senzie Fair is described in the ratification of the privilege made by parliament in October 1581: 'Our Souverane Lord and thrie estaitis of parliament, vnderstanding that the provest, bailleis, counsall and communitie of the cietie of Sanctandrois and thair predicessouris hes bene in vse and possessioun of ane publict fair and mercat, callit the seinzie fair, beginnand vpoun the mononday efter pasche mononday zeirlie and continewand to the space of xv dayis nixt thairefter within the said cietie and cloister of the abbay situate within the samin In all tymes bigane past memorie of man. be the quhilk fair our said Souerane Lordis liegis hes grite commodite baith by bying and selling of all kynd of wairis . . .'[272]

HERESY TRIALS

More sombre were the heresy trials which the cathedral witnessed in the final decades of its existence. While these were not numerous by Continental or English standards, they make sad reading nowadays. On 23 July 1433, Paul Kravar was burned at St Andrews: his trial probably took place in the cathedral but on this point the extant records are silent. Patrick Hamilton's trial did take place in the metropolitan church. The preacher on that occasion was Alexander Campbell, prior of the St Andrews Blackfriars.[273] The sentence of Hamilton's condemnation was read by Archbishop James Beaton 'at our metropolitan church of St Andrew, the last day of the month of February, 1527, there being present the most reuerend fathers in Christ and lords; Gawand, bishop of Glasgow; George, bishop of Dunkeld; John, bishop of Brechyn; William, bishop of Dunblane; Patrick, prior of St Andrews; David, abbot of Abirbrothoke; George, abbot of Dunfermline; Alexander, abbot of Cambuskenneth; Henry, abbot of Lendors; John, prior of Petenweme; the dean and sub-dean of Glasgow; Master Hugh Spens, Thomas Ramsay; Allane Meldrum, etc., in the presence of the clergy and people.'[274]

270. Cal. Scot. Supp., i, 109.
271. George Martine, Reliquiae, 188.
272. Acts Parl. Scot., iii, 239.
273. Pitscottie, Historie, i, 308.
274. S. R. Cattley (ed.), Foxe, iv, 561.

The trial of Henry Forrest, about 1533, was also presumably held in the cathedral and he suffered death ' at the north church-style of the abbey church of St Andrew, to the intent that all the people of Forfar might see the fire and so might be the more feared from falling into the like doctrine.'[275]

For these *autos-da-fé* elaborate preparations were made. A grand-stand was erected to accommodate the civic and ecclesiastical dignitaries. This stand would be constructed against the chancel screen.[276] Alongside the stand was set up the rostrum for the ' accuser, clad in a surplice and red hood ' and another pulpit, or rostrum, was prepared for the accused and there would be ' a great congregation of the whole people, in the body of the church, standing on the ground.'[277] Such trials were regarded as social occasions and, at the trial of David Straton and Norman Gourlay in the abbey church of Holyrood in 1534, it was remarked that King James V was dressed ' altogether in red apparel.'[278]

When the accused was not present in person, the proceedings were less formal. The trial of Sir John Borthwick, at St Andrews on 28 May 1540, was not held in the metropolitan church but in a chamber ' in the cloister of St Andrews '[279] and though King James V was living at the priory at the time he did not attend.[280] But, when Borthwick was condemned to be burnt in effigy, his portrait had to be paraded through the city to the cathedral for the public pronouncement of the sentence and taken thence to the mercat cross to be burned.[281]

George Wishart was tried in the cathedral before Cardinal David Beaton. On that occasion the pulpit, or rostrum, was first occupied by the subprior, John Winram, who preached on the parable of the wheat and the cockle, after which Wishart ascended the rostrum to answer the charges.[282] The last heresy trial conducted in the cathedral was that of Walter Myln who, on 20 April 1558, appeared before Archbishop John Hamilton, the bishops of Moray, Brechin, Caithness and Athens, various abbots and masters of the university and John Winram, the subprior of St Andrews.[283] The preacher on this occasion was Symon Maltman, warden of the St Andrews Greyfriars.[284] There is some evidence in this trial as to the excellent acoustics of the building, for the eye-witness tells how, after the octogenarian Myln had with some difficulty climbed up into the rostrum, he spoke with surprising vigour and ' made the church to ring and sound again.'[285]

275. *Op. cit.*, iv, 579.
276. The arrangement of seating for the various dignitaries is given in the account of the trial of Adam Wallace at the Blackfriars church in Edinburgh in 1550 (Cattley's *Foxe*, v, 636-7) and, on that occasion, the making of the grandstand cost 51s. and 4d. (*Treasurer Accts.*, ix, 435). In Cardinal David Beaton's accounts, £4 10s. was expended on the construction of a grand-stand (*magna scala*) in Holyrood abbey church for a heresy trial in March 1539 (*St Andrews Rentale*, 64, 93).
277. S. R. Cattley (ed.), *Foxe*, v, 637.
278. *Op. cit.*, iv, 579.
279. *Op. cit.*, v, 607.
280. *St Andrews Rentale*, xxxvii.
281. S. R. Cattley (ed.), *Foxe*, v, 621.
282. *Op. cit.*, v, 627-8.
283. *Op. cit.*, v, 644-5.
284. Pitscottie, *Historie*, ii, 131.
285. S. R. Cattley (ed.), *Foxe*, v, 645.

NATIONAL CHARACTER OF THE CATHEDRAL

One aspect of the cathedral of St Andrews which must be mentioned is the importance of the place in the development of Scottish national feeling. Without in any way attempting to discuss the origin of the foundation-legend of St Andrews, one can simply state that the legend was current by the end of the Dark Ages and was accepted as a faithful account of how the Scottish nation was chosen by the apostle Andrew as the people among whom he wished his relics to be kept and honoured.

In the progress of nationalist sentiment in Scotland during the past half century, much attention has been directed towards the Declaration of Arbroath of 1320 as if it was the most important document of Scottish nationhood. Bernard de Linton's manifesto is impressive by any standard, but I doubt if any medieval Scotsman would have agreed with this modern assessment. For the medieval Scot, the most fundamental and influential document in the formation of the Scottish nation would have been the St Andrews legend. Nineteenth-century men tended to underrate the value and power of legend, but no one today who considers the influence of romantic legends on our international conflicts or even on the development of our international tourist traffic would discount the importance of such legends and fantasies.

The St Andrews legend has not a little in common with the contemporary legend of Santiago Matamoros, whose story rallied the Christians of Spain into one nation and finally brought about the Reconquista. Similarly, the claim to possess apostolic relics and the subsequent pilgrimage helped to bring together the inhabitants of North Britain into one nation and, in the political upheaval which followed the death of King Alexander III, the St Andrews legend provided a potent unifying force.[286]

The influence of the St Andrews legend became immensely important during the War of Independence when the whole future of the nation was in jeopardy. It features in the Scottish case against Edward I of England, which was argued before Pope Boniface VIII by three prominent clerics of St Andrews, led by Master Baldred Bisset. We may not be greatly impressed nowadays by the argument, drawn from the legend, that as the chosen people of St Andrew, the Scots had a very special claim on the pope, who was the successor of St Andrew's brother, Simon Peter, and it behoved the pope, as representative of St Peter, to safeguard the independence of his brother's chosen people the Scots nation, but it was a telling argument in the fourteenth-century context.[287]

286. For medieval Scotsmen, St Andrew's protection and patronage was something unquestioned and very real. At popular level it finds expression in such stories as the intervention of the saint in the battle of Athelstaneford (*Chron. Bower*, i, 191), and, at more official level, it finds expression in such documents as the appeal of Archbishop Alexander Stewart against the exemption of the bishop of Moray from his jurisdiction: ' *Neminem regnicolarum latet qualiter miraculose Sancti Andree totius regni et Regis Serenissimi patroni reliquie has ad oras per Sanctum Regulum Angeli Dei admonitione delate sunt. Iterum quot triumphi, quot vero victorie crucis Sancti Andree signaculo in aere diuinitus ostenso Scotorum Regibus et regnicolis contra Anglorum rabiem eiusdem Sancti Andree meritis concesse sunt, nemo sane mentis ignorat* ' (Robertson, *Concilia*, cxxv, note 1).
287. *Chron. Bower*, ii, 198-9.

In the course of the war, the opposing leaders both acknowledged the unique historical importance of the church of St Andrews and its legend. King Edward took an early opportunity of holding a parliament there in 1304 and, pious Christian that he was, he and his queen made suitable offerings at the relics of the apostle. Five years later, the devout and astute Bruce held his first parliament at St Andrews, in 1309, and the declarations in his favour made by the clergy and nobles, which were issued on that occasion, must have gained additional sanction in the eyes of the Scottish people by being promulgated from the shrine of the apostle.

For a brief moment the bishopric of St Andrews came to the forefront of the struggle to maintain national independence when, about 1305, the English king made an unsuccessful attempt to oust Bishop Lamberton and replace him with one of his own supporters, William Comyn, brother of the earl of Buchan.[288] King Edward claimed that Comyn had been elected by the cathedral chapter and it seems that the temporalities had in fact been made over to him for a time, but this move was thwarted by Sir William Wallace and his army when

'Upon the morn to Sanct Androwis thai past,
Owt of the toun that byschop turnyt fast.[289]

Sincere in his devotion to the saints, Bruce was especially grateful for the part that St Andrew had played in saving the Scottish nation from extinction. Within four years of the victory at Bannockburn, the great church at St Andrews was completed and made ready for its solemn consecration on Friday, 5 July 1318. The late-medieval chroniclers all record the event.[290] Abbot Walter Bower writes: ' That same year [1318] on July 5th, the high kirk of Saint Andrew the apostle in Scotland was consecrated by its bishop William Lamberton. In the course of the ceremony of consecration, King Robert, there in person, in the presence of seven bishops, fifteen abbots and nearly all of the nobility of the kingdom, earls as well as barons, offered one hundred merks sterling to be paid each year from the royal coffers in thanksgiving for the notable victory granted to the Scottish people by the blessed Andrew, protector of the realm. Afterwards the cathedral was given the perpetual advowson of the parish church of Fordun in the Mearns with all its emoluments in exchange for the said hundred merks.'

Modern writers have perhaps not fully appreciated the significance of this offering mentioned by Bower. For the lawful consecration of a church, canon law required that the place should have an adequate endowment to ensure the maintenance of divine worship. Usually this consisted of some grant of rent or land, given by the landowner of the district, and signified in the consecration ceremony by the landowner

288. Palgrave, *Docs. Hist. Scot.*, 332.
289. *Schir William Wallace* (ed.) James Moir (STS, 1889), 270-1.
290. *Chron. Bower*, ii, 271-2: *Chron. Pluscarden*, i, 251: *Chron. Wyntoun*, v, 371-3.

111

placing a knife or a stick or some other symbolic object on the altar of the church. The rubric in Bishop David de Bernham's *Pontificale* runs as follows: *Finita hac oratione, exigatur dos a domino fundi, sine qua, ecclesia non potest nec debet dedicari. Concessa vero dos, offeratur ab ipso domino super altare per cultellum vel per baculum.*[291] In the case of the cathedral of St Andrews, the offering of the endowment was designed to imply something greater than the normal endowment of a church, for Bower speaks of two other gifts made that same day and for the self-same reason—*eodem die et eadem ratione.*[292] One of these donations was actually made by the consecrating prelate, William Lamberton, who gave the churches of Dairsie and Abercrombie. The other benefactor was Duncan, earl of Fife, who granted the church of Kilgour. The only satis- factory explanation of this seems to be that, at the normal point in the ceremony of dedication, when the high altar had been duly consecrated and made ready for the celebration of mass, King Robert, acting as ' *dominus fundi* ' and representing the people of Scotland, presented an endowment to the cathedral in thanksgiving to St Andrew for the victory at Bannockburn. Then Bishop Lamberton, not as bishop of St Andrews, but as the principal ecclesiastic, representing the Estate of the Clergy, donated the churches of Dairsie and Abercrombie. Lastly, Duncan, earl of Fife, who was first among the ' seven earls ' of Scotland, makes the offering of the church of Kilgour on behalf of the Estate of the Nobles. In other words, in this unprecedented gathering, in which were present practically all the available bishops and abbots of the *Ecclesia Scoticana* and ' nearly all the nobles of the kingdom,' the king, the bishop and the earl, acting as representatives of the Three Estates of the Realm, symboli- cally endowed the new cathedral in thanksgiving to St Andrew for the successful vindication of Scotland's independence.[293] We can imagine the enthusiasm and emotion with which the antiphon was sung: *Confirma hoc Deus, quod operatus es in nobis,* and never, in the consecration of any church, could the accompanying psalm have seemed more appropriate, the great hymn of thanksgiving for victory: *Exurgat Deus et dissipentur inimici eius* . . . It would be difficult to find in any other kingdom of the medieval world a church that was so clearly intended as the thank- offering of an entire nation for the survival of its independent existence. The two external consecration crosses on the east gable of the chancel and on the gable of the south transept would be anointed with chrism by Bishop Lamberton in the course of the consecration and they are the sole remaining memorials of the impressive ceremony of 1318.

St Andrews cathedral probably had many relics of the great national struggle. Robert Bruce, we know from Boece, distributed the spoils of

---

291. *The Pontifical Offices used by David de Bernham, Bishop of St Andrews,* (ed.) Chr. Words- worth (Edinburgh, 1885), 22.

292. *Chron. Bower,* ii, 272: *Chron. Pluscarden,* i, 251, has ' *eadem racione et causa.*'

293. Actually these churches were all given at different times to St Andrews (see Ian B. Cowan, *The Parishes of Medieval Scotland* (Scottish Record Society, 1967), but the formal and sym- bolic donation of all of them was made in the course of the ceremony of consecration.

Bannockburn among the churches of Scotland.[294] As late as 1549 an inventory of Aberdeen cathedral still lists an ancient set of high mass vestments made of cloth of gold, which came from Bannockburn—*ex spolio conflictus de Bannokburne*.[295] The cathedral of St Andrews would certainly have some of this spoil but none of the medieval inventories has survived to tell us. The only relic of which we have any information was a precious cross of rock crystal, which Richard Augustine Hay assures us, was preserved in the cathedral and came from the spoils of Bruce's victory.[296] One should add that the principal images of the cathedral were probably also memorials of that heroic age. They would date from about the time of the consecration of the church and were apparently the gift of the Douglas family, perhaps of the Good Sir James Douglas himself, since the statue of Our Lady was called ' le Douglas Lady ' and the statue of St Andrew was graced with a lamp maintained by a Douglas bequest, which had been made early in the cathedral's history.

The commitment of the whole nation to the upkeep of the shrine of the patron saint can be seen, sixty years later, after the serious fire which damaged the cathedral in 1378. In the work of reconstruction each section of society made its contribution: the bishop, Walter Trail, provided ' twenty or more ' of the huge and expensive beams which had to be renewed in the roof of the nave: [297] the king, King Robert II, for his part paid the wages of two stonemasons for a period of three years: [298] and nine pillars, which had to be rebuilt in the south arcade of the nave, were each sponsored by individual noblemen, whose coats of arms were carved on the reconstructed pillars as a memorial of their benefaction.[299]

The cathedral, as we have seen, had its share of indulgences, granted by papal letters, urging the faithful to visit and contribute towards the upkeep of the building, such as the letters of Pope Clement VII of 1381[300] or of Pope Benedict XIII in 1418.[301] It had also the endowment of other churches appropriated to the maintenance of its fabric. In addition it benefited from fines levied in ecclesiastical courts[302] and often from penalty clauses for failure to fulfil contracts.[303] In the very earliest extant Scottish will, Sir James Douglas of Dalkeith, writing in 1390, makes

---

294. Boece, *Historiae*, fo 303v.
295. *Aberdeen Registrum*, ii, 189-90.
296. ' Scotia Sacra,' NLS, Adv. MS 34.1.8. fo 144: *" Pulchra hic crux christallina atque aliae exuviae in victoria ad Banoci Ripam parta quae inter illustriores eiusdem domus notas commemorantur?*
297. *Chron. Wyntoun*, vi, 312 note 604.
298. *Exch. Rolls*, iii, 70, 674.
299. *Chron. Wyntoun*, vi, 311. Wyntoun's reference seems to suggest that these coats of arms, carved on the columns and brightly coloured, were a feature of the cathedral pointed out to visitors. This may have set a fashion for later benefactions to churches in Scotland: the ' Cathcart Pillar ' in the nave of Paisley abbey church is an example; the rebuilt south west pier of the crossing at Jedburgh abbey with Abbot Thomas Cranston's coat of arms and the pillar built by John Foular and his wife, Mariota, in the choir of St. John's church, Perth, also follow this fashion.
300. *Moray Registrum*, 348-9: *St Andrews Copiale*, 114-5.
301. *Op. cit.*, 115-8.
302. See, for example, Robertson, *Concilia*, i, cclxxviii; ii, 67: *St Andrews Formulare*, i, 29.
303. See, for example, *Yester Writs*, nos. 204, 341; *Hist. MSS Comm.*, 4th Report (1874), 494; *Balmerino Liber*, 41.

a bequest towards the fabric of St Andrew's shrine: ' Item do lego ad sustentacionem fabrice Sancti Andree sex libras, xiij s, iiij d ': [304] and that bequest was only an early example of many subsequent legacies. In his appeal for funds to complete the renovation of the cathedral in the second quarter of the fifteenth century, Prior James Haldenstone makes it clear that the proper maintenance of the fabric of the cathedral reflects the sincerity of the nation's love for St Andrew,[305] implying, once again, an accepted relationship of an entire people towards the national shrine of their patron saint which can hardly be paralleled elsewhere in Christendom, save in Spain.

PERSONNEL

To keep the daily, complicated life of the cathedral going without a hitch and to keep the fabric in good condition must have required the continuous and devoted attention of many men of varied disciplines and skills. Unfortunately little information has survived about these men. We do have a list of names of the diocesan officials who conducted the legal business of the diocese, sometimes from the chapels in the Archdeacon's Aisle. How learned they were we can only guess, but before we dismiss them all as provincial nonentities, we should pause to consider the fact that one late thirteenth-century official, Baldred Bisset, apparently made such an impression on the Roman Curia by his exposition of the Scottish case against King Edward I of England that, when the scandalous, posthumous trial of Pope Boniface VIII was forced on the papacy by King Philip the Fair of France, Bisset was chosen to lead the defence of the dead pope in the consistory at Avignon on 16 March 1310.[306]

Some of the priors seem to have been men of real distinction, who well deserve the praise with which Bower recalls their names, but even the very names of lesser men are hard to come by. The central area of the south transept seems to have been the place of burial of some special members of the Augustinian community. The Rev. C. J. Lyon copied some of the still legible inscriptions in the early nineteenth century.[307] One tombstone was that of Dene Robert Cathull, a canon of the priory who died in 1380. Another stone marked the grave of Dene James Elioly, another canon of the metropolitan church. This last stone is of some interest because it showed a calvary cross on a stepped base, with the canon's initials I E, a chalice and host and a missal to indicate that he was a priest. Above the cross there was the device of the priory, a crowned

---

304. *Bannatyne Misc.*, ii, 108; see also Robertson, *Concilia*, ii, 39.
305. *St. Andrews Copiale*, 122-3.
306. Pierre Dupuy, *Histoire du différend d'entre le pape Boniface VIII et Philippes le Bel* (Paris, 1655: Reprint, Tucson, 1963), 370. By 1310 Baldred Bisset had become a canon of Glasgow.
307. Rev. C. J. Lyon, *The Ancient Monuments of St Andrews* (Edinburgh, 1847). The symbol of St Augustine and of the Augustinian order was a heart transfixed by an arrow or by arrows. This symbol appears on one of the tombstones copied by the Rev. C. J. Lyon: it also explains the lead heart which was found in 1904 in one of the priors' coffins in the chapter house. This heart (illustrated in David Hay Fleming, *Museum*, 203) has a hole near the base. It probably had a wooden arrow fixed in it and it would be placed in the coffin simply as a symbol of the Augustinian order and not as ' an amulet to ward off the evil-eye or to cure some disease.'

St Andrew's cross, for the priory of St Andrews, and a heart pierced by crossed arrows, for the order of St Augustine. The third gravestone, sketched by Lyon, was that of: [*Robertus*] *Graie quondam vitriarius et plumbarius huius almi templi* — Robert Gray, sometime glazier and plumber of this holy church. Gray's tomb has the calvary cross, but no chalice or missal: he does have, however, the crossed arrows of the Augustinian order, so we have to conclude that this glazier and plumber of the church was a lay brother of the priory. Another of these tombstones, which Lyon found in St Leonard's chapel, provides further evidence that the canons were actively involved in the maintenance of the fabric: it commemorates a canon, William Ruglyn, master of works of the cathedral—*magister fabrice*—who died in 1502.[308] The constitutions of the Augustinian canons entrusted the maintenance of the church fabric to the sacrist[309] and this was obviously the practice at St Andrews, for in 1435, one of the canons, Robert Brog, witnesses a charter as ' sacrista et fabrice illius ecclesie magistro.'[310] From the account given in the Scotichronicon, it would seem that William Bower, another canon, was probably the designer, or master of works, when the new rood loft and altar were erected in the early fifteenth century. All of this confirms the tradition, still alive in Martine's day, that ' many of the channons wer artizans, especiallie masons, and wrought at the work, which was no wayes inconsistent with their office.'[311]

The name of another master of works of the cathedral of St Andrews occurs in a well-known inscription in the south transept of Melrose abbey, in which John Morow speaks of the various church fabrics that were confided to his care sometime probably in the reign of King James IV:

> ' John morow sum tym callit was I
> and born in parysse certanly
> and had in kepyng al masoun werk
> of santandroys ye hye kyrk,
> of glasgw, melros and paslay,
> of nyddysdayll and of galway:
> I pray to god and mari bath
> and sweet s john kep this haly
> kyrk fra skaith.'[312]

One would like to know more about the bedellus of the cathedral who, in May 1505, after three years' work, completed ' the gret portuous [breviary] ' for King James IV, for which the king, in instalments, paid a total price of £22.16.0.[313] The king, who commissioned from the foremost atelier in the Low Countries the splendid Book of Hours to com-

---

308. Rev. C. J. Lyon, *History of St Andrews* (Edinburgh, 1843), ii, 158.
309. John Willis Clark, *The Observances in use at the Augustinian Priory . . . at Barnwell* (Cambridge, 1897), 73.
310. *St Andrews Liber*, 419.
311. George Martine, *Reliquiae Divi Andreae*, 185.
312. P. Macgregor Chalmers, *A Scots Medieval Architect* (Glasgow, 1895), 11.
313. *Treasurer Accts.*, ii, 39, 342, 352, 376, 427: iii, 141, 180

115

memorate his marriage to Margaret Tudor, is not likely to have employed a second-rate calligrapher and miniaturist for his personal breviary.

There is much else that one would like to know. For example, did the cathedral staff include a hermit? A croft in the Swallowgait at St Andrews went by the name of *Crofta Angury* in 1562.[314] If this was an anker's croft, the anker may have performed the useful function of maintaining the harbour light in the tower immediately north-east of the cathedral in much the same way as the Augustinian canons of Holyrood kept a hermit at Seacliff in East Lothian to maintain a navigation light on that dangerous coast.[315]

FINALE

By the mid-sixteenth century a new breed of religious were asserting their influence among the conventual brethren at St Andrews. Like most gradual developments, this influence is undocumented: we can only examine the few facts and surmise the trends. The trends were real enough and we can discern their effects in the career of the nonagenarian subprior, John Winram, whose long life spanned the entire final chapter in the story of the metropolitan church.[316] John Winram was born in the year 1492. Between 1513 and 1515, he was at St Leonard's college, where he became a colleague of Master Gavin Logie, who is credited by John Knox with secretly propagating, among the novices of the cathedral priory, the new theological opinions from the Continent.[317] By 1532, Winram had become a canon of St Andrews: two years later he had become third prior and, in 1536, he was subprior of the cathedral priory, a position he retained for the rest of his life. In 1559, he openly threw in his lot with the reformers, attended the Reformation parliament as prior of Portmoak, helped to draft the 'Confession of Faith' and the 'Book of Discipline' and, in the organisation of the new Church, he was appointed superintendent of Fife.

During all this time the position of the medieval church in St Andrews was being steadily eroded. The novices entering the community at the cathedral were being indoctrinated by Gavin Logie at St Leonard's college and, if we understand Knox correctly, Logie was being aided and abetted by Winram who, when he took his doctor's degree in theology in 1540, accepted a gift of £20 from Cardinal David Beaton.[318] The cardinal was possibly too preoccupied with affairs of state to notice the serious deterioration of religion in his own cathedral city and the gossip that circulated about his personal moral conduct was far from helpful. The cynical appointment by King James V of his seven-year-old bastard son as prior of St Andrews in 1538: the unheroic death of the king in 1542:

314. *Reg. Mag. Sig.*, iv, no. 1917.
315. *Cal. Scot. Supp.*, ii, 172. The sixteenth-century panoramic view of St Andrews shows some kind of lantern or beacon on the tower of Prior Hepburn's wall immediately north east of the cathedral.
316. *Collections upon the Lives of the Reformers* (Maitland Club, 1834), i, 119-30.
317. Knox, *History*, i, 15.
318. *St Andrews Rentale*, 107.

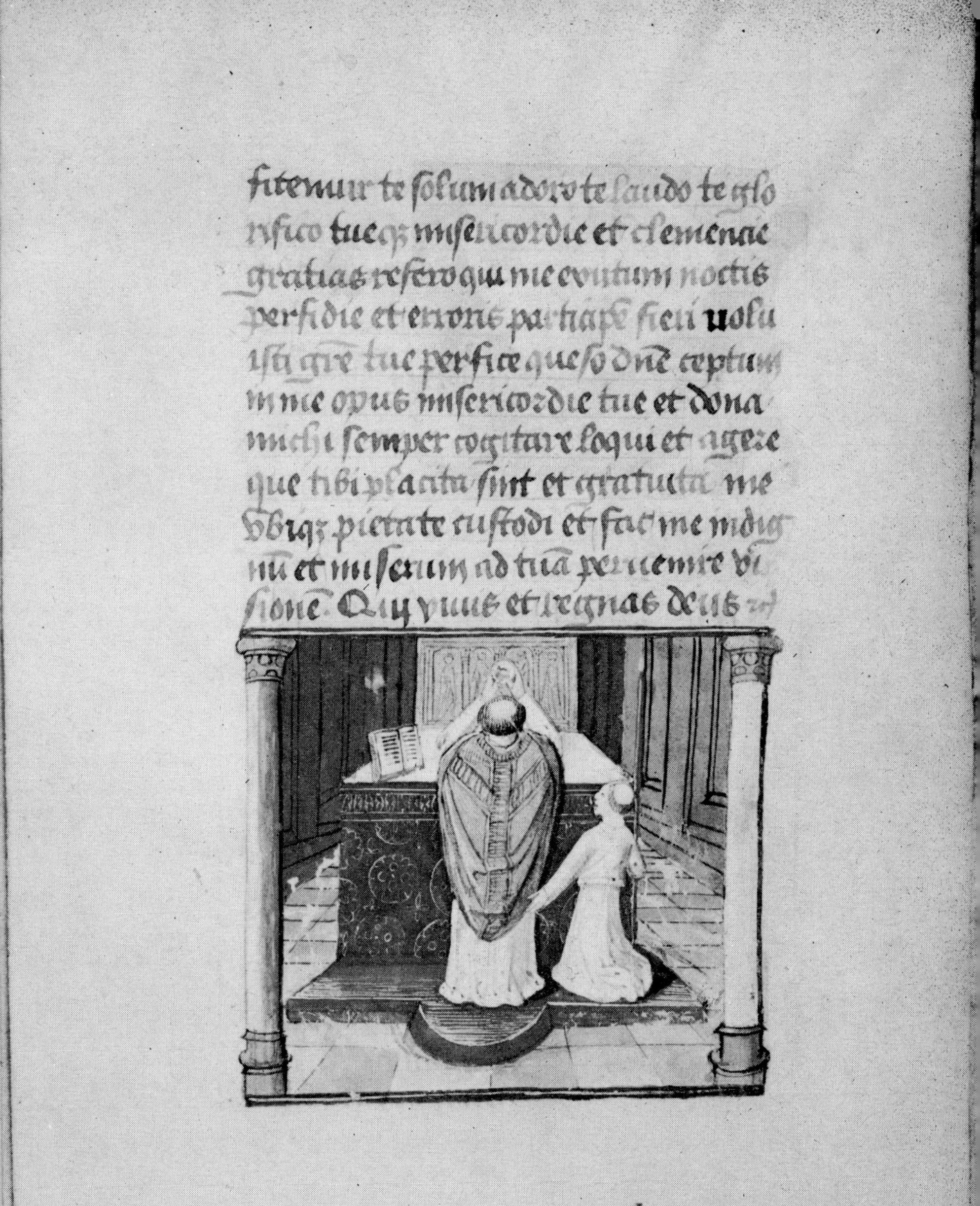

fitemur te folum adoro te laudo te glo
rifico tue q mifericordie et clemencie
gratias refero qui me eontium noctis
perfidie et errore participe fieri uolu
ifti q̄re tue perfice q̄ fo dn̄e ceptum
in me opus mifericordie tue et dona
michi femper cogitare loqui et agere
que tibi placita fint et gratuita me
dbiq̄ pietate cuftodi et fac me indig
nu et miferum ad tua peruenire vi
fione. Qui yuue et regnas deus ...

PLATE XVII.   CELEBRATION OF LOW MASS.

his late fifteenth-century miniature depicts the celebration of Low Mass and illustrates what
me of the lesser altars of St Andrews cathedral would have looked like. The miniature occurs
fo 45v of a Book of Devotions (National Library of Scotland, Ms Acc. 6236) which belonged
Archbishop Alexander Stewart of St Andrews (1504-1513) and which had originally been
ritten and illuminated in the west of Scotland for Robert Blackadder who became Archbishop
Glasgow (1483-1508).

PLATE XVIII.

DAVID BEATON, CARDINAL ARCHBISHOP OF ST ANDREWS, 1539-1546.

This portrait now preserved at St Mary's College, Blairs, came originally from the Scot
College in Rome. It is a 'martyr-picture,' painted about the year 1600 and it is based on
contemporary portrait which seems to have existed in the Scots College at Paris, probabl
bequeathed to that institution by Archbishop James Beaton of Glasgow. A straight copy o
the lost Paris original, made in the eighteenth-century, is the well known Balfour portrai
of Cardinal Beaton.

the burning of George Wishart and the murder of the cardinal in 1546: and the subsequent siege of the Castilians by the French were dramatic highlights in a rapidly changing situation which must have overturned the traditional religious and political views of many people, and the preachers of the new doctrines took full advantage of the opportunities.

As the effective superior of the cathedral priory, John Winram held a key position with regard to the future of Catholicism in St Andrews and, to some extent, in Scotland. One would very much like to know what religious convictions he really held, if any.[319] He was prominent in heresy trials and Church councils yet, in spite of that, Knox asserts that, during this period, he was promoting the Protestant cause. One can sympathise with the exasperated parson of Ballingry, who described Winram, the recently appointed superintendent, as 'that fals, dissaitful, gredy and dissimblit smayk (poltroon), for he wes ane of tham that maist oppressed, smored and held down the Word of God and now he is cum in to it and professis the same for grediness of gayr, lurkand and watchand quhill he maye se ane other tym.'[320]

As subprior, Winram would have some influence in forming the ideas of the new prior, James Stewart, at least during his childhood years. The revenues of the priory, of course, were siphoned off to the royal coffers until the demise of James V, after which they seem to have gone to the young prior's mother, Margaret Douglas, at Lochleven. In spite of his dutiful presence at heresy trials, Lord James, like Winram and his friends, Erskine of Dun and James Sandilands of Calder, was sympathetic to Protestant ideas long before he was converted by John Knox in the winter of 1555. Also, despite his deacon's orders, he apparently had a mistress living at the priory. We catch a glimpse of her in the narrative of Marcus Wagner's visit to St Andrews priory in 1553: Lord James, the prior, was sitting jesting at the dinner table with his friend Erskine of Dun when 'Lady Venus' entered by a door behind the prior and took her seat at the table. She was wearing a gold chain round her neck and a silver girdle round her waist and her fingers were decked with rings, 'indeed from her modest bearing she might have been taken for the Mother of God.' She ate nothing and drank little but sat smiling and gazing at the prior 'with her brown falcon eyes.'[321] Wagner seized the first opportunity of slipping away from the table to see what further manuscripts he could filch from the priory library.

A Catholic satirist, writing a few years later, reflecting anxiously on the rumours that James Stewart, the prior of St Andrews, not only aimed at governing the kingdom as regent but had ambitions of founding, in his own person, a new royal dynasty and reflecting on the appalling ruin

---

319. He is reminiscent of his contemporary, Hermann von Wied, archbishop of Cologne, who was described by the Emperor Charles V as 'neither a Protestant nor a Catholic but a proper heathen.'
320. *St Andrews Kirk Session Register* (SHS, 1889), i, 86.
321. *St Andrews Copiale*, xxvi-vii.

I

which he had brought upon ' the far-famed monastery of St Andrews,'[322] exclaims:

' A cowle, a cowle for such a Greek[323]
    Were fitter far to wear,
Than this Apostate deacon should
    Such princely rule to bear!
But where is now true discipline?
    Dare no man take on hand
To teach such false Apostate monks
    Their faults to understand?
And make this base born Deacon come
    Home to his former state
From whence the Lither Lozell[324] fled
    Lest he should live too straight? '[325]

With such a prior and subprior, the canons, largely trained by Gavin Logie, could hardly be expected to be fervent Catholics. The situation was akin to that of which St John Fisher complained to his fellow bishops at the climax of the Reformation in England: ' The fort is betrayed even of them that should have defended it.' In spite of the self-complacent account of his own heroism which he gives in his ' History,'[326] Knox was well aware of the state of affairs in St Andrews priory in June 1559, and, with the armed followers of Lord James, Argyll, Ruthven, Erskine of Dun, Wishart of Pittarrow and others of the Congregation occupying the town, he knew he could safely defy the futile threats of Archbishop John Hamilton, when he entered St Andrews and preached in the parish church on the ejection of the buyers and sellers from the temple. This was apparently on Sunday, 11 June 1559. Knox preached on the following three days and, on Wednesday 14 June, the work of destruction began. The ' Historie of the Estate of Scotland ' says that ' the sermon was scarcely downe when they fell to work to purge the kirk and break down the altars and images and all kind of idolatrie . . . and before the sun wes downe there wes never inch standing bot bare walls. Bot the idols that were in the Abbay were brought to the north part of the said Abbay, in the same place where Walter Milne wes burned (a year or thereabouts before) and there they burned the whole idols.'[327] Knox suggests that this was done by the townsfolk of St Andrews with the consent of their magistrates but it seems fairly certain that the destruction was carried out by the brethren, that is, by the retainers of the Lords of the Congregation, following the pattern that had emerged in Crail, Perth, Lindores, Scone and other places.[328] Far from being a spontaneous popular rising against the Old Faith, the whole business has the appearance of an organised and

322. ' In famosissimo sancti Andreae coenobio ' (Richardinus, Commentary, 159).
323. Oxford Dictionary, Greek = cunning person.
324. Scot. Nat. Dict., lither losel = lazy scoundrel.
325. ' A Rhime in defence of the Queen of Scots against the Earl of Murray,' in Satirical Poems of the time of the Reformation (STS, 1889), i, 76-7.
326. Knox, History, i, 181-2.
327. Wodrow Misc., 60.
328. Knox's manipulation of facts to suit his polemic, has been discussed recently by Maurice Lee, ' John Knox and his History ' in Scot. Hist. Rev., xlv (1966), 79-88; Andrew Lang, John Knox and the Reformation (London, 1905) examined the question from another viewpoint.

well-directed operation to destroy altars, images of saints, vestments, liturgical books and other equipment of the traditional liturgy, the 'monuments of idolatrie' to use the jargon of the revolutionaries. The church buildings were left, except in the case of the Greyfriars and Blackfriars, who apparently had to be taught a stern lesson for daring to challenge the new theology.

At the metropolitan cathedral the conventual buildings were left undisturbed. Lord James continued to occupy the prior's house, a well-appointed place, judging from the inventory of 1565.[329] The canons still continued to occupy their houses and gardens, John Winram among them, and the Novum Hospitium was able to accommodate Knox and his family during their long sojourn at St Andrews in 1571-72. Knox must have been curiously selective in identifying the buyers and the sellers in his famous sermon. The fate of the metropolitan church itself was very different: the main object of the revolutionaries was to defy Archbishop John Hamilton and for ' reformation to be made in his cathedral church.'[330] The furnishings of the cathedral were broken and burnt. A fine thirteenth-century head of Christ, which survives, and the fifteenth-century fragments of Bishop Wardlaw's tomb indicate the fine quality of some of the sculptured stone that was ruthlessly smashed. Nothing survives to show the quality of woodcarving or painting, manuscript illumination, stained glass or embroidery. One senses a faint twinge of regret when John Foxe's Scottish correspondent, reporting the destruction of the cathedral furnishings, reflects that ' the images of the great church of the abbey ... (sur)passed both in number and costliness.'[331]

The crypto-Protestants of the Augustinian community now came out into the open. Describing these events to Mrs Anna Lock, on 23 June 1559, Knox asserts that ' Diverse channons of Sanct Andrewes have given notable confessiouns and have declared themselves manifest enemies to the Pope, to the masse and to all superstitioun.'[332] Those who proved less tractable were bullied into ' altering the habit '; in fact, the well-informed governor of Berwick, reporting to the English government, gives pride of place to this part of the proceedings at St Andrews.[333] On that summer

329. Printed in David Hay Fleming, *The Reformation in Scotland* (London, 1910), 608-12.
330. Knox, *History*, i, 181.
331. S. R. Cattley (ed.), *Foxe*, v, 647.
332. Knox, *Works*, vi, 26.
333. Sir James Croft to Lords of Council, 20 June 1559: ' Since the matter pacified at St John's Town, the earl of Argyll, the prior of St Andrews, the Lord Ryven and others have held a council at St Andrews how to proceed in matters of religion. They have put down the priory of St Andrews in this sort: altering the habit, burning of images and mass books and breaking of altars ' (*Calendar of State Papers, Foreign Series, Elizabeth*, i, 321).
' Altering the habit ' meant forcing the canons by bullying and threats to don secular dress to symbolise that they were apostatising from their religious order. An important document, describing this procedure from the point of view of one of the victims, is in *Peebles Chrs.*, 259.
In the breakdown of law and order which occurred there seems to have been a considerable element of unrecorded brutality and intimidation. In a relevant document, some monks of Melrose made a public declaration, on 18 September 1569, that they had signed a feu at the command of their commendator, the earl of Bothwell, ' for werray dredour and feir of our lyfis and tynsyll of our levyngis qua said In presens of diuers honorable men that he suld exyle ws of the place of Melros, tak the keis of our chalmeris frome [ws] and schortle burne and mark ws with het keis on our chykkis with mony vther Iniurious wordis. And therfor as we sall ansuer befor the eternall our God quhateuer we did in his fauouris, we did the samyn for werray feir of our lyffis, nocht haiffing respect to God nor gud consciens, common weill of the cuntre, nor zit our awin wyllis, bot as said is, for werray feir ' (*Morton Registrum*, i, 44).

day in 1559, there came to an abrupt end the liturgical worship of God, which had been carried out uninterruptedly in the great medieval cathedral church of St Andrews for well-nigh four centuries and for at least as long again before that in the old cathedral and its predecessors at Kinrimund.

No doubt the cold and calculating prior had removed, before the attack, all items of precious metal from the cathedral and, in the following months, like his half-brother at Melrose,[334] he would not overlook the lucrative disposal of bell-metal, brass lairs, lead, timber, slates and other building material from the now derelict cathedral.[335] There is ample evidence in a surviving register of the priory that, over these years, he disposed of lands and revenues of the priory in wholesale fashion for his own personal advantage and gain.[336]

Soon they were all gone. James Stewart, the prior, was assassinated at Linlithgow, in 1570, by a Hamilton. Archbishop John Hamilton was hanged at Stirling, in 1571, revenge being one of the motives. John Knox died in Edinburgh, in 1572, and, ten years later, in 1582, John Winram ended by death his long occupancy of the subprior's ' duelling hous within the abbay of sanct androis,' leaving his nephews and his stepsons to squabble over his ample worldly gear.[337]

Gradually the masonry of the great medieval cathedral was demolished by the elements and by the citizens of St Andrews in their search for building materials and, early in the seventeenth century, the former magnificence of the church was but a memory. Habakkuk Bisset, describing the place about the year 1620, speaks of ' the auld Rewynous wallis of the Cathedrall and sumtyme maist Magnifik kirk of the Archibischoprie of St androis.'[338] The glory had departed and the Scottish nation had lost irrevocably not just a splendid church, not just a great accumulation of its historic treasures and of its artistic heritage, but part of its very soul.

---

334. *Melrose Recs.*, iii, 158, 218.
335. James Stewart's successor as commendatory prior, Robert Stewart (1570-1586), apparently continued the work of demolishing the cathedral. A reference in the forthcoming volume of *Treasurer's Accts* (xiii, 156) is dated 20 February, 1576/7 and reads: " Item the said day to William Rankelour, messinger, passand of Edinburgh with letters to charge the priour of Sanctandrois and all utheris demolesaris of the cathedrall kirk thairof to desist and ceis fra all forder douncasting thairof . . . iij li." I have to thank Dr A. L. Murray for bringing this reference to my notice and Dr John Imrie, Keeper of the Records of Scotland, for permission to anticipate its publication.
336. NLS. Adv. MS. 17.1.3. The most recent biographer of James Stewart (Maurice Lee, *James Stewart, Earl of Moray* (New York, 1953), 98) remarks that ' it is a pity that our knowledge of Lord James' transactions in real estate is so fragmentary, since he was obviously a gifted, and sometimes unscrupulous, operator in this field.'
337. John Winram's last will and testament is printed in *Collections upon the Lives of the Reformers* (Maitland Club, 1834), i, 463-9.
338. *Habakkuk Bisset's Rolment of Courtis* (STS. 1922), ii, 345.

THE AUGUSTINIAN CHAPTER OF ST ANDREWS

by

MARK DILWORTH, OSB

The cathedral priory of St Andrews was in many respects the most important ecclesiastical corporation in the country. It shared in the prestige of the ancient see, a prestige that was enhanced by St Andrews becoming the first university seat and the metropolitan church of Scotland in the fifteenth century. One should not be misled by the fact that the house was only a priory into under-estimating its importance. As with the cathedral priories in England, there was evidently a feeling that it was more fitting for the superior not to be an abbot, but this was apparently a matter of sentiment and tradition, a survival perhaps from the time when the bishop was the superior of such a religious community and held the office of abbot. Certainly there was no cogent objection to having more than one mitred prelate in the cathedral church. From 1418 the prior of St Andrews enjoyed the use of *pontificalia,* as was considered only fitting, since in Parliament he preceded all the other monastic superiors and all ecclesiastical dignitaries except bishops;[1] the dignity of his office was called *major post pontificalem,* a description that occurs frequently in the fifteenth and sixteenth centuries. The priory was described by James V as the first and most famous monastic house in Scotland.[2]

The priory had a two-fold status and function: it was a community of regular canons following the rule of the Order of St Augustine and at the same time was the cathedral chapter of the diocese. There must have been both identity and conflict of interests, and a varying measure of harmony and disharmony between the two orientations of the same body of men. When the historian sets out to investigate this situation, however, he is confronted at the start with one great difficulty, namely the lack of any surviving constitution of the priory chapter. This is not quite so serious as appears at first sight, because the constitution could not be presumed to have actually operated that way in practice and would have to be tested against what we know of life in the priory and the proceedings

---

1. *CSSR,* i, 9-10; *CPL,* vii, 78; *Chron. Bower,* i, 367; *St A. Lib.,* 23, 412.
   Abbreviations of sources are taken from *Scottish Historical Review,* xlii (1963), with a few from D. E. R. Watt, *Fasti Ecclesiae Scoticanae Medii Aevi* (1969) [Watt, *Fasti*], xiv-xxi. Any others are explained when first referred to.
   The following abbreviations are used for frequently cited manuscript sources:
   SRO, B 65/22 is a collection of charters concerning the town of St Andrews.
   SRO, RH 6 is the collection of Register House Charters.
   NLS, Adv. 17.1.3 is a mid-sixteenth-century cartulary of the priories of St Andrews and Pittenweem.
   NLS, Adv. 15.1.8 is the collection of Denmylne Charters.
   I wish to thank the staffs of the Scottish Record Office and of the Manuscripts Department of the National Library of Scotland for much kind help in making original source material available.
2. *James V Letters,* 259.

of its chapter. But at least there would be a model to work with. There is the further difficulty that no extended records of the priory and its chapter have survived.

The only course open to the investigator is therefore to collate the individual surviving documents in order to form what picture he can, and to compare this with the constitution and proceedings of similar institutions.[3] It is clearly a procedure fraught with difficulties and determined in its scope by the nature of the sources one uses. The present essay must be regarded as limited in its extent and depth and tentative in many of its conclusions but will perhaps serve as a basis for further work.

The model which seems closest is that of the Benedictine cathedral priories in England. The original idea behind regular chapters was that bishop and religious were of like nature and integrated, so that he was their superior while they served the cathedral and formed his chapter. In the English cathedral priories the monks elected the bishop since he was also their abbot, and he in turn then appointed the prior and other officials. When the bishop was no longer a monk, it was natural that the community should wish to control their own affairs. They achieved emancipation from non-monastic bishops and by the fifteenth century there were few notable quarrels between bishops and their monastic chapters.[4]

A regular chapter must have had a cohesion that was not to be found among secular canons. The canons at St Andrews lived in community according to the rule of St Augustine. Unlike secular canons who had their individual prebends and lodgings, they were provided for from the common fund.[5] That at least was the ideal, and in 1418 James Haldenstone, newly elected prior of St Andrews, declared that he had no means of support save the capitular *mensa*.[6] In 1443 another man explained to Rome that he had only his place as a canon, which meant his food and clothes when he was resident and nothing when he was absent.[7]

We do not know to what extent the proceedings of chapter dealing with monastic and diocesan affairs were integrated, whether for instance they could turn in the same sitting from priory affairs like admitting a novice or leasing monastic land to diocesan affairs such as consenting to some act of the bishop. Certainly, however, in the few signed monastic documents which are known to exist, the secular officials who held a capitular seat did not sign, from which one infers that they were either not present or were present only as witnesses. As a religious house, the

3. I am grateful to Dr Marinell Ash for allowing me to read her thesis, ' The administration of the diocese of St Andrews 1202-1328,' in which pp. 147-55, 221-42 deal with the chapter and afford a basis of comparison with later times.
4. D. Knowles, *The Religious Orders in England*, i (1948), 254-60. Mentions of the author and English cathedral monasteries refer to this source.
5. J. Dowden, *The Medieval Church in Scotland* (1910) [Dowden, *Medieval Church*], 89-90.
6. *CPL*, vii, 69.
7. *CPL*, ix, 350.

priory shared in the trends and characteristics of the other monasteries: the benefice hunting of individual canons revealed in the papal documents of the fifteenth century, the encroachment by crown and papacy on the right to free election of priors, the feuing of monastic property in the decades before 1560, and so on. The powers and duties of the monastic chapter with regard to the affairs of the priory can be presumed to have been the same as in other Augustinian houses, and there seems little point in commenting on the documents concerning property, numerous at St Andrews as in other monasteries, issued by prior and chapter. Two particular aspects of the priory to be considered are the functioning of the diocesan chapter and the features which characterised the priory as a religious house. There can be no hard-and-fast delineation between these two areas, but two of the main sections of the present article will take each in turn, and a third will attempt to assess the state of the priory at the time of the Reformation.

I. THE DIOCESAN CHAPTER

The relationship between bishop and chapter was no doubt extremely complex, but some general principles can be stated. The chapter's chief function centred on the cathedral, where it was their task to maintain the fabric and provide the services. Any body of regular canons would have had these duties in their own church, but at St Andrews the monastic church was also the cathedral of the diocese. Their interests here coincided with those of the bishop, for if it was their church in which they performed their monastic office, it was also his church where he carried out his principal liturgical functions and where he would eventually be buried. It was in addition the seat of his government and the administrative centre of the diocese. The interests of bishop and chapter coincided in general as well as in the particular province of the cathedral and they were joint custodians of the integrity of the see: hardly surprising, since it was the chapter that administered the diocese when the see was vacant or the bishop was absent. There was need of a permanent working relationship between bishop and chapter. The chapter was in fact a permanent advisory body, able to provide assistance to the bishop in various unofficial ways as occasion arose in addition to the matters in which its co-operation and consent were legally required.[8]

It is clear from surviving documents that chapter's consent was required for anything affecting the integrity or permanent status of diocesan institutions. The various matters can only be touched on lightly here, as treatment in depth would be far beyond the scope of this article. But first, two rather technical points should be mentioned. Presumably whenever chapter consented to an episcopal act its seal was hung with the bishop's as a sign of consent; usually the document says so explicitly but in some transcripts the seals are not referred to, while occasionally

---

8. This paragraph relies much on Dr Ash's thesis.

in a calendar the seal alone and not the consent is mentioned. The other point is that there seems to be no significant difference between the consent of chapter and the consent of prior and chapter. The two formulas are apparently quite interchangeable.

Consent of chapter was required for matters affecting parish churches: the erection of one into a collegiate church,[9] the foundation of chaplainries or additional grants to chaplainries in them,[10] alterations to the status of a parish church or vicarage,[11] confirmation to a religious house of its rights over a church.[12] By far the most documents concern deals over land, since alienation of church property, at least in legal principle, had to be guarded against. Thus the chapter's consent was needed for tacks and feu charters granted by the bishop,[13] and the latter became increasingly common in the middle of the sixteenth century. It was by no means a new temptation: in 1451, at the petition of Bishop James Kennedy and the chapter, a papal mandate was issued for the recovery of the fruits of both the episcopal and the capitular *mensa* which had been alienated, and bishops were inhibited from making similar alienations even with consent of chapter.[14]

Some less usual acts add to the picture. The grant by the bishop of the office of Great Customar of St Andrews, to which chapter consented in 1556,[15] would seem to be in the same category as a grant of land. The vicar general too needed chapter's formal consent even though he was himself a member of chapter and their representative.[16] Most documents show chapter consenting to an episcopal act, but sometimes bishop and chapter acted together, for instance in an agreement with Balmerino abbey over a baptismal font[17] or in consenting to charters granted by one of the archdeacons[18] or by the parson of a parish church.[19] The act of April 1512, by which the archbishop in presence of his chapter united a parish church to the Pedagogy of St Andrews, looks like a particularly solemn occasion but is probably nothing of the sort. The document portraying it is a notarial instrument testifying to the occasion as it happened, and a charter in the usual form (that is, issued by the archbishop with consent of chapter) was then drawn up. That at least was the kind of document issued when the same parish church was later united to the New College in 1558.[20]

---

9. *CPL*, viii, 461; x, 64; xi, 289; *St A. Form.*, i, 349.
10. SRO, B 65/22, nos. 22, 24, 43, 48, 86, 97, 133, 143.
11. *St A. Form.*, i, 142, 145, 148, 169.
12. SRO, RH 6/282; *CPL*, xii, 731.
13. *RSS*, ii, 3622; *RMS*, iii, 2662, 2985, 3029; Herkless & Hannay, *Archbishops*, ii, 256-57; *St A. Form.*, ii, 228; SRO, RH 6/869, 1210, 1348, 1544, 1561; SRO, GD 1/208/9; NLS, Adv. 17.1.3, fos 304 ff.
14. *CPL*, x, 477.
15. SRO, RH 6/1984.
16. SRO, RH 6/910.
17. *Balm. Lib.*, 63.
18. *RMS*, iv, 2837; SRO, GD 1/208/1; NLS, Adv 17.1.3, fo 345.
19. *RMS*, iv, 1656.
20. *RMS*, iv, 1742.

It is sometimes difficult at first sight to judge whether the chapter was acting as the diocesan or the monastic body. When it consented to an act by the vicar of one of its own appropriated churches it did so as a monastic chapter in its capacity of ' patrons of the said vicarage.'[21] In these documents the term *conventus,* not *capitulum,* is used for the chapter.[22] It was in his capacity of parson that the prior in 1527 gave consent to arrangements made by the bishop for St Andrews parish church.[23] When in 1557 chapter consented to the exemption from various jurisdictions granted by the bishop to Patrick Learmonth of Dairsie, it apparently did so as the cathedral chapter, but a clause was added safeguarding the monastery's jurisdiction.[24] On the other hand the charter of August 1512 erecting St Leonard's hospital into a university college was issued by archbishop and conventus, for it was monastic, not diocesan, property that was concerned and the endowment was given in a charter issued by prior and conventus alone.[25] All the foregoing instances can only be taken as a series of pointers to the undoubtedly complex relationships of bishop and chapter, but it is perhaps significant that the sole case of dispute noticed among them concerned the presentation of a vicar to an appropriated church, a matter in which chapter acted in its monastic capacity.[26]

The cathedral chapter had less than the usual number of dignitaries, or rather, it would be truer to say that if the posts existed they were held by regular canons whose names have not been recorded. In some ways it is a meaningless concept. Revenues were allotted for the offices of precentor and sacristan[27] but these were offices which would have to be filled in any monastic community anyway and the holders were members of chapter whether they held them or not. For instance, John Law, a regular canon, was sacristan in the sixteenth century.[28] Some dignities are, however, consistently recorded. The prior was head of chapter and was often explicitly called dean.[29] The archdeacon of St Andrews and the archdeacon of Lothian, both of them secular clerics, had seats in chapter from early times and retained them in the late middle ages,[30] though it was only at a late date that they assumed the same obligations to this chapter as archdeacons in secular chapters. In the fifteenth century they were required to take an oath to respect the rights of the church of St

21. *RMS,* iv, 1730, 2691; SRO, RH 6/1993; NLS, Adv. 17.1.3, fos 127v, 131v, 166.
22. The terminology slips after 1560 (e.g. *RMS,* iv, 2837). Sometimes prior and convent are mentioned as patrons of a vicarage and then as prior and (diocesan) chapter consent to an act affecting it (SRO, B 65/22, no. 16; *St A. Form.,* i, 135-38).
23. SRO, B 65/22, no. 240.
24. SRO, RH 6/1704.
25. *RMS,* ii, 3812.
26. *CPL,* xiv, 286.
27. *RMS,* iv, 1917.
28. St Andrews University Archives, Acta Rectorum, i, 83, 87. I owe this reference to Dr John Durkan.
29. e.g. *St A. Form.,* i, 227; *James V Letters,* 342.
30. *CPL,* viii, 155; *RMS,* iv, 1742.

Andrews and the Augustinian order.[31] The secular dignity of chancellor existed for a mere twenty years in the fifteenth century. The only other secular dignitary with a seat in chapter was the provost of St Mary on the Rock, a survival from the days of the culdee community in St Andrews.[32] The bishop himself was apparently never a member of chapter.[33]

One most important duty of the chapter was to rule the diocese when the bishop was not in a position to do so. Some general principles can again be stated. The chapter, and in particular the prior, always took the bishop's place when the see was vacant and normally when the bishop was absent *in remotis*. The official administrator was called vicar general, but must not be regarded as similar to a present-day vicar general, who is a permanent official as long as, but only as long as, the bishop who appointed him is in office. The medieval vicar general, on the contrary, did not usually function except when the bishop ceased to administer: he had roughly the same office as his present-day counterpart during any lengthy absence of the bishop, but he corresponds to the official now known as vicar capitular during the vacancy of the see. The prior and chapter ruled when the see was vacant, but *in spiritualibus* only, for the crown had rights over the temporalities after a bishop's death or translation. When the bishop was in office but absent, it was normal for the prior and chapter to rule and for the prior to be vicar general, and they exercised a large measure of control even when the bishop had appointed someone else as special commissioner or vicar general.[34] The commonest duty which the vicar general is found performing in any of the situations above-mentioned is collating to benefices, a function of the spirituality. The phrase ' vicar general *in spiritualibus* ' often appears in papal documents, but the reason for a vicar general being in office is not always apparent and the date may not provide much guidance if the case in question took some time to find its way to the Roman courts.[35]

Prior David Ramsay is found as vicar general during the vacancy of 1465.[36] John Hepburn held the office during the vacancies of 1497,[37] of 1504,[38] of 1513[39] and of 1521[40]—a remarkable record, and he was himself a claimant for the see (or for more power) in the latter two.[41] In the vacancy of 1546, since the prior was in his early teens, the subprior John

31. Dowden, *Medieval Church*, 86; *St A. Lib.*, 425.
32. For these secular dignitaries, see Watt, *Fasti*, 301-14.
33. M. Ash, 233.
34. Dowden, *Medieval Church*, 221-22; M. Ash, 151-52, 230, 239; D. Knowles, 257. It can be seen, however, that the three vicars general appointed by Archbishop Forman on account of pressure of business approximate to their modern counterparts (*St A. Form.*, i, 20, 123).
35. *CPL*, x, 561, 563; xi, 447.
36. *Arb. Lib.*, ii, 145; *Yester Writs*, 127; *CPL*, xii, 466, 469, 635.
37. Herkless & Hannay, *Archbishops*, i, 183-84; SRO, RH 6 Suppl., 8.6.1498.
38. Herkless & Hannay, *Archbishops*, i, 226; *RMS*, ii, 2769-2892.
39. *RMS*, iii, 9-51; *RSS*, i, 2570, 2612; *Glas. Reg.*, ii, 525; *Midl. Chrs.*, 290; SRO, RH 6/816, 840.
40. *RMS*, iii, 203-19, 276, 1707; *Laing Chrs.*, 327, 329, 333; *St A. Acta*, 340; *St A. Form.*, i, 3; SRO, RH 6/933; SRO, GD 28/399.
41. Watt, *Fasti*, 297; Herkless & Hannay, *Archbishops*, iii, 75, 96-97.

Winram was vicar general with him[42] and surely was the person actually operating. These were all the vacancies from the episcopate of James Kennedy to the Reformation, except for 1478 and 1539 when coadjutor bishops were in office.[43]

The prior was vicar general while the bishop was *in remotis* in 1460,[44] but others are found holding the office. Not long before November 1451 the archdeacon of St Andrews was vicar general,[45] in 1471-72 the man appointed by Patrick Graham was the abbot of Scone,[46] and William Scheves in 1491-92 appointed Bishop Elphinstone.[47] The chapter still had rights and duties, however, no matter who was vicar general, for it consented to a charter of confirmation by the vicar general in 1521,[48] and when Patrick Graham was excommunicated, at some point before October 1477, it appointed one of its members, not the prior, as its vicar general,[49] an act that is difficult to explain unless the prior himself was unable to function.

The most important single right of the chapter was that of electing the bishop. Though this may originally have been theirs because the bishop held the place of abbot, the right was maintained through the principle of capitular election.[50] There was an obvious drawback as regards St Andrews, namely that a body of religious, forming an Augustinian community and not recruited in any systematic way, should elect to one of the most important positions, certainly the principal ecclesiastical office, in the kingdom. In practice chapter's right was whittled away in the late middle ages, the crown insisting on its own right of nomination to important positions in the church, while the Holy See reserved to itself the provision to major benefices. Chapter's power became a mere formality, since their candidate stood little chance without crown support and their election was ineffective without papal ratification.

One can see the gradual erosion of the right. The chapter elected candidates in 1401-03 but the bishop eventually provided was not one of them.[51] They elected James Kennedy in 1440, though it is claimed that Rome provided him independently of this.[52] James Stewart was elected in 1497. In the vacancy after Flodden the chapter elected William Elphinstone, who died, and then their own prior, John Hepburn, but it was Hepburn's rival who succeeded. All successful candidates received

42. *ADCP*, 565; *RSS*, iii, 2513; SRO, B 65/22, no. 299; SRO, RH 6/1435.
43. Reference to unnamed vicars general in September 1539 (*RSS*, ii, 3138) offers no relevant evidence.
44. Fraser, *Keir*, 235.
45. *CPL*, x, 563.
46. *Scone Liber*, 194, 196; *CPL*, xiii, 329
47. *St A. Acta*, xlv, n; *HMC*, viii, App. 305
48. SRO, RH 6/910.
49. *CPL*, xiii, 613.
50. Dowden, *Medieval Church*, 91; D. Knowles, 254, 257.
51. Information on these bishops is found in Watt, *Fasti*, 294-99. I use the word ' elect ' even if, technically, some were postulated.
52. *St A. Cop.*, 477.

papal provision, and at least the later ones had been nominated by the crown (the complex struggle after Flodden is somewhat of an exception). Probably, however, the role of chapter did not entirely disappear. When a successor had to be found after the execution of John Hamilton in 1571, royal licence to elect was given to the chapter and this was duly followed by royal confirmation of the election of John Douglas.[53] But in a St Andrews cartulary is found an instruction from the crown to elect Douglas,[54] while a formulary of the reformed Kirk preserves a standard document for royal nomination of the candidate to be elected.[55] One presumes that the procedure current in 1560 was being continued, with chapter playing its traditional but now merely honorary part.

II. THE PRIORY AS A RELIGIOUS HOUSE

In considering St Andrews priory as a religious house, it is natural to look closely at its relations with the bishop, and something of the same difficulty arises as in examining its capitular functions. It is not always clear whether the bishop was acting in his capacity as ordinary towards a religious house in his diocese or whether he stood in a particular relationship to his cathedral monastery. Almost certainly powers of control were not exercised in one direction only, and as the chapter could limit the bishop's acts because its formal consent was so often necessary, so would one expect to find the bishop possessing jurisdiction in various ways over the priory. Originally the bishop had acted as abbot of a cathedral monastery and in England he continued to carry out visitations of the house; indeed Dom David Knowles declares that an exempt cathedral priory would have been almost a contradiction in terms.

The evidence at St Andrews is scanty and not very clear-cut. In 1443 the bishop appointed three canons to inspect the teind sheaves, evidently over the chamberlain's head, for this monastic official protested that he should be cleared of any negligence.[56] This took place when the priorship was vacant that year. The same bishop, James Kennedy, had full powers to govern the priory in 1457 while the prior was abroad, but he claimed these because the prior had appointed him and not in virtue of any right.[57] On the other hand it was the subprior who acted for the absent prior a century later in 1558.[58] During the power struggle in the years after Flodden, the archbishop reminded the prior, John Hepburn, of his obligations: on the day of my installation in the archbishopric (he said) you, for yourself and the chapter, humbly swore obedience, kneeling with your hands joined and placed between mine.[59] This may not have been a special act by the head of chapter, for in another document the arch-

53. *RSS*, vi, 1458, 1473.
54. NLS, Adv. 17.1.3, fo 367.
55. *BUK*, i, 217.
56. NLS, Adv. 15.1.8, no. 90.
57. NLS, Adv. 15.1.8, no. 25.
58. See note 104 below.
59. *St A. Form.*, i, 239-40.

bishop, calling Hepburn his obedientiary, speaks of the same obedience being rendered by other prelates too.[60] It would appear, however, that at St Andrews the bishop had at least some rights of jurisdiction or visitation when the priorship was vacant.

In the days when the bishop was elected by the monks as their abbot, he appointed the prior and other monastic officials. When the prior became in effect their religious superior it was natural that the monks should claim the right to elect him as in other monastic houses. The bishop had a considerable interest in the matter, for the prior was the head of his chapter, but in general the community's right was recognised. At St Andrews the bishop granted the right of free election in the twelfth and thirteenth centuries.[61] In the later middle ages, however, the Scottish crown and the Holy See encroached on this right in monasteries as in bishoprics: papal provision became an indispensable condition, though royal nomination (as far as one can judge) only gradually became the custom and was perhaps never indispensable.

William de Camera in 1416,[62] James Haldenstone in 1418,[63] probably David Ramsay in 1462,[64] and William Cameron in 1469[65] were all canons of St Andrews elected prior by their brethren. William Bonar in 1443 was a canon of St Andrews nominated by the king with the support of Bishop James Kennedy; when the chapter presented the canon of their choice, David Ramsay, the pope replied that he had already made provision of Bonar and could not revoke it.[66] This was a sign of things to come. In 1469 Ramsay resigned the priorship in his last illness to the subprior and chapter, whose candidate was in fact provided, but a secular cleric fought his own claim persistently and was given a pension as a consolation prize.[67] At the next vacancy, in 1483, although a canon of St Andrews, Walter Monypenny, was elected and obtained papal provision,[68] the successful candidate (also of course with papal provision) was John Hepburn, of the great Hailes-Hepburn family. He took the Augustinian habit, made his profession and was prior for forty-three years.[69]

That was the end of free election of the prior. When Hepburn died in January 1526[70] his nephew Patrick Hepburn had been provided as coadjutor and succeeded him.[71] In 1538 Patrick was made bishop of

---

60. . . . quam obedientiam ceteri regni prelati indifferenter prestant (*St A. Form.*, i, 227).
61. *St A. Lib.*, 126, 171.
62. *Chron. Bower*, i, 374.
63. Ibid.; *CPL*, vii, 63; *St A. Cop.*, 20-23.
64. His provision is not found in *CPL*. John Law's MS (Edin. Univ. Lib.), fo 21, is no help as every prior is there called ' electus.'
65. *CPL*, xii, 318.
66. *CPL*, viii, 269; ix, 350, 354.
67. *CPL*, xii, 318, 328; xiii, 15, 319.
68. *CPL*, xiii, 139, 169; xiv, 98.
69. *CPL*, xiii, 840-41; *SP*, ii, 147.
70. *Taymouth Bk.*, 119.
71. *HMC*, ix, App. 191; *SP*, ii, 142.

Moray, James Stewart, the king's five-year-old bastard son, became commendator of the priory and remained in office until after 1560.[72] Some attempt should be made to assess the effect of these intruded priors on the religious life of the community. The two Hepburns belonged to one of the most powerful baronial families; John was ambitious and Patrick notoriously incelibate, while James Stewart was a mere infant when appointed. As religious superiors they were eminently unsuitable. Yet the impression one gets is that in general the rank and file of religious communities led their life independently of who was their nominal superior, and in fact the more exalted the superior, the less were their lives affected by him. John Hepburn was powerful enough to prevent Andrew Forman from assuming office as archbishop for a considerable period, Patrick Hepburn was a man of affairs, James Stewart became a public figure. It is not far-fetched to suggest an analogy with non-indigenous landlords (say, in the Highlands): their policies might cause hardship to tenants, but life on their estates could go on virtually un-influenced by them. To judge from the absence of dispute, though there are exceptions, imposition of superiors from outside had singularly little effect on the internal life of religious communities. When the infant James Stewart was appointed, his administrator was Alexander Milne, abbot of Cambuskenneth, who can hardly have spent much time on the day-to-day affairs of the priory. Almost certainly the subprior, John Winram, dealt with these, just as he actually acted for Stewart as vicar general of the see after Cardinal Beaton's death.

It is interesting to note who did not become priors of St Andrews. While many monasteries in Scotland had bishops as commendator abbots or priors, this never happened at St Andrews, where it would have resulted in the bishop of one diocese holding the position of head of chapter in another. Nor did the bishop of St Andrews himself ever become prior *in commendam*, which would have meant that he was his own dean. Similarly, no dignitary of a secular cathedral chapter was ever prior at St Andrews, though it happened at other monasteries. In fact, no prior of St Andrews seems ever to have combined the office with any other dignity; Patrick Hepburn held the abbacy of Scone, but only after he had demitted the priorship of St Andrews to become bishop of Moray. The prior of St Andrews must have been one of the very few church dignitaries in Scotland who was never a pluralist. The crown officials were undoubtedly well aware of this, and James V in requesting the priorship for his son pointed out to Rome that the prior was dean of the metropolitan chapter and the appointment would therefore safeguard the ecclesiastical condition of Scotland. There is little evidence never-theless that the king's motive was other than avarice. Financially as well as otherwise, it was worth renouncing pluralistic ambitions to become prior of St Andrews.[73]

---

72. *James V Letters*, 342-43.
73. *James V Letters*, 342. But cf. James Bisset in 1411 (*CPP*, i, 597).

A subsidiary but still important question was the appointment of monastic officials. Presumably the bishop, when he ceded the right to free election of the prior, allowed to him when elected the right to choose his own officials. In St Andrews priory the chain of command was prior, subprior, *tertius prior.* The real monastic superior in the mid-sixteenth century must have been the subprior, appointed (to the best of our knowledge) by the prior. It is not altogether idle to speculate that if the system of commendator or intruded abbots had gone on longer, the Scottish monasteries might have adapted to it as the cathedral monasteries had done to a not dissimilar situation some centuries before when the priors took the place of bishop-abbots who were no longer religious superiors. The chain of command at St Andrews would then have developed into subprior (elected), third prior, fourth prior. The situation in the priory in the 1540s shows that the suggestion is by no means absurd.

Another matter with importance beyond the community was the recruitment of novices, for they would form the chapter of the future. The bishop had a particular interest here, since the chapter's co-operation was necessary to him and in secular chapters it was the bishop usually who appointed the canons.[74] Nevertheless bishops with regular chapters did in the main concede the right to admit aspirants to clothing and profession. At St Andrews in 1457 Bishop Kennedy gave leave to the subprior and chapter to admit recruits, but he stated explicitly that he did not intend to establish any claim in the matter for himself or his successors and was acting solely in the name of the absent prior who had committed the power to him.[75] In fact Rome in 1475 granted a petition from the priory for various rights and privileges, including that the prior should not accept novices without consent of the community.[76] Danger, it would seem, was threatening from that quarter rather than from the bishop.

III. THE PRIORY AT THE REFORMATION

St Andrews priory did not diminish in significance in the decades before the Reformation. If anything it grew in importance and prestige. It was still the chapter of the primatial see, its church was the metropolitan cathedral and a place of pilgrimage housing the relics of the national saint. It not only took precedence over other religious houses but had the largest revenues of any.[77] It was well endowed with appropriated parish churches, some of which were served by a vicar from the community,[78] who may have lived there with a couple of fellow canons.[79] It had two dependent houses, Pittenweem and Portmoak, the former of

---

74. Dowden, *Medieval Church,* 90.
75. NLS, Adv. 15.1.8, no. 25.
76. Vat. Arch., Reg. Supp., 725, fo 22.
77. Easson, *Religious Houses,* 82. *CPP,* i, 597.
78. References are not infrequent, e.g. *CPL,* xiii, 378; C. H. Haws, *Scottish Parish Clergy at the Reformation,* 1540-1574 (1972) [Haws, *Clergy*], 67, 94, 213.
79. Dowden, *Medieval Church,* 91

which had actually in living memory returned to the jurisdiction of the priory and become once more a monastery with a community of its own.[80]

No other house of monks or regular canons in Scotland was situated in a university town. In the fifteenth century the prior and canons of St Andrews had no official standing in the university, but in 1512 St Leonard's college was founded by them, within the confines of their monastery[81] and supported by the endowments they bestowed on it. The principal was to be a canon of St Andrews, appointed by and responsible to the prior, and documents issued by the principal with the consent of prior and conventus as patrons or superiors and bearing their seal show that this was in fact the case until after 1560.[82]

The prestige of the priory in the 1550s must have been increased by the calibre of its prior, James Stewart, ironically the bastard infant imposed on it some twenty years before. Whether he considered himself to be a cleric or not, the queen (if we accept John Leslie's story) considered him to be one and refused to grant him any secular title.[83] It is surely significant that in spite of a contract of marriage,[84] James did not attempt to marry before 1560 but did so after that date, and the same is true of his brothers in the like situation.[85] The priorship of St Andrews remained his only title though he was the queen's half-brother, his character commanded respect and he was considered a likely claimant for the throne. Anyone saying ' the Prior ' or ' the Lord Prior ' was known to be speaking of one of the chief men in the kingdom and a leader of the lords of the congregation.[86]

The English cathedral monasteries were wealthy and at the centre of things, and so their interests were more varied, recruitment was better and there was more intellectual activity. The same would seem to be true of St Andrews immediately before the Reformation, certainly as regards its recruitment. In comparison with other major religious houses, very few documents signed by the canons have survived; leaving aside one document signed by part of the community in the late 1540s, all we have are two of 1555 and then none until 1566. The priory had thirty religious in 1555,[87] which is more than in any other Scottish monastery of the time. There were also nine other canons who are found in documents after the Reformation but were surely admitted to the community before August 1560. The number in 1560 was thus less than thirty-nine (on the supposition that some of those recorded in 1555 had died or dropped out) but at least thirty-two (the sum of those documented after

---

80. Appendix IV, 159-160.
81. . . . intra septa monasterii (RMS, iv, 1917; NLS, Adv. 17.1.3, fo 299).
82. St A. Acta, xliii—l; RMS, iv, 2750; NLS, Adv. 17.1.3, fo 2 and passim.
83. Lesley, De Origine, 538.
84. SP, ii, 269; vi, 316; Mort. Reg., i, 9.
85. Dunbar, Scot. Kings, 238-39.
86. CSP Scot., i passim.
87. SRO, B 65/22, no. 323; NLS, Adv. 17.1.3, fo 11, with addition of James Baldowy found in 1553 (SRO, B 65/22, no. 316) and 1557 (Haws, Clergy, 94, 213).

PLATE XIX.   SEAL OF CARDINAL DAVID BEATON.

This fine seal of David Beaton proclaims his position in the Scottish Church: ' The Most Reverend Father and Lord, David Beton, Cardinal Priest of the Holy Roman Church of the title of St Stephen on the Coelian Hill. Archbishop of St Andrews, Primate and Legate *a latere* of the Apostolic See.' The figures of St Peter and St Paul which are featured on this seal and on other late medieval seals of the bishopric of St Andrews are intended to emphasise the dignity of the archbishops as legates of the Apostolie See.

PLATE XX. JAMES STEWART, PRIOR OF ST. ANDREWS, 1538-1570.

The appointment by King James V of his seven-year-old son, James Stewart, as prior of S
Andrews in 1538 was fatal to the medieval Church in St Andrews. How far James Stewar
was motivated by political ambition or theological conviction we shall never know but h
adherence to the Knoxian party spelt final ruin to the ancient cathedral priory of St Andrew
From the contemporary portrait at Darnaway Castle.

1560).[88] All these, it must be emphasised, were canons of St Andrews only, for Pittenweem remained a separate community and has not been included.[89]

Whatever the reason might be, absence or anything else, not all members of a community signed all documents, and it is therefore unsafe to say that the nine canons found only after 1560 had not been professed by 1555. One can, however, get some indication of their ages and dates of entry. Men of their names, and reasonably to be identified with them, matriculated at St Andrews: Alexander Spens in 1552; John Simson, Alexander Jardine and Peter Watson in 1555; Thomas Biggar, William Bradfute and John Rule in 1560. All but one matriculated at the priory's own college of St Leonard.[90] Thomas Biggar was born in 1540.[91] John and Ninian Rule are probably the John and Ninian, sons of John Rule, prior of Pittenweem, who were promised pensions for their education by the St Andrews community in 1550.[92] It would seem, therefore, that at least eight of the nine were young and newcomers in the 1550s. Recruitment at St Andrews continued right up to 1560, as indeed it did in several other Scottish monasteries. At St Andrews, too, a high proportion of the canons were university men, a fact that can be ascertained by scanning the university lists or noting the canons who used the title of Master.

This should not be considered surprising, for if the priory had not possessed vitality right up to the end it could hardly have made the outstanding contribution which it did to the reformed Kirk. From the community came a superintendent, fifteen ministers, five readers or exhorters[93] and David Peebles, who was one of the composers of the music for the Scottish psalter.[94] The priory also made an important financial contribution to the new Kirk. In 1566-67 all the canons were given a pension, correspondingly larger if the recipient was a minister or reader;[95] their servants were rewarded, and occasionally too a minister in one of their appropriated churches who was not a member of the community.[96] In 1562 they gave a generous endowment to St Leonard's college[97] and in 1570 they united Portmoak priory to it to form a *gymnasium* or school to help establish Reformation principles, as they said in

---

88. Twenty-six in 1566 (SRO, RH 6/2015; *Laing Chrs.*, 809) with the addition of three in *BUK*, i, 222, one each in *RMS*, iv, 1730, and NLS, Adv. 17.1.3, fos 371-73, and William Wilson, who married and so can be presumed to have lived until 1560 (D. H. Fleming, *The Reformation in Scotland*, 613). John Allanson, found only in a transcript of a document of 1584 (*Laing Chrs.*, 1082), is probably a ghost, a mis-reading of John Duncanson.
89. See Appendix IV, 160-162.
90. See *St A. Recs.* for these years.
91. Scott, *Fasti*, v, 93.
92. *May Recs.*, ciii.
93. See Haws, *Clergy*, 250 ff, for a convenient list.
94. C. Innes in *PSAS*, vii (1866-68), 447-58.
95. NLS, Adv. 17.1.3, fo 138 ff and passim.
96. Ibid., fo 202v.
97. *RMS*, iv, 1917

language that was unequivocally anti-Catholic and most unlike the usual monastic document concerning property.[98]

Some idea of the possibilities open to a canon of St Andrews can be got by looking at the career of John Winram. He determined at St Leonard's in 1515,[99] took a doctorate in theology in 1540[100] and was deputy rector of the university in 1550.[101] He was subprior from 1535[102] and thus was superior in effect of a large monastic house, and while the prior was under age he was dean in effect of the metropolitan chapter. In the vacancy after Cardinal Beaton's murder he was vicar general of the primatial see. As subprior he carried out a visitation of Pittenweem priory in 1554 and acted with vigour in his disciplinary measures.[103] In 1558 he took over the reins entirely as commissary of James Stewart, absent in France,[104] and in 1570 he was administrator of the priory after Stewart's murder.[105]

Not all his prestige wins our approval nowadays: there was a certain element of the mammon of iniquity. He was vicar of the appropriated church of Dull but can hardly have resided there, and he remained usufructuar or liferenter after demitting the vicarage.[106] He was also well endowed by the community after 1560 and became a man of property able to benefit his relatives.[107] As prior of Portmoak he sat in the Parliament of 1560, and was a lord of the articles,[108] though this would seem to be an instance of packing as no prior of Portmoak is recorded as sitting before then. In political circles he was 'the Subprior,'[109] just as James Stewart was 'the Prior.'

Dom David Knowles makes an interesting judgement on cathedral monasteries, to the effect that the lack of abbatial dignity made the prior less cut off from his community and produced a more co-operative and democratic spirit. A letter of James Stewart to Winram in 1567 seems to bear this out for St Andrews.[110] Stewart wanted his subprior to bring him in Edinburgh the rental-books and seals of St Andrews and Pittenweem. Evidently he expected Winram to drop everything and obey; after all, if Winram was now superintendent of Fife, he himself was soon to be regent of Scotland. But he addresses him as 'traist freind,' states plainly what his intentions are and signs 'Your assured freind, James Stewart,'

---

98. NLS, Adv. 17.1.3, fo 299; cf. *RMS*, v, 1.
99. *St A. Recs.*, 104, 211.
100. *St A. Rent.*, 107.
101. *St A. Recs.*, 253.
102. SRO, RH 6/1117.
103. *Essays on the Scottish Reformation* (1962), 225.
104. NLS, Adv. 17.1.3, fo 267v ff; NLS, Chrs. 6113; SRO, GD 147/17/1.
105. NLS, Adv. 17.1.3, fos 299rv, 360rv, 387.
106. Ibid., fos 193, 372; *RMS*, iv, 1730.
107. NLS, Adv. 17.1.3, fos 115, 195v, 370v, 372v; SRO, E 14/2, fos 87, 62.
108. *APS*, ii, 525, 606, 544; *CSP Scot.*, i, 458.
109. *CSP Scot.*, i, 461, 477.
110. *HMC*, vi, App. 642-43.

then in a postscript tells him to be sure to get the Pittenweem seal from Barty Forman. This was Dene Bartholomew Forman, subprior of Pittenweem. We get a glimpse in the letter of the working relationship between Winram and his prior. In John Winram the Reformation gained a man of theological learning and much experience in affairs, who had developed his considerable talents as an Augustinian canon of St Andrews.

After 1560 the priory and chapter of St Andrews continued in being. There is nothing surprising in this, for it happened with all the other Scottish monasteries. Nevertheless St Andrews was a special case, not only because more than half the religious served in the new Kirk, which probably was not the case anywhere else, but also because it was an executive body in the diocesan and parish structure which the Reformers planned to take over. While Archbishop John Hamilton was alive, chapter proceedings were probably much as before. The flood of documents issued by prior and community concerning property continued unabated after 1560, though it may be that the phrase in them, *capitulariter congregati* or *chaptourlie gadderit*, was a mere formality.[111] In April 1570, when Winram was administrator in place of the assassinated James Stewart, the chapter decided that it would meet twice a year, after Easter and Michaelmas, to consider matters concerning the good of the place and the brethren (that is, monastic affairs), and it appointed Winram and five others to deal with anything occurring between times.[112]

It was the execution of Hamilton and the necessity of using the chapter in the election of his successor that brought about a more radical change. The convention of Leith in January 1572 decided that only those who had professed the Reformation and were ministers should have a voice in electing bishops, and it listed fourteen capitulars who qualified at St Andrews: the commendator (Bishop Robert Stewart), John Winram and twelve other canons. One can note in passing that a great deal of the old position had already been eroded when a bishop was made prior and thus dean of chapter. Nominating these fourteen, however, was a merely temporary arrangement, and a chapter of twenty-one ministers (or more technically nineteen ministers and the priors of St Andrews and Portmoak, who would be serving in the Kirk as Stewart and Winram were) was to take over when the present community died out. Even before this happened, the new chapter was to deal with spiritualities, while the old chapter continued during the lifetime of its members to control temporalities as before.[113] The distinction between temporal and spiritual affairs was not the same as the distinction made in the foregoing pages between monastic and diocesan affairs: for example, presentation

---

111. NLS, Adv. 17.1.3 passim.
112. Ibid., fo 355v.
113. *BUK*, i, 221-23

to a benefice in the patronage of the priory, a monastic matter, was surely considered by the Kirk to pertain to the spirituality and thus to be withdrawn from the competence of the old chapter. It is beyond the scope of this paper to say how the new arrangement worked. In October 1572 the commendator agreed not to make any grants of property without consent of his monastic chapter[114] and in 1586 nine canons signed a monastic document granting a tack.[115] The monastic chapter continued until the old community died out. The diocesan chapter would endure, in one form or another, while episcopacy lasted.

---

114. NLS, Adv. 17.1.3, fo 391v.
115. SRO, RH 6/2818.

ST ANDREWS IN THE JOHN LAW CHRONICLE

by

JOHN DURKAN

John Law is a person of whom we know remarkably little: like many another teacher, his work was unadvertised. He first emerged to light as a student in Paris from the Glasgow diocese; surfaced again a few years later as schoolmaster in Ayr; was compiling his little chronicle in St Andrews in 1521; with a group of other canons regular was incorporated in the university there some years later; took his master's degree in theology before 1545; and succeeded John Annand as principal of St Leonard's college a few years later, a post he occupied till his death.

He was among the bachelors received to the arts faculty in the German nation of the university of Paris in the period 1508-1509, after the first account of the bursar, Henningus Schultetus. He is there described as ' of Glasgow diocese' and a fellow bachelor was William Manderston, while the nation's procurator was John Mair (Major). In 1509-1510 he appears as a licentiate.[1] Our next reference to his existence is at Ayr. On 3 August 1515, ' Maister Johne law feit to mak seruice at ye trinite altare and in ye queir *sicut solebat* and to haif xii markis of fee of ye commone purss and to haif ye scuyll for five zeris with ye profettis yairof.' He was therefore a chaplain of the kirk of St John Baptist before this date and presumably for some years after, though by May 1519 he had been succeeded as chaplain and schoolmaster by the notary public, Gavin Ross.[2] He was writing his chronicle by 1521, for he says (f. 141), ' Et tantum de regibus et temporibus regum scotorum ad annum nostre salutis 1521.'

The presence of Mair and Manderston at St Andrews may have attracted students of theology, for several canons regular, including Law, matriculated.[3] He appeared as an intrant for the nation of Britain (in which Glasgow diocese was included) at the rectorial election of 1527 and again at Manderston's election as rector in 1528 when he was described as sacrist of St Andrews; while in the election of 1545 he was rector's assessor and professor of theology.[4]

He succeeded John Annand as principal of St Leonard's college in 1549, after Whitsunday. He was paid his fee for Martinmas of that year (11 November) and next year, as principal, received the college accounts. He was still alive in May 1553, but must have died shortly afterwards.[5]

---

1. Paris, University Archives (Sorbonne), Régistre 91, ff. 100v, 109.
2. Scottish Record Office, Alloway Court Book (paged), pp. 94, 112.
3. *St Andrews Univ. Recs.*, p. 220.
4. St Andrews University Archives, Acta Rectorum, i, 83, 87; ii, 29.
5. St Andrews University Archives, Liber Computorum Collegii Leonardi, ff. 5, 7, 14.

Presuming that he was about fifteen when he arrived at Paris about 1508, his date of birth would perhaps be 1493. If this were so, he would be about sixty at the time of his death.

There are echoes of his origins in the west here and there in the chronicle. For instance in 1451 he records the arrival of the privileges of Glasgow university with the greatest indulgences granted by Pope Nicholas at the king's request and that of Bishop William Turnbull. He records the latter's death under 1456 (*sic*): ' hoc anno obiit Willelmus trumbil episcopus glasguensis qui impetrauit indulgentias ciuitati glasgwensi.' (ff. 130v, 128v).

He had a great admiration, it would seem, for Bishop Elphinstone whom he compared to Nicholas of Cusa. He gave a very sympathetic account of the first archbishop of St Andrews, Patrick Graham, who emerges in a less favourable light in the standard histories. He also records gifts of Bishop Kennedy to his cathedral.

No attempt has been made to compare Law's work with that of Bower and Wyntoun, although it is clearly related to Bower, echoing and abbreviating his account. Here and there it may illuminate where Bower is ambiguous. For instance, in the latter's account of Prior William de Camera we are told how the new prior took ill while awaiting the ship for Scotland at Bruges. We are then told he was buried before St Andrew's altar in the church of St Giles, and this has been interpreted as a church in Bruges.[6] But Law makes it clear that it was St Giles in Edinburgh.

For the rest, it is clear that he made use of Carion's chronicle: at one point he writes ' hucusque Carion ' and adds an appendix for 1533-1536. Under the latter date he writes: ' thomas morus anglie cancellarius et Roffensis (episcopus) una cum aliquot primariis innocentibus monachis capite truncantur ' (f. 152). The last Scots entry seems to be for 1528 (f. 146), although a reference is made to ' this present year 1541 ' (f. 149).

Attention might be drawn to the claim by Thomas Dempster that he possessed a fragmentary manuscript which gave details concerning the priors of St Andrews. It is possible that Dempster's manuscript was a copy of John Law's chronicle, but the evidence seems rather to indicate that it may have consisted of extracts from the Scotichronicon. Certainly, in one instance, some imaginary details have been added and the language has evidently been remodelled by Dempster to suit seventeenth-century classical taste. Speaking of Prior James Haldenstone, he writes (Vat. lat. 7805, f. 259), ' Ecclesiam Monasterii mirifice decorauit, cum chori sedilibus et seliquastris caelatis, cum imaginibus insignibus dedicatis, nouam Ecclesiam, quam Jacobus Biset decessor inornatam deseruerat omni cura finire sategit, cui fenestras picturis elegantissimis insignitas prouidit, ut in Europa vix ulla Ecclesiastica fabrica ornatior, nam et fastigium puro auro

---

6. *Chron. Bower*, i, 374; cf. *St Andrews Copiale*, p. 396.

caelauerat, et pauimentum opere tesellato et musiuo, quod nonnulli Muscarium vocant, constrauit, aras sacras adiecit veteribus, dedicauitque, ornamenta pleraque addidit, orientalia seliquastra omnia priori et suis Decanis a fundamentis excitauit, atque eo opere superne concamerato inclusit.'

THE MANUSCRIPT

Only a brief notice is possible here. The manuscript is in small octavo format and is bound in a modern binding along with a printed book and this occupies the first eleven leaves. It is *Cathalogus summorum pontificum*, Paris (J. Petit), 1518.[7] Though the binding is modern, it probably replaces an older binding. At the start of the text of the chronicle is the inscription, ' Editum per Johannem law canonicum Sanctiandree.' In the seventeenth century it was owned by a George Wood and donated to Edinburgh university library by Master Andrew Cranston, student in theology, 27 May 1680. Its present shelf number is Dc.7.63.

f. 12.   Nomina episcoporum.
f. 12v. Nomina priorum.
f. 13.   De episcopis.
f. 18.   De prioribus.
ff. 21v - 24v. Blank.
f. 26.   Scocie prioratus.
f. 26v. Prefecture scocie.
f. 27.   Monasteria monialium.
f. 28.   De supplemento Cronicarum.
f. 42v. Blank.
f. 43.   Genologia (*sic*) regum scocie.
f. 43v. Ducatus scocie.
f. 44.   Initium Scoticronicon [*or*] De Cronicis Scotorum breuia.
f. 141v. Nomina regum anglie.
f. 142. Nomina regum francie post sanctum ludouicum.
f. 142v. Imperium romanum.
f. 143. Continuatio cronicarum.
f. 146v. Language notes in later hand.
f. 147v. Note of ownership by Georgius Sylvius (Wood).
f. 148. Continuatio cronicarum.
f. 148v. Historical notes.
f. 150. Blank.
f. 150v. De regno neapolitano.
f. 152. '. . . hucusque Carion.' Appendix to 1536.
f. 152v. Homo sanguinese complexionis (notes).
f. 153v. Historical memoranda.

---

7. For another printed book owned by Law, see Durkan and Ross, *Libraries*, p. 121.

f. 154v. De regibus anglorum ex diuersis nationibus.

f. 155v. See ballad as mentioned in R. L. G. Ritchie, *The Buke of Alexander* (Scottish Text Society, New Series 17, 1925), page cxxxiii.

f. 156v. De sancto kentigerno (published in *Glasgow Registrum*, i, pp. xcix - c).

NAMES OF BISHOPS AND PRIORS

(f. 12) Nomina episcoporum sanctiandree post aduentum canonicorum.

Anno domini 1159 obiit Robertus eiusdem episcopus.
Anno 1162 obiit ernaldus fundator noue ecclesie.
Anno domini 1175 obiit Richardus episcopus.
Anno domini 1185 obiit Hugo episcopus.
Anno domini 1202 obiit Rogerius.
Anno 1238 obiit Wilelmus malvesone.
Anno 1253 obiit dauid de berham.
Anno 1254 obiit abel de golyn.
Anno domini 1271 obiit gamelinus.
Anno 1279 obiit Wyllelmus Wischard.
Anno 1296 obiit Willelmus fraser.
Anno domini 1328 obiit Willelmus de lamberton.
Anno domini 1332 obiit Jacobus ben.
Anno 1375 obiit Willelmus de landalis.
Anno 1401 obiit Valterus trail.
Anno 1440 obiit Henricus wardlaw.
Anno domini 1465 obiit Jacobus Kennydy.
Anno domini 1496 obiit Willelmus scheuez.
Anno domini 1503 obiit Jacobus stewart.
Anno domini 1513 obiit Alexander stewart.
1521 obiit Andreas forman xii marcii festo gregorii.

(f. 12v) Nomina priorum post aduentum canonicorum.

Anno domini 1160 obiit Robertus prior sanctiandree.
Anno domini 1186 obiit Valterus prior eiusdem.
Anno 1199 obiit gilbertus prior eiusdem.
Anno domini 1211 obiit Thomas prior.
Anno domini 1222 obiit Symon.
Anno domini 1236 obiit henricus.
Anno domini 1258 obiit Johannes.
Anno domini 1264 obiit gilbertus secundus.
Anno domini 1304 obiit Johannes secundus.

Anno domini 1313 obiit Adam.
Anno domini 1322 obiit Johannes de forfar.
Anno domini 1340 obiit Johannes de gowry.
Anno domini 1354 obiit Wyllelmus de laudonia.
Anno domini 1364 obiit Thomas bisset.
Anno domini 1385 obiit Stephanus pay.
Anno 1393 obiit Robertus de montross.
Anno 1416 obiit Johannes (*sic*) bisset.
Anno 1423 (*sic*) obiit Jacobus haldeston.
Anno domini 1462 obiit Willelmus bonar.
Anno 1469 obiit dauid ramsay.
Anno domini 1482 obiit Willelmus cameron.

PRIORS OF ST ANDREWS

(f. 18) De prioribus sanctiandree post aduentum canonicorum.

Quamquam religiosus quisque subsequi debet abbatem ex ordine Prior tamen sanctiandree speciali ex prerogatiua uniuersos abbates scocie antecedit atque precellit quamius abbas de calco ex antiquis solebat allegare preuilegiis se omnibus abbatibus scocie et prioribus esse preferendus.

Conclusum fuit in parliamento coram Jacobo primo rege scotorum per tres regni status quod prior sanctiandree post episcopos primum obtinebit locum omnes ante abbates.

1140: Robertus prior de scona electus et vocatus per Robertum episcopum sanctiandree ad prioratum eiusdem hic bene rexit conuentum sibi creditum et stetit prior viginti duobus annis.

1162: Valterus eiusdem loci canonicus sedit prior 13 annis obiit apud clakmanane in hostilagio.

1200: Thomas eiusdem loci supprior religionis exemplar hic valedicens fratribus anno 1211 ipsis renitentibus ac iugiter flentibus de priore et prelato canonicorum factus est in cupro humilis nouicius monachorum.

1211: Symon eiusdem ecclesie canonicus per 14 stetit annos tandem curam prioratus sanctiandree reliquit et consilio episcopi et canonicorum de louchleuyn suscepit [prioratum].

1225: henricus de norham eiusdem ecclesie canonicus xi sedit annis curam renuncians domum debitis oneratam reliquit.

(f. 18v):

1236: Johannes quhit eiusdem ecclesie canonicus henrico successit cuius prouidencia bona loci et possessiones dissipatas ad pristinam statum redegit stetit xxii annis hic dormitorium refectorium et magnam aulam hospitum edificare fecit et alia plura fecit bona.

1258: Gilbertus eiusdem loci terrarius et canonicus Johanne (*sic*) successit qui stetit v annis cui successit.

141

1263: Johannes de hadingtona eiusdem loci camerarius hic construxit magnam cameram in orientali plaga monasterii iuxta cimeterium sedit xl annis sepultus in capitulo cuius est ephitaphium.

Corpore efficitur custos hec petra Johannes
Quadraginta domus prior huius qui fuit annis.

1304: Adam sanctiandree archidiaconus qui rexit prioratum ix annis sepultus in capitulo iuxta predicessorem (*sic*) suum.

1313: Johannes forfar canonicus vicarius de locris hic ampliauit seu nouiter erexit cameram quam priores habere consueuerant / hic stetit ix annis et primus sepultus est in nouo capitulo cui successit

1321: Johannes gowre terrarius eiusdem hic impeditioris lingue fuit bene tamen prioratus officium rexit per xvii annos Compulsus tempore belli per eduard(um) vindesor regem anglie et eduard(um) de balliolo scocie exposuit in constructione unius porte (f. 19) de perth 280 markas sepultusque est in nouo capitulo.

1340: Willelmus de laudonia supprior eiusdem loci stetit 14 annis hic dormitorium intus tabulis dolatis et exterius plumbo sumptuose vestiuit veterem ecclesiam cameram orientalem australem partem refectorii et quatuor partes claustri magnis tegebat expensis ac cameram a Johanne forfar constructam muro lapideo vallauit Monasterium reliquit bene prouisum bordis ferro et sale ac omni sine debito cum centum libris in deposito sepultus in nouo capitulo iuxta predicessorem suum.

1354: Thomas bisset nepos comitis de fyf supprior eiusdem hic regularem obseruantiam et sanctorum patrum instituta pre oculis gestabat amator et diligens custos fratrum per ix annos locum regens. decidens in egritudine curam prioratus pure et simpliciter resignauit in manibus Willelmi landalis episcopi honesta sibi per dictum episcopatum prouisione concessa. Cui successit

1363: Stephanus pay supprior eiusdem vir omnium morum honestate preditus hic magnam ecclesiam infortunio combustam anno 1368 in tecturis opere lapideo in tantum reparauit ut in expensis eiusdem cum reedificacione duarum columpnarum in australi parte iuxta altaria sanctorum michaelis et laurentii 2200 markas exposuit hic xx stetit annis prior tandem episcopus eiusdem electus dum romam proficisceretur in anglia captus ibidem finiuit cui successit

(f. 19v):

1385: Robertus de monte rosarum canonicus eiusdem loci predicator egregius et regularibus intentus obseruanciis hic neque bonos grauauit nec malos palpauit habuit fratrem claustralem minus disciplinatum nomine Thomam platar correctione supprioris et ordinis contemptibiliter aspernantem ydeoque quicquid pater prior ei satagebat incendere ad emendam induratus filius tetendit ad noxam et dum prior reuolueret quomodo fratrem lucretur peruersus discipulus spirituali patri mortem machinatur Nam sero quod cum prior solus ut solitus erat dormitorium ad pernoctandum ascenderet oportunitate explorans iniquus religiosus prelatum aggredere et extracto pugione suum patrem priorem letaliter wulnerauit qui triduo superuixit et valedicens fratribus obdormiuit in domino sepultus in nouo capitulo Valtero trail episcopo sermonem faciente solempnem patricida captus et presentatus coram omnibus perpetuis carceribus deputatus est ubi pane doloris et aque tristicie tantum sustentatus moritur et in sterquilinio sepelitur. Prior iste construxit nouum opus in corpore ecclesie maximas per expensas stetit prior 14 annis.

1393: Jacobus bisset canonicus eiusdem licentiatus in decretis et nepos thome bisset prioris superscripti hic nauem ecclesie tignis et tecturis solemniter consummauit chori stallis et claustrale tetragonum tecturis et pauimentis (f. 20) decenter reparauit sicque utramque ecclesiam forinsecam materialibus decorauit ornamentis et conuentum spiritualibus instituit disciplinis quicquid de loci redditibus acquirere potuit preter vite stipendia ad fabricam ecclesie et usus pauperum seu hospitii reseruauit. Plures etiam discipuli eius canonici electi sunt in pastores quorum unus fuit episcopus rossensis. Alii duo abbates unus in scona alius in emonia preferuntur Tres eorum successiue priores in monimusk intitulantur Nec mirum ex industria prioris duo eorum erant magistri in theologia quorum unus sibi successit in prioratu et alter in scona prefectus duo etiam licentiati erant in decretis et quinque bacularii extiterunt Tunc claustrum sanctiandree suauem paradisi odorem vernantibus undique documentorum floribus redolebat.

Post hunc electus est Willelmus de camera qui ad romam pro confirmacione accessit rediensque infirmitatem incurrens obiit edinburgh et in ecclesia sancti egedii (*sic*) sepultus est.

(f.20):

1417: Jacobus haldenston doctor in theologia canonicus eiusdem loci xiiii annis (*sic*) sedit prior hic indumentis ac eloquentia ornatissimus extitit ipsum stall(os) picturis et imaginibus decorauit nauem ecclesie tanquam vacuam sinagogam cum luminariis vitreis et altarium ornamentis decenter illustrauit gabellum orientalem cum archuali volta construxit reuestiarium cum reliquis (*sic*) studiose perornauit larem cori (*sic*) cum capellis et capitulo duobus lateribus complanauit domestica maneria de ballone (f. 20v) pilmuir sygoir (*sic*) a fundamentis reedificauit Insignia pastoralia scilicet mitram baculum et anulum primus usus est et sequacibus usum impetrauit missam nostre domine in capella eiusdem instituit In cuius tempore Willelmus bovar vicarius sanctiandree solium crucis cum imaginibus et Willelmus balvoty supprior eiusdem larem dormitorii decenter ut apparet perfecerunt et Willelmus de camera refectorium lateribus poliuit Obiit anno domini 1443 sepultus in capella nostre domine cuius extat epitaphii versus

Qui docui mores mundi vitarum fauores
Inter doctores sacros sortitus honores.

THE MEDIEVAL CHURCH OF ST ANDREWS

(f. 20v):

1443: Willelmus bonar canonicus sanctiandree electus prior post Jacobum haldenstone prefuit 19 annis vir simplex et deuotus chorum libris necessariis decenter ornauit et plurima in usus pauperum exposuit Organa magna et parua horecudium chori non sine magnis sumptibus et labore comparauit Optimam cappam rubeam seu totum vestimentum in principalibus festis usitatum auro dupliciter intextum asportauit. fecit enim diebus suis bona plurima Obiit anno domini 1462 sepultus [ad *omitted*] aspersorium ubi aqua benedicta aspergitur sub sigillo ereo ut apparet ascultantibus.

1462: dauid ramsay canonicus eiusdem loci electus prior vir mansuetus et fratribus suis canonicis multum amabilis hic construxit librarium ex quadratis et politis lapidibus asportauit tabernaculum magni altaris Plura bona fecit in diebus suis et ampliora fecisset si vixisset stetit prior 7 annis.

1469: electus ad prioratus officium fuit Willelmus Cameron eiusdem loci canonicus regularis vir quidem simplex et deuotus Obiit anno salutis nostre 1482.

1483 [But 1482 in right-hand margin]: Cui successit vir generoso sanguine propagatus Magister Johannes hepburn germanus nobilis patricii hepbron comitis de bothwell. vir quidem prudentissimus electus ad prioratum sanctiandree prior sane celeberrimus in toto regno religionisque cultor integerrimus habebatur tante namque constantie extitit ut ecclesiastica sub se beneficia et officia non nisi religiosissimis et doctis viris unquam concedere voluit Sic ut totum quasi monasterium muro lapideo decenter vallauit exterius interius lapidibus viuis: et per viros in diuinis tum et humanis literis imbutos ornauit accuratissime [rest blank to f. 25].

BISHOPS OF ST ANDREWS
(f. 13):

De episcopis Sanctiandree post Kenedem regem Pictorumque expulsionem.

Primus episcopus fuit auites fothad qui antiquum euangeliorum textum dedit argenteum. Sic scribitur: hanc euangelii thecam construxit auites ffothad qui primus scotus episcopus est [*added*, summus scotorum] deinde kellach post quem maleseus qui sedit annis viii post illum kellach 2us et primus episcopus qui adiit roman pro consecratione hic sedit annis 35 deinde Maldinor Maleseus 2us et albinus qui tribus sedit annis post quem Malduvinus filius gillandris tuthaldus quatuor annis postea fothade gregorius cathre edmarus et godericus Obierunt electi.

Turgotus prior dunelmensis sedit annis vii in episcopatu sanctiandree qui obiit anno domini 1109.

Robertus prior de Scona electus postea et consecratus sanctiandree episcopus sedit annis 34 hic electus propter fauorem regis alexandri primi

144

qui terram qui cursus apri dicitur ecclesie sanctiandree restituit ea sub ordine ut inibi constitueretur religio canonicorum regularium Ipse enim equum suum arabicum frenum et sellam ac regio coopertum pallio precioso cum lancea (f. 13v) argentea que nunc est hasta crucis usque ad altare adduci fecit et ecclesiasticis libertatibus regalibus pariter et consuetudinibus ecclesiam inuestiri precepit hic obiit diebus macolmi (*sic*) regis sepultus in veteri ecclesia.

1159: Post hunc Valthenus abbas melrossensis electus est hic ex nobili veterique northumbrorum comitum sanguine descendens Cuius proauus Swardus (*sic*) northumbrie comes cuius auus valdenus comes eiusdem fuit vir animosus quare rex anglie terrore perculsus neptem sibi nomine Iulitam tradidit maritandam ex qua valdenus unam suscepit filiam nomine Matildem Valdenus tandem mandato regis morti adductus et non sine martyrii opinione occidere Matildis vero nupsit symoni samlize comiti de hundyngton de quo duos generauit filios scilicet symonem primogenitum et valthenum hunc abbatem sed primogenitus militari cinctus honore moritur Et pater regis henrici primi incurrebat indignationem quia exheredatus versus Ierusalem cruce signatus diem clausit extremum Valthenus istus electus tantam accipere curam similiter recusauit cuius corpus sanctissimum melrossensi ecclesia sepelitur [*Added at foot*, Valtheni Cuius mater matildis quia consobrina regis anglie traditur in matrimonio dauid regi scotorum una cum comitatu de hundyngton nomine **dotis.**]

1160: Ernaldus electus est episcopus sanctiandree sedit annum unum x menses et xvii dies hic cum rege macolmo fundauit (f. 14) nouam ecclesiam sepultusque est in veteri iuxta predecessorem suum.

1162: Richardus electus est et sedit tam electus quam consecratus per annos xiiii obiit in infirmatorio canonicorum sepultus est in veteri ecclesia cum predecessoribus suis anno 1177 Epitaphium:

> Qui peregrinus ades respice primo
> Robertum ernoldum reliquum dat tumba ricardum.

1177: electus est magister Johannes scotus archedianus (*sic*) sanctiandree cui restitit rex Willelmus quia hugonem capellanum suum consecrari procurauit hinc inde grauis euasit contencio et res ecclesie atque redditus confiscantur quo se uerteret seruus christi Johannes non habebat sed sedem ad apostolicam appellauit et causam suam pape alexandro in protectione commisit ac singula per ordinem veraciter exposuit hiis auditis admirans papa quod vir tante prudentie tamquam canonice electus exulari permitteretur Sed literas apostolicas statim direxit cum ligato (*sic*) quatenus sub excommunicationis et interdicti sententia super regem et sedem ipsum Johannem in episcopum sancti [andree *omitted*] consecrari permitteret Sic cum difficultate in monasterio sancte crucis consecratus. sed regis indignationem pertimescens romam conscito perrexit Cui et papa dixit mane nobiscum et nunquam a latere nostro discedes unum erit nostrum commune marsupium sed et totum regnum scocie sub interdicto papa supponere diffiniuit. Cui Johannes inquit Malo pater sancte episcopalem in vestras resignare manus digni- (f. 14v) tatem quam misse pro animarum redemptione unica die obmitterentur sicque tantam in summi pontificatus postmodum consecutus est gratiam ut quicquid iuridice postularet statim consequeretur. In fauorem regis tandem receptus ad regis saluandum iuramentum episcopatum dunkeldensem tunc vacantem libera permutatione accepit Verum quia linguam populi unius partis diocesis sue ignorabat precauens animarum periculum honestum clericum suum heroldum illius lingue peritum ad apostolicam direxit sedem quatenus episcopatum dunkeldensem in duas diuideret sedes scilicet argadiensem et dunkeldensem perlectis utique literis admirans summus pontifex circumstantibus ait hodie Johannes dunkeldensis episcopus absens corpore nobis literatorie presentatur. Nam quod ceteri moliuntur prolongare solus nititur breuiare. Alii student redditus et pontificatum suum ampliare. Ipse tamen episcopatum satis tenuem conatur dimediare scio quod non cessabit donec mentis assequetur conceptum Et Clerico heroldo vacato episcopum ergadie consecratum ad scociam cum peroptatis remisit literis Johannes item in senectute sancta apud neubotil monachus obiit nec sine opinione sanctitatis.

1178: hugo accessor eius sedit annis decim (*sic*).

(f. 15):

1185: Ricardus (*sic*) rogerus filius comitis leycestre stetit annis xiii sepultusque in veteri ecclesia sanctiandree.

1202: Vilelmus malus vicinus dictus electus instantia regis Willelmi sedit xxxv annis hic ablata a sede et alienata reuocare studuit et episcopatum ampliando ad pristinum reducere statum Voluntarie tamen abstulit a dunfermlyng vicariam de kynglasse et de halis eo quod sibi defecisset vinum dum semel ibidem pernoctasset sepultusque est in noua ecclesia.

1238: dauid per viam compromissi inter ipsum et gaufridum dunkeldensem successit hic ecclesiam de Inchtur a canonicis abstulit sed parum lucri reportauit quia incidit in morbum incurabilem et restituta canonicis ecclesie quanta eiis rex Willelmus dederat moritur et in calco contra morem ecclesie sanctiandree sepelitur.

1253: Abel archidiaconus eidem successit gratia principum et canonicorum electus sed de romana curia infulatus diuertens in ualuis ecclesie scripsit

hec mihi sunt tria lex canon philosophia

Ante crastinum alius subscribebat cuius nomen ignoratur

Te tenent absque bria fraus fauor vana sophia.

Sed imposterum episcopus canonicos suspectos pariter et exosos habuit parum tamen vixit scilicet x mensibus et ii septimanis sepultus in noua ecclesia anno 1254.

(f. 15v):

1254: gamelinus cancellarius alexandri 3 regis scocie sedit xvii annis bene rexit ecclesiam sepultus est ante magnum altare Cui successit Willelmus Wischard vir prudens.

1271: Willelmus Wischard glasguensis episcopus electus et sedit vii annis et sex mensibus hic primus exclusit keledeos ab electione et occidentalem ecclesie plagam vento ad terram derectam de propriis eschaetis sumptuose erexit his temporibus nemo contra ecclesiam aliquid mouere audebat canonicos summe dilexit In noua ecclesia ante magnum altare sepelitur.

1279: Willelmus fraser electus et consecratus sedit annis xviii hic regis anglie declinans tyrannidem secessit ad galliam et ibidem obiit cuius cor ad ecclesiam sanctiandree delatum est et in pariete collocatum est iussit expellere omnes anglicos beneficiatos de scocia cuius executor fuit nobilis vilelmus vallace.

1297: Willelmus lamberton keldeis ab electione penitus exclusis quare eorum prepositus Willelmus cummyng electioni opponens romam adiit sed nihil preualuit Iste episcopus construxit nouum capitulum et multa cetera reparacione monasterii exposuit. Insuper edificauit proprium palacium in sancto andrea Palacium de inchemurdach manerium de monimeil darsy thorry mukkardy carness Munimusk lynton leswade et ly stou de Wedail Preterea pretiosum rubeum vestimentum imaginibus contextum cum (f. 16) mitra et baculo pastorali et plures libros valde bonos eiusdem canonicis reliquit sepultus in boreali parte magne ecclesie sedit annis xxx et totidem septimanis.

1328: Jacobus ben archidiaconus sanctiandree sedit annis quatuor et ii septimanis Iste coronauit regem dauid bross et postea anglorum furiam declinans gallias petiuit et in brugis flandrie obiit sepultus in monasterio canonicorum sancti Augustini ibidem.

1332: Willelmus bel decanus dunkeldensis electus sed variis afflictus incommodis electioni cessit canonicus eiusdem efficitur regularis.

1342: Vyllelmus landalis vir doctus et mansuetus hic rexit sedem 44 annis sepultus in pauimento in ecclesia coram ostio vestibuli in tumba ex ere fabricata.

1385: Valterus trail pugil ecclesie et censor ecclesie hic commendatus a clemente papa descendente linealiter a maria comitissa bolonie filia sancte margarete et macolmi regis scocie de valtero episcopo sic inquit idem papa Iudicio meo dignior es papatu quam episcopatu Iste valterus inter cetera laudabilia vite sue opera construxit castrum sanctiandree sepultus in parte aquilonali sanctiandree.

1401: electus est dominus thomas stewart filius regis roberti et vir columbine simplicitatis qui electioni similiter renunciauit post quem valterus danzelston postulatur hic castrum de dumbertan none sine displicentia regis tenuit vir quidem magnanimus atque viciosus [sic sed recte virtuosus] post illum postulatur (f. 16v) gilbertus grenlaw episcopus aberdonensis sed non consecratus fuit.

1404: Henricus wardlaw doctor iuris nepos magistri valteri vardlaw cardinalis glasguensis episcopi sedit xl annis inter quem et valterum trail sedes vacabat 3 annis hic fundator extitit uniuersitatis sanctiandree qui etiam construxit le gairbrig obiit anno 1440 sepultus in ostio capelle nostre domine.

1440: Jacobus kennydy nepos regis Jacobi primi sedit annis 25 hic construxit collegium saluatoris in ciuitate sanctiandree quod pluribus iocalibus pariter et redditibus dotauit cuius ossa ibidem quiescunt obiit anno nostre salutis 1465 [Added at foot of page: Item episcopus Jacobus kennydy dedit nostre ecclesie vestimentum album optimum cum omni suo apparatu usu in solemniis b. v. marie Item duas nouas cappas rubras deauratas Item mattam magnam rubram bisso intextam que sternitur coram magno altari in principalibus festis et alia plura contulit].

1465: Patricius grame episcopus brechinensis nepos Jacobi predicessoris sui electus in roma archipresul primus in toto regno scocie efficitur Vir corporis forma pariter et scientia clarissimus Hic indulgentias efficacissimas sancti michaelis sedi et ecclesie sanctiandree obtinere promeruit perpulcrum etiam sancte margarite iocale fabricare fecit Insuper infectum pontis opus scilicet le garbrig siue gramis brig perficere mandauit similiterque compleuit fecit enim mirabilia in tempore suo pluraque fecisset si pacifice sedisset Sed innumeris pene fatigatus iniuriis sedem utcunque declinauit ac in insula lacus levin non sine sanctitatis opinione multorum obiit prefuit annis 13 [in margin: sedit annis].

(f. 17):

Consecratus 1477 Willelmus schewess medicus gratia principis electus sedit annis quasi 19 hic primus fuit primas in regno scocie et legatus natus maxime libros diligebat plurimaque comparauit volumina obiit anno virginei partus 1496 sepultus in pauimento ante magnum altare sub decenti tumba.

1496: Jacobus stewart filius regis Jacobi 3 et germanus regis Jacobi quarti dux Rothiacensis electus archiepiscopus sanctiandree necdum consecratusve sacerdos stetit annis nouem hic plures cappas sericas et duo iocalia reliquiarum composuit canonicos summe dilexit plura fecisset inuida nisi mors impedisset Sepultus ante reliquias.

1503: Alexander stewart filius regis Jacobi quarti electus nec tamen consecratus stetit annis 10 morte preuentus in anglia obiit anno 1513.

PLATE XXI. TOMBSTONE OF JOHN WINRAM, ST ANDREWS.

The remains of John Winram's tombstone in St Leonard's college chapel, St Andrews.

L

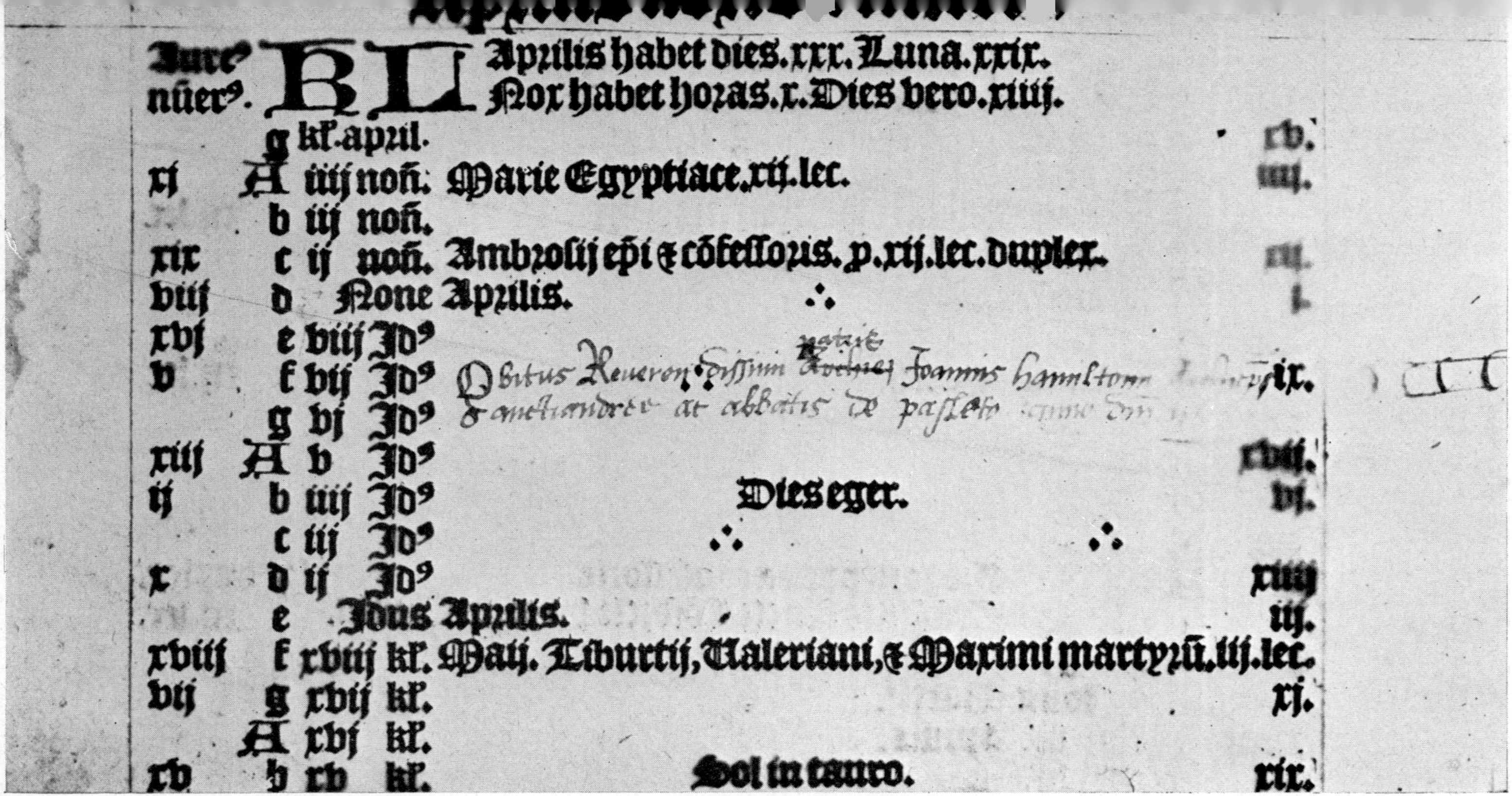
Aure' nūer'. KL Aprilis habet dies.xxx. Luna.xxix.
Nox habet horas.x. Dies vero.xiiij.

g kl.april. xv.
xi A iiij non. Marie Egyptiace.xij.lec. iiij.
b iij non.
xix c ij non. Ambrosij epi & cōfessoris. p.xij.lec.duplex.
viij d None Aprilis.
xvj e viij Id'
v f vij Id' Obitus Reverendissimi patris Joannis hamilton ... Sancti Andree ac abbatis de paslay anno dni ... ix.
g vj Id'
xiij A v Id' xvij.
ij b iiij Id' Dies eger. vj.
c iij Id'
x d ij Id' xiiij
e Idus Aprilis. iij.
xviij f xviij kl. Maij. Tiburtij, Valeriani, & Maximi martyrū.iij.lec.
vij g xvij kl. xj.
A xvj kl.
xv b xv kl. Sol in tauro. xix.

PLATE XXII. OBIT OF ARCHBISHOP JOHN HAMILTON, 1571.

Along with the primatial see of St Andrews, Archbishop John Hamilton held the abbacy of Paisley. In the calendar of a missal, which was apparently still in use in the abbey church at Paisley in 1571, a monk has noted the death of his abbot on 7 April 1571.

1513: electus fuit venerabilis in christo pater Johannes hebron eiusdem ecclesie prior et decanus qui electioni renunciauit Post quem postulatus est Willelmus elpheston episcopus abirdonensis qui paulo post obiit et sedes ad biennium quasi uacauit electus fuit Andreas forman episcopus morauie nec tamen redditibus admissus pacifice usque ad annum domini 1515 hinc e roma rediens archipresul sanctiandree commendatarius perpetuus de dunfermlyng (f. 17v) primas legatus natus cum plena potestate legati a latere in uniuerso regno scocie Quanta bona faciet ecclesie non est mee facultatis euoluere quia futurorum ignarus uiuat feliciter deo gratias [*Added*] sedit annis sex obiit anno domini 1521 xi martii sepultus in pauimento ante magnum altare iuxta predicessorem suum Willelmum scheweze.

OTHER ST ANDREWS REFERENCES

(f. 90v):

1114: Rex alexander apud sconam ecclesiam monasterialem fundauit et eedem terras de lyf et invergory in dotem contulit hic rex dotauit dunfermlyng a patre fundatum Emonia insula sancti columbe fundatur ab eodem hic ecclesiam sancti andree dotauit et canonicos regulares inibi locauit cum preuilegiis regalibus.

(f. 93v):

1159: Obiit Robertus episcopus noster sanctiandree cui successit ernoldus ab alexandro pontifice maximo legatus creatus.

1162: Hoc anno fundata est noua ecclesia Sanctiandree a rege Macolmo et episcopo arnaldo quo etiam anno obiit arnoldus.

(f. 123):

Eodem anno [1411] fundata est ecclesia parochialis sanctiandree cuius primus erat vicarius Willelmus bouar canonicus regularis eiusdem.

(f. 126):

1436: Eodem anno obiit Robertus de cardine episcopus dunkeldensis qui nauem ecclesie dunkeldensis construxit Cui successit Jacobus kenedy nepos regis ex sorore eius comitissa de angus qui post duos annos electus est episcopus sanctiandree.

(f. 132v):

1469: hoc anno 3 aprilis obiit venerabilis pater dauid prior sanctiandree vir mitissimus et cantor egregius.

L

(f. 135v):

1503: hoc anno obiit Jacobus dux et archipresul sanctiandree commendator de dunfermlyng Cui successit alexander filius regis Jacobi quarti et domine margarete boyd amasie regis et sedit decem annis neuter istorum consecratus est.

(f. 137v):

Hac tempestate Magister andreas forman episcopus morauiensis et commendatarius de petwenynin [sic] existens in gallia tanquam procurator et orator regis scocie ac pacis reformator inter regem gallie et pontificem maximum huic rex gallie archiepiscopatum bituricensem tunc vacantem tanquam dilecto clerico regis scotorum ambassiatori gratanter concessit quem episcopatum post mortem regis et belli de flodon exitum idem andreas resignauit in manus summi (f. 138) pontificis in fauorem nepotis eiusdem pape qua de re promotus pontifex idem Leo decimus creauit hunc andream archiepiscopum sanctiandree et commendatarium perpetuum de dunfermlyng et legatum a latere in regno scocie cum plena potestate ad patriam remisit.

(f. 144v):

1523: Jacobus beton archiepiscopus glasguensis translatus est ad metropolim sanctiandree in solemnitate corporis christi.

The Sixteenth-Century Panoramic View of St Andrews

The curious sixteenth-century panoramic view of St Andrews, which was first published in the form of a line-drawing as the frontispiece to the first volume of the Rev. C. J. Lyon's *History of St Andrews* (1843) and of which copies have appeared in subsequent publications, has always been something of a mystery. Lyon (vol. I, p. 4) suggests that it represents the town about the year 1530 to 1540, but he does not disclose the source of this ' bird's-eye view.' The provenance of the drawing was unknown to David Hay Fleming, *Handbook to St Andrews and Neighbourhood* (1894), p. 63; to the Royal Scottish Geographical Society's *The Early Maps of Scotland* (1936), p. 146; to J. B. Salmond and G. H. Bushnell, *Henderson's Benefaction* (1942), opposite p. 17; and to all others who have dealt with it in any way.

The source of Lyon's drawing was quite certainly the panoramic view which is now reproduced as the frontispiece of the present volume. This is a large, late sixteenth-century, or early seventeenth-century engraving ($19\frac{1}{2}$ x $13\frac{3}{4}$ inches) in contemporary colouring, which was bought in 1958 by the National Library of Scotland and is now Ms Acc. 2887 in that collection. This engraving of St Andrews is from the atelier of Georg Braun and Franz Hogenberg who, in 1572, at Cologne, published their celebrated *Civitates orbis terrarum*, or collection of views of the great cities of the world, which was followed, during the next three decades, by a further five volumes of topographical collections. A panoramic view of ' Edenburg,' or ' Edenburgum Scotiae Metropolis ' appears as plate 4 in Braun and Hogenberg's third volume, published in 1581 and, like the other views, it has descriptive letterpress on the back, the letterpress, in this case, being based on the description of Edinburgh by Alexander Alesius, first published in 1550. While it is not so detailed, the Edinburgh view is similar in style to the St Andrews panoramic view and it is likely that both date from approximately the same period. The St Andrews view does not appear in any of the six volumes of the great atlas and the fact that no descriptive letterpress appears on the back of the print suggests that it is not extracted from any atlas volume but rather that it is an isolated broadsheet and the copy in the National Library of Scotland seems to be the only known copy. Where this engraving was, before it was acquired by the National Library, we do not know. It was presumably in some private collection in Scotland in the early nineteenth century when C. J. Lyon had a line-drawing made of it for his *History of St Andrews*. It will be noted that Lyon's nineteenth-century line-drawing has taken some liberties with the original engraving: the ' Ecclesia Perochiae civitatis ' becomes ' ecclesia parochialis sancti [sic] Trinitatis ' and the incorrect ' collegium D. Mariani ' for St Mary's College is simply changed to ' divae Mariae.'

Lyon guessed that the original drawing was made about 1530 or 1540. This is probably too early. It seems reasonable to assume that it was made before the events of June 1559 which destroyed the houses of the Greyfriars and the Blackfriars and also that it could hardly have been made before the early 1550s when, under Archbishop John Hamilton, St Mary's college finally took shape. The fact that the Pends are represented without a vaulted roof is not evidence of destruction but is rather the cartographer's convention to show the street continuing through the barrier. The date when the material for this view of St Andrews was collected would appear to be the mid-1550s. Dean Georg Braun invited scholars, if their city was not already represented in his collections, to send him sketches of their towns so that engravings could be made and published. Material sent to him at Cologne might lie unused for many years before the artist could find time to work it up into a finished engraving or found opportunity for publishing it. Many of the views in the volumes of the great atlas are from drawings at least two decades older than the eventual date of publication.

The probable sequence of events is that some scholar of St Andrews, in the 1550s, responded to Georg Braun's invitation and made sketches and notes of the town which were duly sent to Cologne. (It is unlikely that Alesius provided this material because he had been out of touch with St Andrews since 1532.) At some later date one of the artists of the Braun-Hogenberg publishing house worked the sketches up into this panoramic view which has preserved for us the appearance of the pre-Reformation city of St Andrews. In spite of the distortions made by the artist in his efforts to combine a bird's-eye view with a ground plan of the town, we have the feeling that a serious attempt is made to delineate with some accuracy the little tenements and gardens and public buildings of the city. In spite of their elongated towers, the college kirk of St Salvator, the parish church and the old cathedral are all easily recognizable. The Cologne artist has had some difficulty in interpreting the sketch of the metropolitan cathedral and seems to have decided that an arrangement of prominent corner towers would be appropriate; this was an architectural feature which would be familiar to him in such cathedrals as Speyer, Worms, Mainz, Bonn, Bamberg and other famous churches of the empire. He has also misread the note attached to the Collegium Marianum and produced a 'collegium D. Mariani' but, on the whole, one lays down this strangely effective plan with increased respect for its accuracy.

It seems clear that in St Andrews, in the 1550s, there was sufficient interest in cartography, and sufficient skill in the style of technical drawing required, to supply Braun and Hogenberg with accurate material for the plan of St Andrews. That interest in cartography may have continued at St Andrews and, in the next generation, it probably provided the stimulus for the work of Timothy Pont, who studied at St Leonard's college in St Andrews in the 1580s.

DAVID McROBERTS.

Comparative Interior Dimensions of Some Other Medieval Cathedrals*

Canterbury - - - - - - - -	517 feet
Florence - - - - - - - -	490
York - - - - - - - - -	486
Milan - - - - - - - - -	486
Cologne - - - - - - - - -	468
Rheims - - - - - - - - -	452
Amiens - - - - - - - - -	438
Chartres - - - - - - - -	427
Durham (excluding galilee) - - - - -	418
Paris - - - - - - - - -	402
St Peter's, Rome (the medieval basilica) - - -	400
Toledo - - - - - - - - -	395
Antwerp - - - - - - - -	388
Lubeck - - - - - - - - -	363
Mainz - - - - - - - - -	361

ST ANDREWS:

interior length (excluding narthex) - - -	357
length of nave - - - - - - -	196
length of choir and eastern chapel - - -	125
length of transept - - - - - -	168
overall width of nave and choir - - - -	63
width of nave and choir (centre) - - - -	26
width of aisles - - - - - - -	13
overall width of transept - - - - -	45
height of choir - - - - - - -	63
total area - - - - - - -	- 26,000 sq. ft.

*These comparative interior lengths have been collected from a variety of sources and the exactness of the measurement cannot be guaranteed in each case. While it is true that the interior length of a building is not necessarily related to its actual size, these figures may serve to provide a guide to the comparative dimensions of this representative group of European cathedrals.

Burgos (including eastern chapel) - - - - 357 feet
Upsala - - - - - - - - - 351
Vienna - - - - - - - - - 340
Siena - - - - - - - - - 320
Trondheim - - - - - - - - 317
Santiago de Compostela - - - - - - 315
Pisa - - - - - - - - - 300
Dublin, St Patrick's - - - - - - 300
St David's, Wales - - - - - - - 298
Glasgow - - - - - - - - 285
Roskilde - - - - - - - - 275
Elgin - - - - - - - - - 263
Kirkwall, St Magnus - - - - - - 217
Basle - - - - - - - - - 213
Amalfi - - - - - - - - - 190

RONALD G. CANT.

APPENDIX III

A St Andrews Pilgrimage Certificate of 1333 at Saint-Omer

Pilgrimages in expiation of homicide were an established feature of the judicial system in the Middle Ages. The guilty person was ordered to make a pilgrimage to some distant shrine and bring back a formal certificate stating that the pilgrimage had been duly accomplished. This certificate had to be presented to the judicial authorities who had ordered the pilgrimage and, when accepted by them, the pilgrim was acquitted of his crime. Such certificates are extremely rare but, by good chance, the text of a St Andrews example has survived at Saint-Omer, incorporated in the exoneration of a cleric named William Bondolf of Dunkirk. Bondolf had apparently killed a man named André d'Esquerdes and had been ordered, in expiation of his crime, to pay a fine of twelve livres, to have thirteen masses sung for the soul of the deceased and to make an expiatory pilgrimage to St Andrews in Scotland. The pilgrimage to the shrine of St Andrew was presumably chosen because he was the patron saint of the victim.

Bondolf duly performed his pilgrimage and on 29 May 1333 the Saturday before Trinity Sunday, he received his certificate, certifying the fulfilment of his pilgrimage, from the prior of St Andrews, John of Gowrie. On 26 June 1333, he was back in Saint-Omer, presenting the certificate to the judicial authorities and being absolved from his crime. The document in the Saint-Omer town archives gives the details of the case: it is reprinted here from *Bulletin historique et philologique du Comité des Travaux Historiques et Scientifiques* (1892), pp. 372-373.

*   *   *   *

L'an de grace MCCCXXXIII, le xxvi jour de juing, se comparut devant nous Wille Bondolf, clercs, et présenta unes lettres saines et entières sous la forme qui s'ensuit:

'Universis presentes litteras inspecturis Johannes Dei gracia prior Sancti Andree in Scotia salutem in Domino sempiternam. Cum sit meritorium veritati perhibere testimonium, universitati vestre tenore presentium significamus quod accessit ad monasterium nostrum Sancti Andree, die confectionis presentium, Willelmus, dictus Bondolf, clericus, lator presentium, burgensis et inhabitator ville de Dunkerka, et peregrinationem suam quam subiit pro interfectione Andree d'Esquerdes humiliter peregit in ecclesia nostra conventuali pro anima ejusdem Andree, nobis et conventu nostro presentibus. In cujus rei testimonium, sigillum nostrum presentibus litteris fecimus apponi. Datum apud Sanctum Andream, die sabati in vigilia Sancte Trinitatis anno gracie MCCC tricesimo tertio.'

Et requist li dis Willes, present nous, à Thomas le candeillier, que, comme il eust entièrement parfait toute l'ordenance faite de le pars de le mort Andrieu d'Esquerdes, à savoir est paiiet la somme de xii libvres et fait canter xiii messes pour l'ame du mort, et parfait le voiage de Saint-Andrieu en Escoche, si que il appert par lettres dessus escripte, que li dis Thumas li vausist rendre le chartre faite sus l'ordenance de le pais, et que il remist ledite pais pour bonne et estaule à tous jours, li quels Thumas recognut que lidis Willes avoit bien parfait l'ordenance de ledicte pais, et que le pais tenoit pour bonne et estaule à tousjours, et que ledicte chartre il n'avoit mie, et se il l'avoit il lui rendroit, et quita le dit Wille de tout che dont il avoit esté obligies en l'ordenance de ledicte pais comme celui qui bien avoit tout parfait.

Fait l'an et jour dessus dis.

(Registre G gothique, E moderne, p. 88, aux archives de la ville de Saint-Omer.)

DAVID McROBERTS.

156

APPENDIX IV

The Dependent Priories of St Andrews

I. PORTMOAK

This priory or cell was called variously Lochleven, St Serf's Isle or Portmoak. It had moved from an island in Loch Leven to the nearby mainland and was known by both its old and its new names. The island's culdee monastery was given to the priory of St Andrews in the mid-twelfth century, a grant which was frequently reiterated and confirmed, as the priory register testifies.[1] The dependent status of Lochleven was made clear in 1268 when the prior and convent of St Andrews declared that it was for them in any vacancy to present a new prior from either their own chapter or the Lochleven community. The bishop would then instal him, and the new prior was to be responsible to the bishop as regards spiritualities and to the priory of St Andrews as regards temporalities and regular observance.[2]

According to an old writer, the two houses came to be united and the Lochleven prior to be the *tertius prior* of St Andrews.[3] In 1421 a supplication for papal provision described Lochleven as accustomed to be ruled by canons of St Andrews priory, on which it was dependent.[4] In fact all the priors in the fifteenth century of whom we have certain knowledge were canons of St Andrews. Andrew de Wynton (x1421) significantly continued to describe himself as a canon of St Andrews while in office at Lochleven;[5] perhaps already there was no resident community. The prior provided in 1421 was a St Andrews canon, as was Walter Monypenny, whose term of office spanned at least forty years (1465 x 1506).[6]

Both Michael Donaldson,[7] appointed coadjutor in 1525 and in office in the 1540s, and John Winram,[8] found as prior from 1560, were and continued to be canons of St Andrews. They granted leases and so on with the consent of prior and convent of St Andrews and used the common seal of St Andrews. Significantly, too, they acted in their own name only, with no mention of a community, and in fact some of Winram's documents call Portmoak non-conventual. It had probably been without a community for a century and a half at least. In 1570 the St Andrews chapter, patrons (so they said) of Portmoak for the last five centuries in any vacancy, united it to St Leonard's college,[9] an act that was confirmed by the crown ten years later.

---

1. SRO, RH 6/7; *St A. Lib.* passim. Source references given in Easson, *Religious Houses*, 78-80, will not be repeated.
2. *St A. Lib.*, 121-22, where for *uobis . . . respondere* one should surely read *nobis* and the date 1248 does not fit in with the names.
3. Sibbald, *Fife*, 280.
4. *CSSR*, i, 273.
5. *St A. Lib.*, 6, 11, 15, 19.
6. *ACSB*, 150; SRO, B 65/22, no. 185; *CPL*, xiii, 169, 225.
7. PRO, 31/9/32, fo 79; SRO, E 14/2, fo 336; SRO, NP 1/169, fo 16rv; *RMS*, v 1146.
8. SRO, E 14/2, fos 62, 87v; SRO, E 48/1/1, fo 68v; NLS, Adv. 17.1.3, fos 165, 191; *RMS*, iv, 2934.
9. NLS, Adv. 17.1.3, fo 299.

157

II. PITTENWEEM

This house, originally a Benedictine cell of Reading, was transferred to the jurisdiction of St Andrews and had become a dependent Augustinian priory by the early fourteenth century. At some time, too, the community moved from the Isle of May to Pittenweem on the mainland and thereafter the priory was called by either name. By the early fifteenth century it had declined into being a mere benefice, non-conventual, elective, in the gift of the bishop and chapter of St Andrews and accustomed to be governed by a canon of St Andrews.[10] In less technical language, the St Andrews chapter elected one of its members to be prior of this house lacking a resident community. By this time, of course, chapter's power had been greatly diminished by papal reservation. Nevertheless the four priors from the beginnnig of the century to 1447 were all canons of St Andrews, as were the rival claimants in the vacancies of 1418 and 1421.[11] In 1443 the prior of May is found transacting business as a member of the St Andrews chapter.[12]

A further decline in status took place in 1447 when Bishop Kennedy arranged for the prior then in office to become abbot of Scone while he himself became commendator of May. After Kennedy's death two canons of St Andrews disputed for the priory, but the successful claimant very soon resigned it to the new bishop, Patrick Graham. The priory was annexed to the bishop's *mensa* for Graham's lifetime, during which period a canon of St Andrews, removable at Graham's pleasure, was to be called prior and exercise the cure of souls.[13] Five years later, in December 1472, the union and incorporation of the priory into the episcopal *mensa* was made perpetual.[14] Two canons are found with the title of prior after this date and to the second of these, a canon of Holyrood, Archbishop Scheves pledged that the annexation of the priory to the see would not prejudice his priorship.[15] In 1487, however, Scheves petitioned successfully for the priory to be dissolved and united in perpetuity to the episcopal *mensa*, with only a portion allotted to a canon of St Andrews or other priest appointed at the pleasure of the archbishop.[16] In 1467, 1472 and 1487 the absence of a resident community was stressed, as well as the traditional status of dependence on the priory of St Andrews.

Within ten years, however, Scheves was dead and the status of Pittenweem changed decisively. It is a cogent reminder of the caution with which Roman documents of the period must be received, for papal

10. *CSSR*, i, 9, 260; *CPL*, vii, 292; *CPP*, i, 597.
11. *CPP*, i, 592, 597; *CPL*, vii, 63, 292; *CSSR*, i, 8-9, 89-90, 260; NLS, Adv. 15.1.18, no.15.
12. NLS, Adv. 15.1.18, no. 90.
13. *CPL*, xii, 572-73; *ACSB*, 150.
14. *Vet. Mon.*, 468, *ACSB*, 175.
15. *Cawdor Bk.*, 62; *ACSB*, 189; *APS*, ii, 129.
16. *CPL*, xiv, 157; *ACSB*, 220.

approval, though necessary in the long run, was ineffective unless circumstances in Scotland were also favourable. In 1497 James IV had his brother appointed administrator of the diocese, and it was no doubt by the king's will also that Andrew Forman was made prior of Pittenweem. Forman is found from 1497 as prior [17] and retained the office on becoming bishop of Moray in 1501; from this point on he could only hold Pittenweem *in commendam*. In fact he paid annates for the retention of Pittenweem on being provided to Moray in 1501, and again in December 1513 on being provided to the archbishopric of Bourges.[18]

What happened after Forman was translated to St Andrews in the years following Flodden is not clear, whether he resigned Pittenweem along with other benefices or retained it in virtue of its previous annexation to the see. At some point before his death, however, he seems to have resigned it in favour of his brother Robert, dean of Glasgow. Robert Forman was certainly commendator from 1522 to 1525, when he in turn resigned it to his nephew, John Rule, retaining for himself the fruits and right of regress.[19] Apparently this arrangement was planned in the lifetime of Archbishop Forman,[20] though not negotiated at Rome until October 1525. When Robert Forman died in 1530, John Rule obtained full possession.

These changes were of far-reaching importance. On the surface Pittenweem seems merely to have passed from being a perquisite of the ruling archbishop to being a perquisite of the Forman family. But whereas Andrew and Robert Forman were commendators, John Rule was provided to Pittenweem as a religious prior and was obliged to take the habit and make his religious profession.[21] As a religious superior he was eminently unsuitable, being neither celibate nor law-abiding and of a decidedly bad reputation.[22] In spite of this, Pittenweem had passed from being a mere benefice to having a commendator and now to having an Augustinian prior. Moreover, from being non-conventual it now had a community and it was once more dependent on St Andrews, not by a traditional though empty formula but in reality.

The first indication of a resident community is in 1513 when Andrew Forman and the convent described themselves as *capitulariter congregati*.[23] One must of course be cautious in accepting traditional expressions

---

17. *CDS*, iv, 1644.
18. PRO, 31/9/31, fos, 29, 283.
19. *Fife Ct. Bk.*, 175, 265; *St A. Form.*, i, 171-73, 179-81; PRO, 31/9/32, fo 72.
20. Draft documents of Forman refer to documents of Leo X dealing with the affair (*St A. Form.*, i, 179, 304). Both Forman and Leo X died in 1521. The same draft documents call Pittenweem conventual and mention its subprior, indicating the existence of some community before 1521. (see below.)
21. *St A. Form.*, i, 304-05.
22. Fleming, *Reformation in Scotland*, 188 n; *James V Letters*, 200.
23. NLS, Chrs. 6062.

as corresponding to reality, but in 1522 the chamberlain and two other canons of Pittenweem produced a letter in court and in the following year there is mention of a subprior.[24] Both the chamberlain and the subprior were called Forman. Besides the prior, seven canons signed community documents in 1534 and 1535,[25] and nine in 1541 and 1542,[26] including two formerly at Monymusk. A royal charter in February 1541 referred to the growing number of religious at Pittenweem.[27] Six of the nine were still signing in the 1550s.

The dependent status of Pittenweem at this period is also amply demonstrated. Although Andrew Forman described the priory as a dependent cell of St Andrews with the qualifying phrases *forsan* and *seu olim*,[28] other records make the dependence clear. The prior and convent of Pittenweem leased property with the consent of the prior and convent of St Andrews; this was the case in the transaction of 1513 mentioned above, and so it was with many Pittenweem charters in the 1530s and 1540s. Sometimes the St Andrews seal was hung with that of Pittenweem.[29] That the phrase was no empty one is shown by the king's petition in 1534 (which he afterwards withdrew) asking the pope to allow Pittenweem to lease its possessions without having to consult the prior of St Andrews.[30] In 1550 there was a show of strength when on 15 March the prior of St Andrews canonically summoned John Rule to proffer his obedience in the chapter house at St Andrews in accordance with the status of Pittenweem and the Rule of St Augustine.[31] It seems unlikely that this could have happened had Rule been a commendator and not an Augustinian canon. Some months later, Rule and his community had proffered their obedience, acknowledged their dependent status and renounced any privileges to the contrary, including the use of their seal without the St Andrews seal being hung beside it. The St Andrews prior and community then took Pittenweem under their protection.[32]

There is no doubt therefore that Pittenweem was dependent on St Andrews at this period. The question must also be asked, however, whether Pittenweem retained its separate identity in the years before 1560, since recent writers have asserted that the two communities issued

24. *Fife Ct. Bk.*, 268; *St A. Form.*, i, 54.
25. SRO, GD 147/18; NLS, Chrs. 6089; SRO, GD 169, Inventory of Moncreiff muniments, bundle 28, no. 1 (original seen by kind permission of Miss Moncreiff).
26. NLS, Chrs. 6093, 6097-8, 6100-2; *Yester Writs*, 590-1.
27. *RMS*, iii, 2292.
28. *St A. Form.*, i, 179.
29. *May Recs..*, xxxii, and various sources already cited.
30. *James V Letters*, 259.
31. NLS, Adv. 15.1.18, no. 93, imperfectly transcribed in *May Recs.*, xcv.
32. *May Recs.*, cii.

joint deeds and were integrated at the Reformation. Certainly there are indications, notably the charters issued by James commendator of St Andrews and Pittenweem, that the houses were linked in some way.

In August 1550 the St Andrews community granted pensions to the four sons of John Rule, payment to begin when their prior or another canon of St Andrews obtained possession of Pittenweem after Rule's resignation. The agreement was evidently effective and the resignation was similar to that made by Rule's uncle a quarter of a century earlier. From 1552 Rule is called usufructuar or liferenter of Pittenweem, while James Stewart is designated commendator of St Andrews and Pittenweem. Furthermore, in September 1552 Rule set the priory of Pittenweem in tack to Stewart, with generous provision for himself.[33]

Stewart was superior of both priories for fifteen years, until in September 1567 the crown granted Pittenweem to Sir James Balfour of Pittendreich.[34] For all that, a closer examination of the evidence shows that there was no union of the two priories or their communities. The most that can be said is that they resembled Scotland and England in the seventeenth century when the same sovereign ruled the two countries. In his charters, Stewart was often designated or signed himself commendator of St Andrews and Pittenweem, though often also of St Andrews alone or Pittenweem alone, for there was no consistency in the matter. When the designation was commendator of one house, it was clearly a transaction concerning that house; when the designation was commendator of both houses, it could be a transaction concerning either St Andrews or Pittenweem. But of the many extant documents, not one is a joint deed of the two houses. In fact the pattern is the same as with Stewart's brother, also called James, who was commendator of Kelso and Melrose and issued charters under this joint designation but in the name and with the consent of one community alone.

In Pittenweem charters, whether Stewart was styled commendator of both priories or of Pittenweem alone, the grant was made with the consent of the St Andrews convent while the signatures were those of the Pittenweem convent alone. The register of St Andrews and Pittenweem begun in the 1550s has a separate section for Pittenweem deeds[35] and there was certainly no amalgamation of temporalities. Stewart in 1567 sent for the rental books and chapter seals of both priories, as ' ane dowble procuratorye ' might be needed for resignation of the temporal lands,[36] and later that year he retained St Andrews while James Balfour was given Pittenweem. In this wealth of documentation and varied

33. *May Recs.*, ciii, cviii, cx.
34. *RSS*, vi, 18.
35. NLS, Adv. 17.1.3, fos 197, 206-95 (fos 198-205 were apparently written on later).
36. *HMC*, vi, App. 642-43.

formulas, Stewart is once designated prior of the metropolitan church and of the monastery of Pittenweem annexed to the same,[37] but the word *annexi* used on this single occasion must surely be taken to indicate the dependent status of Pittenweem.

Up to the year 1555 the Pittenweem community is far better documented than that of St Andrews. No new name appears in it after 1541. Of the nine men recorded in 1541 and 1542, Alan Galt and George Nisbet do not appear at any later date and Henry Congilton does not appear after 1547.[38] The remaining six all signed in the years 1548-53[39] and comprised the whole resident community at the visitation of 1554: Patrick Forman, subprior, Robert Wright, Bartholomew Forman, James Murray, Thomas Wright and Patrick Anderson.[40] Of these, all but Patrick Forman are found in 1558.[41] Not a single one of these Pittenweem canons signs with the St Andrews community in 1555 or 1566 or any other year.[42] The signature John Rule in 1566 is not that of the former Pittenweem prior reduced to the ranks as a simple canon but of the St Andrews canon, most probably Rule's son, who is found still signing at St Andrews in 1586.[43]

Strangely enough, the document most likely to mislead belongs to 1568 when Pittenweem once again had a separate commendator, also called James. James, commendator of Pittenweem, and the convent granted a pension with consent of the commendator and convent of St Andrews. James signed J. Balfour; Bartholomew Forman and James Murray also signed. Stewart then signed simply James Stewart, and Peter Ramsay (a St Andrews canon) also signed, but clearly according to the terms of reference these two did so to signify the needed consent. It is not a joint deed even though only three of the five signatories belong to Pittenweem.[44] In fact this post-Reformation document manifests the status of Pittenweem in the decades before 1560, subordinate to St Andrews priory but separate and with a community of its own.

III. MONYMUSK

There is a certain *prima facie* case for considering Monymusk priory a dependent house of St Andrews. It was originally under the church of St Andrews, its original culdee community became Augustinian canons,

---

37. NLS, Adv. 17.1.3, fo 287.
38. SRO, GD 147/19.
39. SRO, RH 6/1428; SRO, GD 147/17, 147/18, 147/19.
40. British Museum, Harley 4637 C, fo 167; NLS, Adv. 29.4.2, Vol. 6, fo 36.
41. NLS, Chrs. 6112 (wrongly attributed to 1548 in *Pitfirrane Writs*), 6768; SRO, GD 147/17.
42. See above, 132-133. One must therefore abandon the views expressed by J. O'Dea in *Essays on the Scottish Reformation*, 238, and by C. Haws in *RSCHS*, xvi, 207. Martine's figure quoted by the former is not taken from a particular document (and so not from a joint deed, as is suggested) but is the sum of the names he found in various sources.
43. For this John Rule see above, 133; NLS. Adv. 17.1.3, fo 196v; SRO, RH 6/2818.
44. SRO, RH 6/2134.

its documents are found in St Andrews priory register. In the early fifteenth century three of its priors were canons of St Andrews and in the sixteenth century Monymusk canons are found signing at St Andrews and Pittenweem. The editor of the St Andrews register (1841) has been followed by later writers in presuming that Monymusk was joined to St Andrews priory.[45]

The evidence to the contrary is nevertheless conclusive. In the first place, Monymusk's subjection was to the bishop, not the priory of St Andrews. According to the chroniclers, King Malcolm vowed the barony of Monymusk to St Andrew, territory that was later described as the episcopal lands of Monymusk granted by Malcolm to the *ecclesia* of St Andrews.[46] It can reasonably be assumed that *ecclesia* bears the common medieval sense of ' see.' Monymusk in the early thirteenth century was included in the possessions of the bishop of St Andrews, who still held the lordship of Monymusk in the sixteenth century.[47]

The bishop of St Andrews subsequently endowed the priory of Monymusk and was considered its founder.[48] In the early thirteenth century he had the final word in selecting the prior, who then swore fidelity to him; the brethren's rule of life was subject to his consent and he was to be received with solemnity if he visited Monymusk. Again, it was the bishop of St Andrews who at the request of prior and community issued a mandate about brethren of Monymusk returning to the world.[49]

The intention here is not to unravel the complicated status of Monymusk priory and parish church. Monymusk became a prebend of Aberdeen cathedral and was also a mensal church of the bishop of St Andrews,[50] and already in early times the bishop of Aberdeen had declared that the priory should be subject to no person but himself.[51] But enough has been said to show that the relations of Monymusk with St Andrews were with the bishop and not with the priory. It is noteworthy that the Monymusk documents in St Andrews priory register never refer to the priory and canons of St Andrews. Perhaps they were included because of the priory's interest as diocesan chapter, and indeed there are references in them to chapter's consent.

45. *St A. Lib.*, xvi. An eighteenth-century account, printed in 1843, gives the same view (*A.B. Coll.*, 169).
46. *A.B. Coll.*, 169, 171.
47. *CPL*, i, 30, 61; *St A. Rent.*, passim; *A.B. Ill.*, iii, 499, iv, 479-81; *Prot. Bk. Cristisone*, 131.
48. *St A. Lib.*, 366, 369, 371. But cf. *MRHS*, 79.
49. *St A. Lib.*, 370-72, 368-69.
50. W. D. Simpson. ' The Augustinian priory and parish church of Monymusk, Aberdeenshire,' *PSAS*, lix, 44-45, 67-70.
51. *St A. Lib.*, 374-75.

Three successive priors of Monymusk in the early fifteenth century were said by Walter Bower to be canons of St Andrews. The context, however, shows that the dependent status of Monymusk was not being demonstrated, but rather the reverse. Bower, himself a canon of St Andrews, was extolling the merits of St Andrews under its prior, James Bisset, many of whose disciples (he said) attained high ecclesiastical office: a bishop of Ross, an abbot of Scone, an abbot of Inchcolm (Bower himself) and three priors of Monymusk in succession.[52] A glance at the Roman curial records shows the somewhat squalid reality behind the chronicler's noble language, as canons of St Andrews, Scone, Holyrood and Inchcolm tried to obtain the priorship of Monymusk in the years 1424-31.[53] The growing tendency towards crown nomination and papal provision, coupled with the benefice hunting of the time, was destroying the traditional system of election, but apparently the routine at Monymusk was nomination (after election) by the community, presentation by the bishop of St Andrews and institution by the bishop of Aberdeen.[54] As before, the priory of St Andrews is not mentioned, while the bishop of St Andrews has rights of patronage.

There is explicit though on the whole negative evidence that Monymusk was in no way dependent on St Andrews priory in the sixteenth century.[55] The induction of a new prior in 1522 was carried out by the treasurer of Aberdeen diocese. When this prior had a new common seal made, the protest considered only the rights of the priory and its residents. A coadjutor prior was put in by papal and episcopal authority (apostolica primo et deinde . . . ordinaria auctoritatibus) and given full power (omnimoda potestas) by decree of the bishop and chapter of Aberdeen. A charter by prior and coadjutor bore the seals of the priory and the coadjutor, while the convent described it as ' giffin be owr suprem heid ' and spoke of ' owir Prior ordinar or administrator haffand jurisdictioun on wss.'[56]

This silence with regard to St Andrews and its rights and its capitular consent is significant, and the same silence speaks even more eloquently in a notarial instrument drawn up after a meeting of the priors of St Andrews and Monymusk. The two met as equals and agreed to cancel their mutual debts; the Monymusk prior on his side had been intromitting with the fruits of St Andrews priory, perhaps its possessions in

---

52. *Chron. Bower*, i, 373.
53. *CSSR*, ii, iii, passim; *CPL*, vii, 513.
54. *CSSR*, iii, 2.
55. Where no reference is given the source is *A.B. Ill.*, iii, 484-99 (also found in *Prot. Bk. Cristisone*); *A.B. Coll.*, 179-84.
56. *A.B. Coll.*, 183, 179, 180, 181.

PLATE XXIII. EARLY THIRTEENTH-CENTURY HEAD OF CHRIST.

Found during excavations at the site of St Andrews cathedral in August 1894.

PLATE XXIV. BISHOP KENNEDY'S MACE.

Upper part of the mace given by Bishop James Kennedy to his college of St Salvator. Elaborate as it is, the design appears to be incomplete in its present condition. A crowning half-length figure of the Eternal Father should probably surmount the mace-head and angel musicians should stand in the battlemented turrets.

the north-east. It is hardly possible that all mention of the relationship of dependence could have been omitted had it existed.

The presence of Monymusk canons at Pittenweem and St Andrews can be given a very reasonable explanation, but first the background at Monymusk must be described. David Forbes was inducted as prior in 1522, his predecessor remaining there as usufructuar and acting as delegated superior while the new prior resided elsewhere. The arrangement does not seem to have worked too well. There was the matter of the common seal, and twice the old prior asked local magnates to honour their guarantee of protection.[57] In 1533 David arrived back on the scene and demanded the obedience of the community. Serious strife ensued, centred on one of the canons, Alan Galt, and in November 1534 divine office was suspended. Galt refused to submit to the penance imposed, most of the community sided with him and office was once more suspended the following June. At this time the community numbered half a dozen besides the prior.

When the internal condition of Monymusk next comes to light, in 1549-50, the community consisted of only two canons and the buildings were in ruins. Practically the whole of Monymusk apart from the monastery itself was set in feu. The internal troubles and ruinous state of the buildings are surely the reason why Monymusk canons are found in other monasteries and not in their own. William Wilson signed at St Andrews in the late 1540s and 1555, while Alan Galt, Patrick Anderson and James Murray arrived at Pittenweem between 1535 and 1541. These are names of four of the six canons known to belong to Monymusk in the 1530s.

Identification based on names alone can never be cut and dried. Wilson's name is a common one and the St Andrews canon is reasonably to be identified with the Dominus Willelmus Wilson who matriculated at St Andrews in 1539,[58] though this does not prevent identification with the Monymusk canon. On the other hand, the James Murray found at Pittenweem from 1541 to 1568 can hardly be the James Murray who was at Monymusk in 1549-50 and was still receiving his Monymusk portion in 1574.[59] Of the other two, Anderson has a fairly common name, but Galt's is distinctive enough to make identification with the man in the trouble at Monymusk reasonably certain. It would therefore seem that, of a community of six, Galt certainly and two others probably are later found at St Andrews or its dependent house of Pittenweem. But the transfer is sufficiently explained without positing any special relationship of Monymusk with St Andrews.

---

57. *A.B. Ill.*, iii, 486-87; *Prot. Bk. Cristisone*, 89.
58. For Wilson at St Andrews see above, 132-133; *St A Recs.*, 243; NLS, MS 73, no. 10 (the transcript of which in *Mort. Reg.*, i, 6, omits Wilson's signature).
59. For Murray at Monymusk, see *A.B. Coll.*, 179, 181; *RPC*, ii, 389-90.

M

The fortunes of Monymusk did not revive. It had been almost entirely burned by 1554, was described as 'distroyit' in 1558 and remained feued to laymen.[60] Of the two canons in 1550 only one remained in 1574.[61] And just as in Monymusk records there is no mention implying dependence on St Andrews, so in St Andrews records there is no reference to Monymusk. The contrast with the priories of Portmoak and Pittenween is striking and conclusive.

MARK DILWORTH, O.S.B.

---

60. SRO, E 48/1/1, fo 389.
61. There can hardly have been four at the Reformation as suggested by C. Haws in *RSCHS*, xvi, 207.

APPENDIX V

Bishop Kennedy's Mace

Apart from a few broken fragments of sculptured stone, nothing survives of the medieval furnishings of the metropolitan church of St Andrews. These furnishings were claimed by contemporaries to be among the finest in the kingdom[1] and, to gain some idea of their quality, we might do well to look briefly at the most important example of the medieval silversmith's craft which has survived at St Andrews, the mace given by Bishop James Kennedy to the college which he had founded in honour of the Holy Saviour. While this mace was never part of the equipment of the cathedral, it does provide us with some evidence for the quality of craftsmanship that a bishop of St Andrews might commission for his cathedral and it illustrates very clearly the amount of theological, as well as of artistic, thinking that went into the production of an ornament for the use or embellishment of a church in medieval times.

The mace presented to St Salvator's college by Bishop Kennedy is the most important piece of late medieval ecclesiastical silver to have survived in Scotland. Commissioned by Bishop Kennedy, it was made in Paris in 1461 by Jean Mayelle who, at that time, was one of the wardens of the Incorporation of Goldsmiths of Paris. In its elaborate design, the mace is typical of late medieval French orfèvrerie.[2]

An intriguing feature of the mace is the fact that the Parisian goldsmith has signed his work in a short inscription, written not in French or Latin as one might expect, but in Scots: ' Johne Maiel Gouldsmithe and Verlette off Chamer til the Lord the Dalfyne hes made this Masse in the Toune of Paris the yher of our Lorde mcccclxi.' The fact that the inscription is in Scots suggests that the goldsmith was a Scotsman and the Frenchified form, Maiel (or Mayelle), probably conceals some Scots name such as Maule or Meile. We need not be surprised at a Scotsman being ' Verlette of Chamer ' to the dauphin since the dauphin's first wife (who died in 1445) was the eldest daughter of King James I, the Princess Margaret, who was incidentally a full cousin to Bishop James Kennedy. This relationship probably explains why the commission to make the mace was placed with Maiel in Paris. The inscription also informs us that the mace must have been finished and the inscription engraved in the early part of the year because the dauphin succeeded to the French throne as King Louis XI on 22 July 1461.

In the year 1892, the *Proceedings of the Society of Antiquaries of Scotland* published a long and erudite article by Alexander J. S. Brook

---

1. Hector Boece, speaking of Prior John Hepburn's extensive restoration of the buildings and furnishings of the priory, remarks ' *basilica maiori interioribus ornamentis (quibus nihil pulchrius ad diuinum cultum) ingenti sumptu comparatis ornata.* '
2. See Plate xxiv.

on the university maces of Scotland.[3] Deservedly this article has since been regarded as the standard account of these national treasures and all subsequent accounts of Bishop Kennedy's mace have been based on Brook's article. Unfortunately, there are two inaccuracies in Alexander Brook's description of the Kennedy mace and these inaccuracies, repeated by later writers, have made it difficult to grasp the unity of design of the mace or to form a coherent interpretation of its symbolism.

The first of these inaccuracies concerns the decoration of the staff of the mace. The staff of the mace is ornamented with spiral bands which display alternating motifs of a columbine flower and a crowned monogram. The letters of the crowned monogram Brook reads as I K and, forty years later, the *Fife Inventory* of the Historical Monuments Commission simply assumes that these are the initials of Bishop James Kennedy who commissioned the mace. This, of course, is quite untenable. If these letters were indeed the initials of James Kennedy, we would expect them to be surmounted by a mitre. Kennedy would never have dared to surmount his initials with a crown: such an action would surely have left him open to a charge of *lèse-majesté*. Kennedy, however, is free from suspicion of any such charge because the letters are quite clearly not I K but Jh. These two letters are used here as the monogram of the name Jhesus, the usual form that the Holy Name assumed in fifteenth-century literature and art. The Holy Name was depicted, for example, as Jhesus on the famous banner, painted in 1429 by the Scots artist, James Polwarth, for La Pucelle.[4] The Jh here represents the name Jhesus and, in the fifteenth century, it was perfectly orthodox, politically as well as theologically, to surmount the Holy Name with a crown. Andrew Melville's thesis of the kingship of Christ was by no means a sixteenth-century innovation in Christian thought.

The second inaccuracy in Alexander Brook's description of the mace is his identification of one of the three figures which stand round the head of the mace. According to Brook, these represent a bishop, a king and a mendicant friar. Brook actually decides that the third figure is clothed in the habit of an Observantine friar. This is also incorrect. This third figure wears a normal form of secular dress such as one sees merchants and well-to-do townsfolk wearing in Flemish altar-pieces, French manuscript miniatures, or in Italian frescoes, which date from the fifteenth century. The three figures undoubtedly represent a bishop, a king and a burgess—the Three Estates of the Christian realm.

Once these inaccuracies are cleared out of the way, it becomes a little less difficult to appreciate the symbolism of Bishop Kennedy's mace. The mace is entirely devoted to one theme, the triumph of Christ the Redeemer, the titular of Bishop Kennedy's college, and the glory of the name Jesus, which Christ bore as Saviour of mankind.

3. Alexander J. S. Brook. ' The University, Civic and Judicial Maces of Scotland ' in *Proc. Soc. Antiq. Scot.*, xxvi (1891-2), 440-474.
4. Francisque Michel, *Les Ecossais en France* (Paris, 1862), i, 174-5.

In working out the design of the mace, Kennedy has turned to that passage in Holy Writ, which was the scriptural foundation for medieval devotion to the Holy Name, the well-known paean of praise in honour of Christ the Redeemer, which St Paul introduces into his Epistle to the Philippians (ch. II, vv. 8-11): ' *Humiliavit semetipsum, factus obediens usque ad mortem, mortem autem crucis. Propter quod et Deus exaltavit illum, et donavit illi nomen quod est super omne nomen, ut in nomine Jesu omne genu flectatur caelestium, terrestrium et infernorum, et omnis lingua confiteatur quia Dominus Jesus Christus in gloria est Dei Patris.'* James Kennedy, the theologian, and Jean Mayelle, the silversmith, between them have produced a mace which is, in effect, an artistic commentary on these words of St Paul.

The central feature of the mace is the figure of Christ, standing on the orb of the world, which is the conventional manner in which Christ is represented as St Salvator, the Saviour of the world. This figure is enclosed within the head of the mace, which is designed as an open architectural shrine. The figure of the glorified Christ is surrounded by three angels on bended knee, holding the Instruments of the Passion. Christ is exalted because he humbled himself to the death of the cross and now the angels of heaven bend the knee in honour of his name Jesus, which signifies Saviour and Redeemer—' *ut in nomine Jesu omne genu flectatur caelestium.'*

The mace-head is elaborate enough in its present state but it would appear that, in the original design, it was even more elaborate. Brook noticed that traces of a figure remain on top of one of the three turrets which project from the head of the mace. The head of the mace is a representation of the Celestial City and, as in other medieval examples of this theme, all three projecting turrets would have angelic figures, carrying musical instruments and looking upwards at some holy image which, in this case, would almost certainly be a half-length figure of the Eternal Father surmounting the main architectural element of the composition. For similarity of imagery, the Kennedy mace might be compared with the magnificent reliquary of the Holy Thorn, made for Louis, Duc d'Orléans, about the year 1400.[5] In the central niche of the Holy Thorn reliquary, the glorified Christ stands on the orb of the world; the crowning finial of the composition is a half-length figure of the Eternal Father and the crenellated turrets, which form the base of the reliquary, have half-length figures of angels blowing the trumpets for the Resurrection of the Dead. Almost certainly, figures of angel musicians and a half-length figure of the Eternal Father formed part of the original design of the Kennedy mace and illustrated St Paul's phrase about Christ being ' in the glory of God the Father,' but, even in its present condition, the mace-head proclaims the veneration of the citizens of heaven for the world's Saviour.

---

5. Illustrated in Joan Evans, *Art in Mediaeval France*, 987-1498 (London, 1948), plate 197.

Before leaving this upper part of the mace, we might note that, on each of the three sides of the mace-head, a flight of steps leads up to the top-most mansion of the Heavenly City. In each flight the number of steps is the mystical number seven. It is unlikely that this number was chosen at random and the probable intention is to teach us that access to the Heavenly Jerusalem is to be sought by way of the seven sacraments.

The homage of mankind—'*terrestrium*'—is indicated by the three figures of bishop, king and burgess, representing the Three Estates of the Christian commonwealth. Lastly, in the lower part of the architectural head of the mace, is placed the dungeon of hell and, at its entrances, can be seen the chained demons, signifying the submission of the powers of darkness to the Holy Name of the Saviour—'*et infernorum.*' But the mace reminds us that the devil is not completely confined to hell and the lions, which appear in front of the gates of hell between the figures of bishop, king and burgess, are probably placed there to repeat the warning, given by St Peter: '*vigilate, quia adversarius vester diabolus, tanquam leo rugiens, circuit quaerens quem devoret, cui resistite fortes in fide*' (I Peter, ch. V, vv. 8-9).

The redemptive work of St Salvator and the glory of his Holy Name continually overflow into the world and regenerate our human existence. For Bishop Kennedy, as for St Paul, this continuation of Christ's saving work is intimately associated with the activity of the Holy Ghost—'*per lavacrum regenerationis et renovationis Spiritus sancti quem effudit in nos abunde per Jesum Christum salvatorem nostrum*' (Titus, ch. III, vv. 5-6). This is indicated by the spiral bands, which decorate the staff of the mace and display the alternating motifs of a columbine flower and the crowned monogram of the Saviour's name. The seven-petalled columbine was used by Flemish artists (and used also in Scotland, where it occurs on the Fetternear Banner) to symbolise the seven gifts of the Holy Ghost. The shaft of the mace represents our life on earth and no doubt, for Bishop Kennedy, the repeated columbine symbol of the Holy Ghost represented his regenerative work in this world, of which the Psalmist speaks: '*Emittes spiritum tuum et creabuntur, et renovabis faciem terrae,*' (Ps. CIII, 30), while the repeated monogram of the Holy Saviour would suggest that the whole earth resounds with the praise of the Holy Name as in that other verse of the Psalmist: '*Domine, Dominus noster, quam admirabile est nomen tuum in universa terra!*' (Ps. VIII, 2). These decorative bands envelop the knops on the staff, with their figures illustrating the Parable of the Talents and the academic figures of scholars and masters. These, it seems to say, while they live their lives in this world, receive in abundance the gifts of the Holy Ghost, but they are warned by the Parable of the Talents of their responsibility to produce the fruits of good works according to their abilities and according to the graces they have received and also, by their learning and scholarship, they must promote on earth the acknowledgement of Christ's glory so that '*omnis lingua confiteatur quia Dominus Jesus Christus in gloria est Dei Patris.*'

Farthest away from the Celestial City, represented in the head of the mace, and beyond the reach of the bands, decorated with the columbine and the crowned monogram of the Holy Name, the mace ends in a splendid *fleuron* of foliage and prancing lions. It might not be too fanciful to imagine that the designer intended the *fleuron* to represent that uncharted and dangerous world that lay beyond the frontiers of Christendom, making it the equivalent of those areas where the early map-makers wrote: ' *Terra incognita* ' or, more picturesquely, ' Here be monsters.' Or again, in this dramatic contrast between the shaft of the mace, with its figures of talented and scholarly men set against a background, permeated with the gifts of the Holy Ghost and resonant with the praise of the Holy Name, and the exuberant vegetation and wild beasts of the *fleuron*, the designer may be suggesting the contrast which medieval men saw between the calm, orderly and pious academic life of the scholar and the ' *fera et agrestis vita* ' of ordinary human endeavour.

The mace of St Salvator's college is not just a commonplace article, purchased without thought by Bishop James Kennedy on a visit to Paris. It is a handsome *jocale,* carefully designed for its future purpose and setting, an ornament on which the purchaser has expended much meditation and the craftsman much skill. It is a permanent sermon in silver, bequeathed by their founder to the foundationers of his college, reminding them of the veneration they must show to the Saviour and his Holy Name and bidding them keep before their eyes the stern lesson of the Parable of the Talents. The dependence of the imagery of the mace on the text of the Epistle to the Philippians might well escape the modern student, for Holy Writ is no longer the all-pervasive influence that it was in medieval thought, but the whole symbolism would be immediately obvious to the early generations of Bishop Kennedy's scholars, especially during the Triduum Sanctum, when the words of St Paul found solemn expression in the *Christus factus est* antiphon of Tenebrae.

Bishop Kennedy's mace is assuredly an item of furnishing which has richness of meaning as well as excellence of craftsmanship. There are indications that these characteristics were not exceptional among the furnishings provided for Scottish medieval churches, and accordingly we can assume that, in the great church of St Andrews, much of the furnishing in metal-work, wood-carving, stained glass, manuscript illumination, in embroidery, painting and kindred crafts, would be of much more than passing interest.

DAVID McROBERTS.

INDEX OF PERSONS

ABEL, MASTER, de GULLANE, archdeacon, 40, bishop, 78, 85, 146
ACCA, bishop of Hexham, 97
ADAM, prior, 141, 142
AED, son of MAELMITHID, 97
ALANE, ALEXANDER (ALESIUS), 107, 151
ALBANY, JOHN, duke of, 45
ALBIN, bishop of Brechin, 40
ALDHELM, ST, 72
ALESIUS, see ALANE
ALEXANDER, of Edinburgh, 43
ALEXANDER I, king, 6, 8-10, 11n, 67, 149
ALEXANDER II, king, 37
ALEXANDER III, king, 26, 37, 39, 69, 110
ALEXANDER, his son, 106
ALLANSON, JOHN, see DUNCAN-SON
ANDERSON, PATRICK, 162, 165
ANGUS I, king, 1n
ANGUS II, king, 1
ANNAND, JOHN, principal of St Leonard's, 137
ANSELM, ST, archbishop of Canterbury, 8
ARNOLD, bishop, 12, 33, 64, 145
ARNOT, JOHN, graniter of Arbroath, 54
ARRAN, EARL OF, 62
AUCHMOWTY, JAMES, chamberlain of Arbroath, 50-51, 54, 56
AUCHMOWTY, ROBERT, 51

BAILIE, BERNARD, chamberlain, 49-50, 53, 54-55
BAILIE, CUTHBERT, commendator of Glenluce, 50
BAILIE, RICHARD, 50
BAILIE, WILLIAM, of Bakky, 50n
BALBUTHY, WILLIAM de, sub-prior, 75, 143
BALFOUR, HENRY, royal chaplain and almoner, 51
BALFOUR, JAMES, 60-1, 161
BALFOUR, MARTIN, canon, provost of St Salvator's, 47-8, 54
BALLANTYNE, JOHN, notary, 54
BALNAVES, HENRY, 48, 55n
BARDE, GILBERT, vicar of Alva, 82

BEATON, ALEXANDER, cardinal's son, 58
BEATON, ARCHIBALD of Capildrae, 49-50
BEATON, DAVID, archbishop, cardinal, 45-62 passim, 92-3, 95, 107, 108, 109, 116
BEATON, DAVID, of Melgund, son of Cardinal Beaton, 49
BEATON, ELIZABETH, cardinal's daughter, 56
BEATON, JAMES, archbishop of Glasgow, later of St Andrews, 45, 49, 50, 52, 53, 92, 94, 108, 150
BEATON, JAMES, nephew of the cardinal, 56
BEATON, JANET, cousin of the cardinal, 50n
BEATON, JOHN, of Balfour, 49, 56
BEATON, MARGARET, 58n
BEATON, ROBERT, of Creich, steward and bailie of the regality, 50
BEATON, WALTER, canon of Glasgow (Govan), 47, 59
BEAUMONT, ROGER, bishop, 20n, 21, 146
BELL, WILLIAM, dean of Dunkeld, bishop elect, 86, 87, 147
BEN, JAMES, bishop, 86, 147
BENEDICT XIII, pope, 104, 113
BERCHAN, 3-4
BERNARD de LINTON, abbot of Arbroath, 110
BERNHAM, DAVID de, bishop, 22n, 33-44 passim, 84-5, 146; chaplains to, 43
BERNHAM, SIR ROBERT, Mayor of Berwick, 34
BERNHAM, WILLIAM, student, 33n
BIGGAR, THOMAS, canon, 133
BISHOPS of St Andrews, 144-49
BISSET, BALDRED, 110, 114
BISSET, HABBAKUK, 120
BISSET, JAMES, prior, 31, 64, 66, 75-6, 81, 105
BISSET, THOMAS, prior, 142, 143
BLAIR, WILLIAM, musician, 55
BOECE, HECTOR, 65
BONAR, DAVID, cardinal's secretary, 60

173

BONAR, WILLIAM, prior, 66, 77, 84, 129, 141, 144
BONAR, WILLIAM, of Rossie, 61
BONDOLF, WILLIAM, 155
BONIFACE VIII, pope, 110, 114
BORTHWICK, SIR JOHN, 109
BOWER, WALTER, 62, 63, 74, 89, 105, 111, 138, 164
BOWER, WILLIAM, canon, 32, 73, 115, 143
BRADFUTE, WILLIAM, 133
BRAUN, GEORG, 151-2
BROG, ROBERT, canon, 22n, 115
BROOK, ALEXANDER J. S., 167-8
BROWN, JOHN, commissary of St Andrews, 49, 54, 152
BRUCE, ROBERT, king, 26, 111, 112
BRUDE, king of Fortriu, 1n
BUTE, Third Marquis of, 32

CADOG, ST, 6
CAMERON, WILLIAM, prior, 129, 138, 143
CAMPBELL, ALEXANDER, OP, 108
CARION, 138
CATHULL, ROBERT, canon, 114
CATROE, ST, 97
CELI DE, see Culdees
CELLACH I, bishop, 3, 6
CELLACH II, bishop, 5, 144
CHAPMAN, JOHN, notary, 54
CHISHOLM, WILLIAM, bishop of Dunblane, 59, 108
CHRISTISON, DAVID, 51, 60
CLEMENT III, pope, 37
CLEMENT VII, pope, 113
COCKBURN, JOHN, merchant, 60
COLET, JOHN, 73
COMYNS, 40
COMYN, WILLIAM, 111
CONGILTON, HENRY, 162
CONSTANTINE, son of Aed, king, 3-4, 97
COOK, GEORGE, secretary to archbishop James Beaton, 49, 53
COUTTS, ALAN, 56
CRANSTON, ANDREW, 139
CRANSTON, THOMAS, abbot of Jedburgh, 113n
CRICHTON, ABRAHAM, official of Lothian, 47-8
CRICHTON, ALEXANDER, chamberlain, 50, 50n, 60
CRICHTON, ALEXANDER of Brunston, 57

CRICHTON, GEORGE, bishop of Dunkeld, 59, 108
CRICHTON, ROBERT, 59
CROFT, SIR JAMES, 119n
CULDEES, 2, 4, 8-9, 21, 38, 126, 157
CULEN, king, 5
CUNNINGHAM, WILLIAM, chaplain, 43

DALZIEL, sons of the baron of, 57
DANIELSTON, WALTER, postulated bishop, 148
DAVID, earl of Huntingdon, 22n, 37
DAVID I, king, 10, 20n, 147
DAVID II, 103
DE MOULINS, M. de, 60
DEMPSTER, THOMAS, 138
DONALDSON, MICHAEL, canon, 56, 157
DOUGLAS, ARCHIBALD, duke of Touraine, 70
DOUGLAS FAMILY, 113
DOUGLAS, SIR JAMES of Dalkeith, 113
DOUGLAS, JOHN, 128
DOUGLAS, MARGARET, mother of James Stewart, 117
DOUGLAS, MARGARET, countess of, 98
DUNBAR, GAVIN, archbishop of Glasgow, 59-60, 108
DUNBAR, JOHN, earl of Moray, 30n
DUNCAN, earl of Fife, 98, 112
DUNCANSON, JOHN (ALLANSON), 133n
DURIE, ANDREW, bishop of Galloway, 48, 60
DURIE, GEORGE, abbot of Dunfermline, 47, 55, 108
DURWARDS, 40

EADMER, bishop, 8-9
EDGAR, king, 8
EDWARD I, king, 26, 69, 88, 102, 110, 111
ELIOLY, JAMES, canon, 114
ELIOT, JOHN, bedellus, 92-3
EPLHINSTONE, WILLIAM, bishop of Aberdeen, 127, 138, 149
ERASMUS, 73, 102n
ERSKINE, JOHN of Dun, 117-18

FISHER, ST JOHN, 118
FLEMING, LORD, 59
FORBES, DAVID, prior of Monymusk, 63, 165

FORBES, RICHARD, dean of Aberdeen, 71
FORD, WILLIAM, sacrist of Arbroath, 54
FORFAR, JOHN OF, prior, 27
FORMAN, ANDREW, archbishop, 58, 82, 92, 95, 107, 126n, 130, 149-150, 159
FORMAN, BARTHOLOMEW, subprior of Pittenweem, 61, 135, 162
FORMAN, PATRICK, subprior of Pittenweem, 61, 162
FORMAN, ROBERT, commendator of Pittenweem, 58, 159
FORREST, HENRY, 109
FOTHAD, bishop, 5, 68, 144
FOTHAD II, bishop, 5-8, 33
FOULAR, JOHN, & MARIOTA, his wife, 113n
FOULAR, WILLIAM, 91
FRANCIS I, king of France, 45
FRASER, WILLIAM, bishop, 26, 88, 147
FREDERICK II, emperor, 35, 37
FRENCH SERVANTS, 55
FURROUR, SANDY, 52

GABRIEL, French cook, 55
GALT, ALAN, canon of Monymusk and Pittenweem, 60, 63-4, 162, 165
GAMELIN, bishop, 22n, 39, 85, 87, 106, 147
GEOFFREY, bishop of Dunkeld, 34, 146
GEOFFREY OF CRAUFORD, chancellor, 42
GELLIN, dewar of The Morbrac, 99-100
GEORGE de BRAMA, bishop of Dromore, 93
GIBSON, WILLIAM, bishop of Libraria, 59, 94, 107
GILBERT, chaplain, 43
GILBERT, culdee, 39
GILBERT, prior, 141
GILLEMUR, dewar of The Morbrac, 99
GODRIC OF FINCHALE, ST, 97
GOLIGHTLY (GALICHTLIE), JOHN, 65n
GOURLAY, NORMAN, 109
GOWRIE, JOHN, prior, 142
GRAHAM, PATRICK, archbishop, 68, 90, 94, 127, 138, 148, 158
GRAY, LORD, 57
GRAY, ROBERT, glazier and plumber, 115

GREENLAW, GILBERT, bishop of Aberdeen, 148
GREGORY IX, pope, 34-5
GRIMANI, MARCO, papal legate, 48, 61
GROSSETESTE, ROBERT, bishop of Lincoln, 35-6
GUTHRIE, AMAND, cardinal's page, 55

HADDINGTON, JOHN OF, prior, 28
HALDENSTONE, JAMES, prior, 18n, 22n, 31-2, 63-4, 66-7, 70, 71, 75, 76, 80, 81, 86, 89, 92, 93, 99, 114, 122, 129, 138
HALYBURTON, ANDREW, 82, 90
HAMILTON, JOHN, archbishop, 54, 59, 92, 109, 119, 120, 128, 135, 152
HAMILTON, PATRICK, abbot of Fearn, 95, 108
HARALD, bishop of Argyll, 146
HARDYNG, JOHN, 99
HAY, GEORGE, secretary, 52, 60
HAY, RICHARD AUGUSTINE, 93, 113
HAY, THOMAS, royal secretary, 53
HEGGIE, FRANCIS, composer, 96
HENRY III, king of England, 37, 39
HENRY VIII, king of England, 57, 103
HEPBURN, JOHN, bishop of Brechin, 59, 108
HEPBURN, JOHN, prior, 30n, 32, 95, 126, 127, 128, 129, 149, 167n
HEPBURN, PATRICK, prior, bishop of Moray, 59, 107, 108, 129
HERMIT, 116
HERTFORD, EARL OF, 61
HILLIARD, RICHARD, 60
HOGENBERG, FRANZ, 151
HUNTINGDON, DAVID, earl of, 22n, 37

ILLYRICUS, FLACIUS, 96, 102
INDULF, king, 4, 97
INGLIS, ALEXANDER, archdeacon, 82, 84
INNOCENT IV, pope, 38, 40

JAMES I, king, 53, 141
JAMES II, king, 106
JAMES III, king, 106
JAMES IV, king, 58, 95, 102, 115, 159
JAMES V, king, 45, 95, 105, 109, 116, 121
JARDANE, SANDY, 62

175

JARDINE, ALEXANDER, 133
JOHN, CARDINAL of ST
LAURENCE, 39
JOHN OF GOWRIE, prior, 155
JOHN OF STIRLING, 103
KENNEDY, JAMES, bishop, 31, 67, 69, 90, 104, 124, 127, 128, 129, 131, 138, 148, 158, 167 sqq.
KELLIE, LAIRD OF, 57
KERSE, ALEXANDER, 56
KINMOND, ALEXANDER, regent in Arts, 49
KINNEIR, KATHERINE, 96
KNOX, HENRY, 56
KNOX, JOHN, 107, 117-20
KNOX, THOMAS, ' writer to the cardinal,' 53-4
KNOWLES, DAVID, 134
KRAVAR, PAUL, 108

LAMBERTON, WILLIAM, bishop, 26, 27, 68, 69, 79, 87, 88, 98n, 111, 112, 147
LAMONT, ALAN, graniter, chamberlain of St Andrews priory, 49
LANDALE, ROBERT, of Grange, 3
LANDALLIS, WILLIAM de, bishop, 29, 30, 31, 68, 69, 80, 86, 87, 103, 104, 142, 147
LAUDER, JOHN, chief secretary to archbishop David Beaton, archdeacon of Teviotdale, 49, 52, 54, 59
LAW, JOHN, canon, 63, 68, 85, 89, 90, 92, 125, 137 sqq
LEARMONTH, PATRICK, of Dairsie, 125
LEOT, 5
LEO X, pope, 58n, 150, 159n
LE ROMEYN, JOHN, 35, 37
LESLIE, JOHN, bishop of Ross, 132
LESLIE, NORMAN, 56, 67
LESLIE, ROBERT, 57n, 67
LINDORES, HENRY, abbot of, 108
LINDSAY OF THE MOUNT, SIR DAVID, 105
LINDSAY, JAMES, bishop suffragan, 93
LINDSAY, ROBERT, master of the stable, 56
LOGIE, GAVIN, 116-18
LORGES, SIEUR DE, 60, 62
LOTHIAN, WILLIAM OF, prior, 29, 66n, 69, 142
LOUDON, WILLIAM, see Lothian
LOUIS XI, king of France, 167
LOWYS, JOHN, the cardinal's fool, 55

LUMSDEN, HENRY, chamberlain, vicar of Tarves, 49-50
LYON, C. J., 76, 114, 151

MACLEAN, RODERICK, bishop of the Isles, 60
McMATH, GILBERT, almoner, 51
MAELDUIN, bishop, 5
MAIEL, see MAYELLE
MAJOR, JOHN, 58, 90, 137
MALCOLM III, king of Scotland, 6, 8, 61-2, 149, 163
MALTMAN, SYMON, OFM, 109
MALVOISIN, WILLIAM, bishop, 20n, 21, 22, 22n, 33, 41, 42, 85, 98, 146
MANDERSTON, WILLIAM, 58, 137
MAR, WALTER, master of works, 51
MARCH, PATRICK, earl of, 69
MARGARET, princess of England, 40
MARGARET, princess of Scotland, 167
MARGARET, ST, queen of Scotland, 6, 8, 37, 68, 72, 98
MARGARET TUDOR, 116
MARIANUS, papal chaplain, 37
MARIE DE LORRAINE, queen, 45, 105
MARJORIBANKS, THOMAS, provost of Edinburgh, clerk register, 58
MARY OF GUELDRES, queen, 102
MAUL, THOMAS, 57
MAYELLE, JEAN, 167
MAYO, of HEREFORD, bishop, 71
MELDRUM, ALANE, 108
MELVILLE, ANDREW, 168
METHVEN, HENRY, bailie of St Andrews, 54
METHVEN, JOHN, chaplain, 51
MILL, WALTER, see Myln
MILNE, ALEXANDER, abbot of Cambuskenneth, 59, 94, 107, 108, 130
MONTROSE, ROBERT, prior, 64, 75, 142-3
MONYPENNY, GEORGE, 55n
MONYPENNY, WALTER, canon, 129, 157
MORAY, EARL OF, 57
MORE, ST THOMAS, 138
MORTIMER, WALTER, 43
MOROW, JOHN, master of works, 22n, 115
MURE, ADAM, schoolmaster, 58
MURRAY, JAMES, 61, 64, 162, 165

MURRAY, WILLIAM, treasurer of Dunblane, 83
MYLN, WALTER, 51, 109, 118

NICHOLAS OF CUSA, 138
NICHOLAS IV, pope, 94
NICHOLAS V, pope, 138
NISBET, GEORGE, 60, 162
NORHAM, HENRY OF, prior, 141

OGILVIE, HENRY, 104
OGILVIE, PATRICK, 83
OLIPHANT, ANDREW, secretary to Cardinal David Beaton, 49, 52, 53, 60, 61
OTTERBURN, ADAM, provost of Edinburgh, 57
OTTO, CARDINAL, 35

PANITER, DAVID, bishop of Ross, 59
PAUL III, pope, 45
PAY, STEPHEN, prior, 30, 64, 87, 142
PEEBLES, DAVID, canon, composer, 96, 133
PETRUS, (PETER), FRANCIS, Cardinal Beaton's French secretary, 54
PITTENWEEM, CANONS, 162
PLATER, THOMAS, subprior, 142
POLE, CARDINAL, 60
POLWARTH, JAMES, 168
PONT, TIMOTHY, 152
PRIORS OF ST ANDREWS, 140-4

RAMSAY, DAVID, prior, 68, 95, 126, 129
RAMSAY, GEORGE, of Clatty, 57
RAMSAY, PETER, bishop of Aberdeen, 35, 35n, 43
RAMSAY, PETER, canon, 162
RAMSAY, THOMAS, subdean of Glasgow, 108
RANDOLPH, THOMAS, earl of Moray, 30n
RANKELOUR, WILLIAM, 120n
RATTRAY, WILLIAM, 60
REGINALD OF COLDINGHAM, 102-3
REGULUS, ST, 2n
REID, ROBERT, bishop of Orkney, 59, 62
RICHARD, bishop, 22, 42, 145
RICHARD, canon, 39n
RICHARD OF NORTH BERWICK, chaplain, 75
ROBERT, bishop, 9-10, 11, 12, 44, 98, 141

ROBERT, prior, 141 (previously prior of Scone), 144
ROBERT, rector of Methven, 43
ROBERT II, king of Scotland, 113
ROGER, bishop, 42, 85
ROSS, ELIZABETH, countess of, 83
ROSS, GAVIN, notary, 137
ROTHES, EARL OF, 82
RUGLYN, JOHN, master of works, 22n
RUGLYN, WILLIAM, canon, master of works, 115
RULE, JOHN, prior of Pittenweem, 27, 58-60, 108, 159, 160-2
RULE, JOHN, canon, son of J.R., prior of Pittenweem, 61, 133
RULE, NINIAN, son of the prior of Pittenweem, 133
RUTHERFORD, DAVID, master of the stable, 56
RUTHERFORD, THOMAS, subprior, 56
RUTLEDGE, scullion, 56

SADLER, RALPH, 57, 59
SANDILANDS, JAMES, of Calder, 117
SCHEVEZ, WILLIAM, archbishop, 90, 93, 106, 127, 148, 158
SCHULTETUS, HENNINGUS, 137
SCOT, JOHN, pilgrim, bishop of St Andrews, 102, 145
SETON, LORD, 57
SIMON, prior, 141
SIMPSON, JOHN, sub-graniter, 51, 56
SIMSON, JOHN, canon, 133
SINCLAIR, OLIVER, 58
SIWARD, earl of Northumbria, 145
SLUAGADACH, 5
SMYTH, ALEXANDER, 96
SPENS, ALEXANDER, canon, 133
SPENS, HUGH, dean of Glasgow, 108
STEWART, ALEXANDER, archbishop, 92, 110n, 148, 150
STEWART, EDWARD, bishop of Orkney, 93
STEWART, JAMES, archbishop, duke of Ross, 68, 84n, 90-1, 127, 130, 148, 150
STEWART, JAMES, commendator of Kelso and Melrose, 60, 161
STEWART, JAMES, duke of Rothesay, 105
STEWART, LORD JAMES, prior, 60-1, 117, 120, 132, 134, 161, 162
STEWART, MARIOTA, 67

STEWART, PATRICK, archdeacon of Lothian, 47
STEWART, ROBERT, postulate of Caithness, commendatory prior, 120n, 135
STEWART, THOMAS, bishop-elect, 147
STIRLING, AMBROSE, castle porter, 56
STRATON, DAVID, 109
STURY, WILLIAM, canon, 75

THEALDINI, ALESSANDRO, 61
THOMAS, prior, 141
THOMSON, WILLIAM, OFM, 60
TOD, THOMAS, 83
TRAIL, WALTER, bishop, 31, 65, 68, 69, 87, 113, 143, 147
TROILLUS, scullion, 56
TUATHALAN, abbot, 1
TURGOT, bishop, 8, 33, 72, 144
TURNBULL, WILLIAM, bishop of Glasgow, 138

'VENUS, LADY,' 117

WAGHORN, ALEXANDER, bishop of Ross, 105
WAGNER, MARCUS, 79, 96, 102, 117
WALLACE, ADAM, 109n, 276
WALLACE, SIR WILLIAM, 111
WALTER, mason, 22n
WALTER, prior, 141
WALTHEOF (VALTHENUS), bishop-elect, abbot of Melrose, 145
WARDLAW, HENRY, bishop, 31, 65, 66, 80, 89, 99, 105, 108, 148
WARDLAW, JOHN, of Torry, 48
WARDLAW, WALTER, cardinal, 148
WARHAM, WILLIAM, archbishop of Canterbury, 73

WATSON, PETER, canon, 133
WAUCHOPE, ROBERT, archbishop of Armagh, 62
WELLS, ROBERT, archdeacon, 66n, 82-3
WEMYSS, SIR JOHN, 83
WESTPUTYWS, ANTHONY, 60
WEYREMENT, RICHARD, culdee, 39
WHITE, JOHN, prior, 21, 28, 38, 141
WIED, HERMANN VON, archbishop of Cologne, 117n
WILLIAM, monk of Bury, 8-9
WILLIAM, king of Scotland, 145, 146
WILLIAM of LOTHIAN, prior (see Lothian)
WILLIAMSON, JOHN, dean of Linlithgow, 48
WILSON, WILLIAM, canon, 64, 133n, 165
WINCHELSEY, ROBERT, archbishop of Canterbury, 70
WINCHESTER, GEORGE, steward and bailie of the regality, 50
WINRAM, JOHN, subprior, 56, 109, 116-7, 119, 120, 127, 130, 134, 135, 157
WISHART, GEORGE, 52, 56, 62, 109
WISHART, ROBERT, bishop of Glasgow, 69
WISHART, WILLIAM, bishop, 23, 26, 65, 69, 77, 85, 147
WOOD, GEORGE, 139
WOOD, THOMAS, 96
WRIGHT, ROBERT, 61, 162
WRIGHT, THOMAS, 61, 162
WYNTOUN, ANDREW, canon, 56, 63, 64-5, 85, 87, 138, 157

YOUNG, WILLIAM, chaplain, 51, 56

DATE DUE

GAYLORD | | | PRINTED IN U.S.A.